PRAISE FOR *PC*

"In her latest book, J
readers and lovers venturing into the uncharted. With great
care and necessary nuance, *Polywise* is a must-read for anyone
navigating open relationships."
—Esther Perel

"In *Polywise's* expansive and eye-opening exploration of the
possibilities of nonmonogamous life, Jessica Fern invites us to
examine our individual and societal beliefs about love and offers
an indispensable guide for newly opened couples' transitions to
their next chapter. If you are ready to think more deeply about
communication, codependency, conflict, and repair in your most
important relationships, *Polywise* is required reading. I am looking forward to recommending this guide to clients and students."
—Alexandra H. Solomon, PhD, author of *Love Every Day*
and host of *Reimagining Love*

"As someone who's experienced a multitude of relationship
transitions throughout the course of my life, I found *Polywise*
to be incredibly profound. This book moves past the polyamory
101 manual into graduate-level territory. It's an exceptional
achievement that will be required reading for anyone practicing
consensual nonmonogamy, from seasoned veteran to timid
newbie alike."
—Emily Sotelo Matlack, co-host of the Multiamory
podcast and co-author of *Multiamory:
Essential Tools for Modern Relationships*

"So often advice about nonmongamy feels like it is addressing the
visible issues at hand—jealousy, boundaries, communication,
etc.—so relationships can survive. In *Polywise*, Jessica Fern
and David Cooley help readers understand the often unseen
root causes of those symptoms and give them the strategies they
need so their relationships can actually thrive."
—JoEllen Notte, author of *The Monster Under the
Bed: Sex, Depression, and the Conversations We
Aren't Having* and *In It Together: Navigating
Depression with Partners, Friends, and Family*

"*Polywise* is an important book for anyone on how we change and adapt. Change is never easy. We need this guide to help us examine our narratives and beliefs around monogamy and create clear relationship agreements, shifting old paradigms of loyalty to structures that more closely resonate with our core values. In fact, this book leads us on a complete overhaul of the relationship foundation, a deconstruction of partnerships as we know them, while at the same time respecting those who want to stay monogamous. No matter where your relationship stands, this book is a necessity for examining your future and creating the life you'll love."

 —Tammy Nelson PhD, sex and relationship expert
  and author of *Open Monogamy; A Guide to*
  Co-Creating Your Ideal Relationship Agreement

"Most of us are thrilled if we can manage the logistical and emotional challenges of polyamory without murder or mayhem. We are content to 'make polyamory work' in our lives and keep ourselves and our partners reasonably happy. Jessica Fern is taking us far beyond that to a much deeper level of understanding of our psyches and the underpinnings of our relationship dynamics. She and her co-conspirator David Cooley have bared their souls about the evolution of their own poly lives and relationships, as well as sharing countless illuminating stories about their clients' struggles. They have truly pulled back the curtain to expose the real truth of how things can go so horribly awry, and exactly *why* poly relationships can so often spiral down into Poly Hell. Required reading and a must-have for your poly bookshelf!"

 —Kathy Labriola, counselor, nurse and author
  of *The Polyamory Breakup Book*

"This book is thorough! There were so many useful tools, concepts, exercises and prompts for personal inquiry that anyone who reads it can walk away with something they can apply to level up their nonmonogamous journey. I often say there's being polyamorous and then there's being polyamorous *well*. I believe *Polywise* can equip you to do just that."

 —Evita Sawyers, author of *A Polyamory Devotional*

pol*wise*

Amanda
To Abundant love!
Jesperm
many blessings on your
relational journey!

David Cool

ALSO BY JESSICA FERN

Polysecure
Attachment, Trauma and Consensual Nonmonogamy

The Polysecure Workbook
Healing Your Attachment and Creating
Security in Loving Relationships

The HEARTS of Being Polysecure
Creating Secure Attachments in Multiple Relationships

polywise

A Deeper Dive into Navigating
Open Relationships

Jessica Fern

with David Cooley

THORNAPPLE PRESS

Polywise
A Deeper Dive into Navigating Open Relationships
Copyright © 2023 by Jessica Fern

Thornapple Press
300 – 722 Cormorant Street
Victoria, BC V8W 1P8 Canada
press@thornapplepress.ca

Thornapple Press is a brand of Talk Science to Me Communications Inc. and the successor to Thorntree Press. Our business offices are located in the traditional, ancestral and unceded territories of the ləkʷəŋən and W̱SÁNEĆ peoples.

Cover design by Brianna Harden
Interior design by Jeff Werner
Editing by Andrea Zanin and Eve Rickert
Proofreading by Alison Whyte
Index by Maria Hypponen

Library and Archives Canada Cataloguing in Publication

Title: Polywise : a deeper dive into navigating open relationships / Jessica Fern with David Cooley.
Names: Fern, Jessica, author. | Cooley, David (Restorative justice facilitator), author.
Description: Includes bibliographical references and index.
Identifiers: Canadiana (print) 20230443095 |
    Canadiana (ebook) 20230443117 |
    ISBN 9781990869143 (softcover) |
    ISBN 9781990869150 (EPUB)
Subjects: LCSH: Non-monogamous relationships.
Classification: LCC HQ980 .F47 2023 | DDC 306.84/23—dc23

10 9 8 7 6 5 4 3 2 1

Printed and bound in Canada.

CONTENTS

FOREWORD

I'm pretty interested in love and relationships. I spend a lot of my time thinking and writing about them, both as a philosophy professor (that's my day job) and as a human.

In fact, it's always felt obvious to me that I can't really separate these things: being a philosopher of love and being a person who experiences love. When I first told people I was polyamorous and some of them told me "That's not real love," that disagreement was philosophical.

More generally, our lived experience of love is deeply bound up with how we theorize about it. Whether or not we *notice* the theoretical frameworks built into our worldview and our culture, the shape of our concepts inevitably manifests itself in our actions, and ultimately our lives. The assumption that romantic love is monogamous is a piece of theory. So is the assumption that love is heterosexual (or sexual at all, for that matter). Assumptions like these delimit how we imagine the possibilities for our own relationships—and how we police other people's.

Attachment theory has been a hot topic for a while now. For those of us who live in relationship-theory land, it's hard to move without running into its characteristic vocabulary. But the practical implications of attachment theory are making themselves felt far beyond the realms of the theoretical. We've been seeing a lot more mentions in the mainstream of what it is to be *secure* as opposed to being *anxious preoccupied, dismissive avoidant*, or the dreaded *fearful avoidant*... (hi)... which I'm constantly reassured is not "the worst one."

It's easy to get caught up in the social media caricatures of what this all means. One thing it certainly *seems* to mean is that secure people—and secure relationships—are monogamous. But this assumption isn't entirely the fault of social media: until a couple of years ago, the literature on attachment theory was tripping along pretty happily with the assumption that monogamy is a baseline for what constitutes a good romantic relationship, without so much as mentioning that alternatives could also be healthy or viable. For those of us who know other love stories than that defined by the monogamous norm, this meant attachment theory was raising more than a few heckles and eyebrows.

Fern's book *Polysecure* burst onto this scene like a breath of fresh air. For the first time, those of us seeking, exploring or living in nonmonogamous relationships had a way to access the wisdom contained in attachment theory without being constantly excluded by the assumption that secure love is monogamous. *Polysecure* became a translation manual of sorts, enabling us to reap the practical benefits of a piece of theory that wasn't previously written in our language.

So don't take it lightly when I say that in *Polywise* we're getting something even deeper and more valuable.

Polywise emphasizes *transitions*—whether from monogamy to nonmonogamy, or from one form of nonmonogamy to another. It is these transitional periods that can easily reveal the grinding mechanisms behind the scenes, and the cracks in a relationship's infrastructure. This is where many of us need the most help, and so *Polywise* goes straight to the heart of the matter, offering balms for healing and genuinely feasible strategies for making these things...not painless, perhaps, but hopefully a little kinder to all involved, and certainly survivable.

As I read, I found myself particularly inspired by the collaborative spirit of *Polywise*, incorporating as it does several sections written by David Cooley, with whom Fern has been "classmates, friends, lovers, husband and wife, co-parents, exhusband and ex-wife, family of choice, housemates, life partners and now, even co-authors." The book's very existence is tangible proof of the general fact that relationship transitions need not be losses.

More generally, you can feel in these pages the accumulated practical wisdom that comes from seeking emergent patterns in the data, rather than simply imposing pre-conceived ideas. And Fern's data are, in a sense, *us*, the nonmonogamous:

this is a book about *our* real lives and real loves, as represented in the kinds of challenges that came up repeatedly for her non-monogamous clients and interviewees.

The practical and the theoretical are integrated seamlessly in this book, just like in real life. Many of us will be visiting the wisdom of *Polywise* over and over again as our relationships grow and change, like the living things they are.

Carrie Jenkins
Vancouver, BC, February 2023

Carrie Jenkins is a professor of philosophy at the University of British Columbia and the author of *What Love Is (and What it Could Be)* and *Sad Love: Romance and the Search for Meaning.*

ACKNOWLEDGMENTS

Dave, we did it! We accomplished our undeniably impossibly incredible dream of one day writing a book together. Thank you for sharing this creative project with me. Thank you for being a true life partner. The birth of this book could not have happened without you. The dyslexic in me eternally bows to the obsessive writer in you.

Mom, thank you so much for stepping up as such an awesome Mima so that Dave and I could have the extra time and space we needed to write this book. It's been beautiful to see you and Diego bond even more over this time, and we are truly grateful for all your support.

John Leporati, your encouragement and help with my writing have been an ongoing gift in my life. Even after 30 years, you still teach me so much about what it means to truly love someone.

John S, our relationship and unique beginning have been the necessary puzzle piece for several significant insights and ideas in this book. Thank you for the gift of all of you.

Jessica Fern
March 2023

Dave here!

Yes, Jessica! What an utterly unpredictable, wild and divinely inspired journey it has been to get to this point. It's hard to believe the intention we set in motion so many years ago of co-authoring together has finally come to fruition. It has been a powerful and cathartic process to revisit some of our most challenging and tender moments together, and such an amazing gift to be able to distill so many of the painful lessons we learned along the way into something that may genuinely serve others in their relational journeys. I will always be so grateful for everything you have been and continue to be in my life!

Diego, it will probably be a few years before you are really able to understand what I'm saying to you here. Being your father has taught me more about what it means to truly commit my heart to loving someone else than any other relationship in my life. The beauty of your presence, humor, joy, empathy and talent is a continuous source of inspiration and renewal for me and has served as a motivation for writing this book in countless ways. ¡Te amo con todo mi corazón, mi amor!

Julia, my love. Being with you has truly been a game-changing relationship for me. I have never felt so safe, seen and securely attached to a partner before. Your love has brought a clarity and groundedness that has helped me navigate the tremendous ups and downs of writing this book, and I'm so grateful to be able to lean into you!

V, your unshakeable enthusiasm and optimism for this project has been an incredible source of support. Thank you for all the ways you have cared for me along the way!

David Cooley
March 2023

Eve Rickert, thank you for all of your fine-comb editing and big-picture thinking. Andrea Zanin, thank you for your substantive editing and crucial input. Both of your perspectives have been necessary enhancements to the book. Hazel Boydell, thank you for all the behind-the-scenes logistics and details that you managed to make this book happen.

Jessica and David

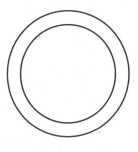

INTRODUCTION

"Aren't you worried about being jealous?"
"Polyamory just seems way too hard."
"Sounds like you just want to have your cake and eat it too."
"Isn't that just an attachment or commitment issue?"
"What aren't you getting in your relationship that makes you want to open up?"
"Isn't that just the first stop on the way to divorce?"
"You know you can always just go back to monogamy."

These are just some of the judgments and discouraging remarks that many people bump up against when they reveal they are nonmonogamous or share some of their nonmonogamous woes. These responses can come from friends, family, professionals, even therapists. Some of these comments are spoken with an insensitive disregard for you, your experiences or your desires, while in other cases, people are just trying to be helpful or protective, or even to sidestep their own discomfort with the topic. Whatever the intention, the person who is sharing about being nonmonogamous often leaves the interaction feeling demoralized and dejected. Here you are, attempting to share something important about yourself with the hope of making a connection, and instead, you are left feeling exactly the opposite: disconnection. Regardless of whether these unwelcome statements are meant to be callous or caring, they hurt precisely because of the ignorance underlying them.

Through no fault of their own, many people are misinformed about what nonmonogamy actually is and why people do it, nor do they understand that for many, it is an orientation or a way of being, as opposed to simply a lifestyle choice. Sadly, there is no shortage of horror stories about the exploits of unfaithful partners, about nonconsenting women and young girls being forced into polygamy, or about couples who, after opening up their marriage, inevitably divorce. These pervasive narratives become the evidence for justifying and reinforcing the mononormative ideal that dominates our society: the idea that monogamous relationships are fundamentally more natural and morally correct. These biased points of view also serve to bolster and legitimize the dominance of the institution of monogamous marriage in our culture, especially a heteronormative view that sees the sacred union between a man and a woman as the goal of any healthy romantic relationship. Because consensual nonmonogamy (CNM) challenges these powerful discourses, many people, whether consciously or not, consider it dangerous—and even potentially contagious. This is not because CNM is inherently dangerous, however, but because it shows us there are other viable ways to love and live out our intimate relationships, which in turn can call into question deeply entrenched ideas about how relationships can or should look in general.

I remember when David and I told his parents we were opening up our marriage and exploring polyamory. My mother-in-law started to cry right there on the spot. She said she couldn't help but recall the havoc and relational devastation she witnessed during the 1960s as people got caught up in the frenzy of the free love movement and suburban key parties. Understandably, because of what she had seen, she feared our polyamorous exploration inevitably meant that we were doomed to divorce. Interestingly, my clients often echo this same fear in therapy and coaching sessions when they are either new to open relationships or making some kind of significant transition in their current nonmonogamous relationships. Even though these people come to me for various reasons, often included in their need for genuine support on how to navigate their transition is the concern of becoming the cliché of the relationship that broke up because of being open. The bad reputation that polyamory and other types of CNM have received over the years for being relationship wreckers, unfortunately, still prevails.

Let's be honest: it does happen. It *is* true that many open relationships do break up, and the easy scapegoat in many cases is nonmonogamy. However, in my experience, the unhappy end of many open relationships actually has very little to do with nonmonogamy in and of itself, and instead is much more related to the powerful influences of the monogamous paradigm that continue to shape our relational templates. Rather than nonmonogamy being the cause of relationship problems or endings, the problem has more to do with the difficulty of trying to make the square peg of a monogamous mindset fit into the round hole of nonmonogamous relationships. Many individuals are simply not aware of the ways that a monogamous or couple-centric perspective continues to linger in the recesses of their minds and hearts, showing up in their new or long-term open relationships in ways that can create significant obstacles. The complexity, change and tumult of CNM often present us with new and unforeseen challenges that are simply not applicable in a strictly monogamous context. As a result, whether you are brand new to or already familiar with CNM, these unique challenges often expose the ways our underlying relational operating system is still rooted in the tenets of monogamy.

Transitioning from practicing monogamy to nonmonogamy means making a massive shift in worldview. It implies living through a new paradigm of relationship, where almost every aspect of love, romance, sex, partnership and family has a different set of rules, expectations, practices, codes of conduct and even language. As Hardy and Easton say in the third edition of *The Ethical Slut*, "...you and your beloved are, like all of us, products of our culture, and it takes hard work to step out of the paradigm upon which your entire previous existence was based." Additionally, this shift is accompanied by stepping into a paradigm of relationship that is still, by and large, mostly misunderstood, feared and stigmatized. This means not only are you navigating the rough and choppy waters of a fundamental shift in your own worldview, but you're also swimming against the social current of acceptability to do so. The scope of this kind of challenge cannot be overstated.

Even after submerging themselves into a thorough and dedicated study of the growing number of quality resources on nonmonogamy, people still reach out to me in the distress of not feeling adequately prepared for this paradigm-altering journey. Others are confused as to why they and a partner are now struggling even though they have been practicing CNM for some time. As one client said to me, "I just had no clue about the depth of process that this would be. I just wasn't prepared for how it would entirely rearrange my whole world."

Many of the available resources for individuals or partners transitioning to CNM focus on how to define what kind of CNM structure you want, how to establish agreements, how to communicate better or how to deal with jealousy. These are extremely important and foundational topics, and they do reflect the majority of the complaints I hear from the people seeking my support. Clients typically begin with telling me that some version of broken agreements, communication challenges, increased conflict or jealousy is bringing them to my office. However, as we get several sessions into the work, it usually comes to light that these are actually just symptoms or secondary manifestations of much deeper issues. These other, more underlying challenges are the focus of this book.

From *Polysecure* to *Polywise*

Polywise could have been my first book. After presenting at CNM conferences for a few years on very practical topics like how to manage emotional triggers or jealousy, it was my talk on couples transitioning from monogamy to polyamory that really felt like my first, original contribution to the world of nonmonogamy. In that talk, I was not just applying something like general trigger management tools or polyvagal theory to a nonmonogamous context, I was actually sharing the specific experiences and insights gleaned from thousands of session hours with nonmonogamous psychotherapy and coaching clients, as well as dozens of qualitative interviews that I conducted with people practicing CNM.* My talk felt like the first time I was actually getting to the root of what so many people struggle with when transitioning to nonmonogamy instead of just dealing with the symptoms, and it resonated deeply with my audiences precisely because it reflected the lived experiences of the people on the front lines of that transition.

In graduate school, I was trained in grounded theory,** a qualitative research method where the theories and ideas that are developed are "grounded" in actual data and emerge from

---

* Over the course of a year, I conducted over 30 interviews with people who identified as CNM. I posted a request for interviewees on social media and local polyamorous groups. Interviews were conducted in person and over the phone to get more in-depth insight into the experiences people had with transitioning to CNM from monogamy and what they experienced as their joys and hardships in being CNM. The interviewees were all adults and self-selecting. They ranged in age from 22 to 71 and varied from people who started CNM within the past year to people practicing CNM for over four decades.

** See, for example, Glaser and Strauss, *The Discovery of Grounded Theory.*

the patterns identified from the narratives of the interviewees. This methodology is in stark contrast to other research
methods, where I as the researcher would first impose my
theories and assumptions before even encountering the
data. I later brought this qualitative research training to my
therapy practice, allowing the personal stories and anecdotes
of hundreds of clients and dozens of CNM people that I interviewed to illuminate the repeating patterns underlying their
nonmonogamous difficulties. Through a grounded theory
approach, I let my clients and interviewees inform me of their
nonmonogamous joys and hardships, and I came to better
understand the root issues beneath the symptoms of broken
agreements, chronic misunderstandings, increased fighting
and persistent jealousy.

When I presented my findings at conferences, people
would regularly approach me afterward, saying it was like I
had a camera in their house because so much of what I shared
was exactly what they themselves had experienced. I, of course,
did not have a camera in their houses, but the intentional
listening I did with my clients and interviewees led me to
identify the principal challenges that people face in their CNM
transitions, whether they are new to CNM or have been nonmonogamous for years. The purpose of this book is to name
these key paradigmatic hurdles to living nonmonogamously,
offer important insights into why these might be showing up
in your relationships, and provide tips and techniques for how
to move beyond them.

When I first met Eve Rickert, publisher of Thornapple
Press, at Southwest Love Fest in 2019, I had 20 minutes to
pitch my potential book ideas to her. While I proposed several
different ideas, I was actually expecting that the book you are
currently holding would be my first. However, Eve, having
her finger on the pulse of what was needed in the different
nonmonogamous communities, thought we were way past
due for a book that connected nonmonogamy and attachment
theory. Even though attachment disruption in nonmonogamy

was only one of the chapter topics that I pitched to her for this book, I agreed I could fill an entire book on attachment and CNM. Thankfully I did, because she was right! The response to *Polysecure* was tremendous. And while by no means perfect, *Polysecure* gave a much-needed voice to so many who were struggling to make sense of their experience as they made their way through the often murky waters of CNM. Most importantly, I think that by anchoring the concept of attachment in a nonmonogamous context, the book provided a scaffolding of meaning and understanding to which readers could connect their own personal stories. With *Polywise*, my hope is to expand the breadth and scope of that initial contribution by offering a new, complementary work that gives readers further insights into what I have come to see as the core challenges many people grapple with when making the profound paradigm shift into nonmonogamy.

This Book is for CNM Transitions

Some parts of the book may speak more to individuals and partners who are currently transitioning (or thinking about transitioning) from monogamy to nonmonogamy, and other parts speak more broadly to the challenges of CNM that I see partners face at any point on their CNM journey. This is because the transition from monogamy to nonmonogamy is typically not linear, nor a one-and-done experience, and the unpacking of the monogamous paradigm often unfolds in various phases over many years, across multiple relationships. For example, I commonly encounter partners or individuals who have technically been practicing CNM for years, but it is not until one of them has a partner who falls in love with someone else, starts dating people more locally or wants to move in with a certain partner that many of the issues presented in this book get exposed. For others, these challenges can emerge immediately after opening their relationship. Similarly, for many CNM people, the pandemic reduced the number of partners they saw or had, or even created a period of temporary exclusivity with one partner. As the pandemic abated and they began to date again, many were surprised by the feeling of being back at square one with open relating, even though they had previously had multiple partners.

When I refer to CNM transitions throughout this book, I am referring to such experiences as:

- Escalations and de-escalations in your or your partners' relationships.
- Changes in the CNM style or structure you or your partners are practicing.
- Transitioning to less hierarchical forms of CNM.
- The introduction of new romantic or sexual partners into your polycule.
- Having partners and metamours who are relatively new to CNM.
- Opening up a monogamous relationship or marriage.
- Being single and starting to practice CNM for the first time.

Transitions like these can be extremely difficult for you as well as highly taxing on your relationships. They can shake up the very foundation of your current relationships, potentially destabilizing your sense of safety and security. A transition to CNM from monogamy or going through a transition within your CNM relationships can activate any and all of your personal insecurities and has an uncanny way of exposing all the ways your relationships have been masking unresolved conflicts, codependency or dysfunctional patterns of communication. For those of you who are already CNM, significant changes in your relationships can also reveal the lingering traces of a monogamous and couple-centric paradigm—particularly in terms of problematic expectations—that no longer serves you or your CNM relationships. For those of you who are newer to CNM, the transition out of monogamy can be particularly arduous because it requires not just behavioral changes, but also a complete revisioning of how you perceive and embody yourself, others and your entire relational world.

A big part of what makes this process so complex is the power of the construct of "the couple." The prevalence of this concept is so ingrained in our relational consciousness that it can be extremely difficult to escape its influence even when we are actively trying to resist or deconstruct it. While it may be tempting to assume that the issues related to shedding the paradigm of coupledom only plague newly opened heterosexual couples, the truth is many of the people who come to me for help are at various stages of their CNM journey and reflect a wide range of identities beyond the mainstream, such as queer, kinky or neurodivergent. Regardless of their starting point or number of current partners, many individuals continue to experience some degree of difficulty in terms of how entrenched they are in the lingering expectations of monogamy or the dynamics of couplehood—so much so that even the people who have intentionally crafted their lives to be less couple-centric, such as those who identify as solo polyamorous or relationship anarchists, often still have to deal with the influence of couple-centrism, either in terms of how much coupleness their partners want with them, or the way their partners' autonomy and availability are limited because of their degree of coupleness with others.

The Title: *Polywise*

The title of this book, *Polywise*, has several meanings. First, it's a play on the title of my first book, *Polysecure*. Second, it's a kind of slang or shorthand that frequently comes up in my sessions with clients. For example, in the first few minutes of a session, before launching into relationship stuff, clients will usually give me recent updates about their life, and then, as a segue, will say something like, "...and then poly-wise, XYZ has been happening." The final meaning of polywise refers to the stage in our CNM journey that comes after we've metabolized the follies and blunders of our initial experiences and have developed a certain maturity in our process.

Being polywise means you are no longer a newbie to CNM and have weathered the storm that can accompany the initial stages of the transition. You have endured and overcome the lack of clarity about where you're going or what you're doing, experienced the escalation of problems in your new relationships, confronted the lingering elements of monogamy from your preexisting relationships that no longer work for you, witnessed the deconstruction and subsequent reconstruction of your sense of identity, and even grappled with the general sense of just feeling lost and overwhelmed by the whole thing. You may have also experimented with the different types of CNM, possibly explored the question of hierarchy in your relationships and, most importantly, no longer feel like your entire relational life is simply one hot, smoldering mess. You have arrived at a place where you have better footing and stability and are navigating the inevitable ups and downs of CNM with relative ease, skill and, yes, wisdom.

I'm not implying that being polywise means that your relationships are perfect, or that you are somehow immune to any relational challenges or mistakes. I'm simply saying that you have traversed the various stages of your own unique journey, going from polyinsecure to polysecure and from polyconfused to polywise. Knowing that it's possible to have the kind of relationship you want is key for staying motivated to continue growing and evolving as a relational being, especially when things get hard. I see the concept of polywise as a beacon, reminding us of what is possible in relationships. The intention of this book is to offer guidance along this journey by posing questions to spark deeper reflection, highlighting the obstacles others have faced so that you may learn from their experiences, sharing insights and theoretical models to expand your perspective, providing techniques and exercises for overcoming your particular struggles, and commiserating with your difficulties so you feel less alone in your process. Whatever your personal version of polywise may look like, my hope is that this book is a resource for helping you get there.

Introducing David Cooley

Finally, I am very excited to introduce my cowriter on this project, David Cooley. Dave and I have been in each other's lives since 2002. In the past two decades, we have been classmates, friends, lovers, husband and wife, co-parents, ex-husband and ex-wife, family of choice, housemates, life partners, and now, even co-authors. More than anyone else in each other's lives, together we have embodied the true meaning of relationship fluidity, where the deep commitment to each other as human beings and the way that commitment is expressed and experienced continually ebbs, flows and evolves throughout the years. Dave and I started our polyamorous journey together, and many of the insights reflected in this book were forged in the anguish and polyamorous life education we accrued in the process of opening up our marriage. Because of this, as I started to write *Polywise*, there were several places along the way where I knew Dave's expertise would be a necessary addition.

After working in the field of restorative justice, Dave created his own restorative conflict model called Restorative Relationship Conversations, which is designed to both address ruptures and traumas in intimate relationships and help partners learn new techniques for healthier communication. His extensive experience teaching CNM partners how to restore and repair relationship conflict, along with his emphasis on the role attachment issues play in conflict dynamics, offers an important and complementary perspective to my own. As you read *Polywise*, the default voice will read as mine, Jessica Fern's, but please know that Dave's contribution appears on every page of this book through his support with the editing, crafting, refinement and elevation of the concepts shared.

While my work has been the driver of the content, this book is undeniably a collaboration between Dave and me. As well, at times within different chapters, I indicate when we switch to a direct contribution in Dave's voice.

Our Bias

Like all of us, the distinctive fingerprint of our multiple biases, identities and unique life experiences is unlike anyone else's, even if we use the very same labels to identify ourselves. Personally, I have never felt comfortably or accurately centered in any one identity label. I am by all appearances white and of European descent, but I was not raised in normative white culture, and I am half Jewish, which at one point was considered a separate race to justify slavery and genocide, but is now typically considered its own ethnicity. I grew up with a single mother in the New York City housing projects buying fast food with food stamps. I grew up in multiple families (biological, step and surrogate) with different religions, cultures and languages. I am technically dyslexic, yet I hold higher education degrees and advanced certificates, and I am mostly physically strong and able-bodied, but I have an autoimmune condition that has at times been life-altering and debilitating.

I have lived inside and outside of the United States, in both rural and urban environments. I am not heterosexual, monogamous, or vanilla. And while I am much more confident claiming that I am polyamorous, saying that I'm fully kinky or queer is not completely fitting, since I am not kinky with all my partners. And as a cisgender woman who is more bisexual, I have on many occasions been objectified and marginalized by queer people or fetishized by straight people. I have navigated multi-generational family trauma, and I still work on healing my own complex trauma and childhood neglect. While most of my achievements and successes have felt like an uphill battle,

I have undeniably benefited from white privilege, legal marriage to a straight white man, eyes that people consider pretty, having English as a first language and owning a US passport. I also came from a family that knows how to laugh—at each other, ourselves and the hardships of life—which I credit as one of my major resiliency factors. I share all of this to disclose the multiple biases, privileges and marginalizations that I am coming from. My life experiences have been mostly on the fringe, rich and complex, which I have come to see as a gift that enables me to bridge multiple identities and paradigms. With that said, I also still have gaps in my knowledge that will inevitably influence my writing.

Dave here!

When Jessica and I first met in 2002 at a residential massage school in the mountains of northern California, we were drawn to each other not only because of a magnetic attraction and curiosity, but also out of necessity. Both of us were fleeing the East Coast in search of healthier ways of living and working in the world, and we were completely new to the peace-and-love culture of northern coast Cali. Despite the fact that we had left the East Coast with the intention of opening our hearts and minds to new ideas and experiences, we couldn't avoid the ways our sarcastic and cynical attitude—so characteristic of the native east coaster—rubbed against all the New Age positivity of the West. While the East Coast had become too intense and abrasive for our nervous systems, the West Coast felt refreshing, but also ungrounded and lacking the straightforwardness that we were accustomed to. The fact that we shared a sense of not fully belonging in either place helped make our transition much more manageable and, later, even continued to be a central theme in our relationship.

Like Jessica, my life has continuously maneuvered in and out of the spaces where various cultures, languages and worldviews intersect. I was born the son of two white, liberal Christian ministers who were passionate about social justice, which granted me an undeniably privileged beginning. However, because my parents were committed to living in service of the poor and marginalized, I was raised in communities where I was situationally in the racial minority. In that context, I was the target of regular bullying and racial violence because I was white. In my search to understand why my "whiteness" was so problematic, I became aware of the larger reality of racial inequality in the United States and the way the concept of white supremacy has been at the center of this injustice.

Later, as I worked in restaurant kitchens to pay for college, I again found myself positioned in between the unearned privilege of my racial status and being a racial minority. Working side-by-side with predominantly Spanish-speaking coworkers sensitized me to a whole new level of social inequity. Over time, witnessing the overt and subtle forms of racism and exploitation that my colleagues endured because of their challenges with English or precarious migratory status motivated me to learn Spanish as a means of creating solidarity and finding a way to cross the cultural divide. Recognizing that the unjust social dynamics of professional kitchens were simply a reflection of much larger social patterns, I felt compelled to do work that promoted cultural bridge-building through the mediums of teaching language, restorative justice facilitation, mediation and advocating for language justice.

My perspective has been further influenced by my complicated relationship to my body. I've had the privilege of being born male and identifying mostly as cisgender and straight. However, in my adolescence, I contracted a severe form of arthritis, and in a matter of months my body went from being young, strong and healthy to skinny, frail and sick. My rapid decline meant I had to give up my athletic pursuits, and my identity as an able-bodied person collapsed, completely calling into question my sense of value and worth as a man. Over the years, my condition created numerous hardships, ranging from the exorbitant costs of medication to inability to work, crushing financial debt, debilitating chronic pain and depression. Additionally, my arthritis created joint deformities, which impacted not just my posture and pain levels, but my body image as well. On the journey back to health, I have taken a long and winding road of deconstructing mainstream notions of gender, sex and health, which further informed my perspective.

While our unique life circumstances have given both Jessica and me an appreciation for people who are marginalized and left out of mainstream discourse, as well as a capacity for holding complexity, making space for nuance and honoring the gray areas of life, our various privileges also mean that we inevitably have certain limitations in our understanding, which can show up in our writing and our perspectives as individuals. In naming these, we intend to take responsibility for the impact they may have on anyone whose voice or experience we have unintentionally excluded.

The Structure of This Book

In the chapters to come, we will systematically address and tackle what I have come to see as the most common, archetypal obstacles for people either new to opening up from a monogamous relationship or people who are already nonmonogamous and struggling with some kind of CNM transition. Regardless of where you are in your particular relational journey, the greater degree of complexity inherent in CNM means you have to keep working on your emotional intelligence to do it well. It is a path that continually stretches and challenges us, changing the way we relate to sex and relationships, always pushing us to become more self-aware. As we grow along this path, often what worked in the past no longer works in the context of our constantly evolving relationships. This is one of the primary benefits of CNM in general, because no matter where you end up on your personal journey, having been exposed to the paradigm of CNM means you are much more likely to have a clearer sense of who you are and what you want. So while this book is intended for a CNM audience, a significant amount of what is covered in the following chapters offers helpful material for anyone in any relationship structure.

In chapter one we define what a paradigm is and explore some of the reasons why making a paradigm shift can be so challenging, even for people who have set the intention to make this kind of shift. We also help examine your lingering monogamous beliefs as well as encourage you to define your nonmonogamous beliefs. We finish by emphasizing the importance of explicitly having consent for making the paradigm shift to CNM, offering ways to support you in getting to your own consent in the context of your relationships.

Chapter two focuses on troubleshooting the uncertainty and resistance to making CNM transitions, offering different ideas and exercises to support you in understanding what might be in the way of getting fully on board with either practicing CNM or making a specific shift in the nonmonogamy you are already practicing, as well as offering reflections on how to figure out if CNM is ultimately right for you.

Chapter three dives into how nonmonogamy can expose all of the cracks in the foundation of the relationship you're currently opening up, or in CNM relationships that are making some kind of significant transition. This chapter covers challenges such as dysfunctional communication patterns, relationship neglect, justice jealousy and being in a companion marriage, as well as the times when the cracks in the relationship are just too big to repair.

Chapter four deals with the issue of conflict in relationships and, in particular, how to successfully address pain and hurt from the past. Dave talks about the importance of making a fundamental paradigm shift in terms of how we think and relate to conflict by moving from an adversarial approach to a restorative one, and how this shift can be a critical first step in handling conflict differently. He also exposes several of the most common obstacles that CNM partners face when trying to deal with unresolved issues from the past. Finally, utilizing his Restorative Relationship Conversations model, he offers some practical ways of working with conflict that will leave partners feeling more confident and capable of managing their own relational conflict.

Chapter five addresses the topic of codependency and enmeshment, exploring the ways that the lingering influence of monogamy and a couple-centric perspective has prevented many CNM partners from going through the necessary relationship phase of healthy differentiation. Much of the mono-romantic ideal encourages forms of codependency, which can remain invisible and even functional for a couple until they open up, or until partners change the level of hierarchy or style of their CNM relationships. Practices for going from enmeshment to differentiation as an individual and in partnership are offered at the end of the chapter.

Chapter six looks at the question of how certain differences between partners can make CNM feel close to impossible, such as in how fast or slow partners move forward with nonmonogamy, or whether a partner identifies as being more nonmonogamous as their orientation or nonmonogamous as a lifestyle choice. The difference in pursuing nonmonogamy as a lifestyle choice versus experiencing it as an orientation usually influences how each person moves forward with and approaches nonmonogamy. This difference can cause conflicts, hurt and many avoidable misunderstandings. Differences in the way people want to practice CNM, and new differences that arise between people through transitioning to CNM, can also make certain relationships no longer viable.

Finally, in chapter seven, we explore how the paradigm shift to CNM can create an awakening of the self, where the previously unexpressed or unrealized parts of the self become conscious and accessible. This radical awakening can potentially turn a person's entire relational world upside down, despite the freedom and expansiveness of the experience. People may be waking up not just to their nonmonogamous desires or orientation, but also to aspects of their sexuality, unexpressed identities, or even forms of oppression they may have denied, exiled, or left completely unacknowledged. We will also examine how CNM can be expressed through the different stages of adult psychological development, and how the shift to nonmonogamy or less-hierarchical forms of CNM can sometimes initiate a painful and destabilizing deconstruction of the self.

Throughout certain chapters in this book you will encounter exercises, questions and prompts to support you in your further exploration and integration of the material. Some of the questions and exercises might feel easy and straightforward, while others might be challenging and bring up pain regarding the hardships you have encountered. As you go through the different prompts, it is normal to experience a mix of insight, relief, anger, overwhelm, or fear; a sense of renewal; or needed release. Please make the space to allow all these different feelings to be present. Holding an attitude of curiosity and courage is important here. I suggest setting aside time for yourself to focus on the exercises and go at the pace that best suits you. Additionally, if you feel called to do so, you can go through these sections with your partners, friends or loved ones, a therapist, or a group of like-minded individuals.

Practicing CNM can expand your life and your entire worldview. It can broaden your experiences of sex, love, self, partnership and family. For that, it is truly incredible. CNM, like a tornado, can also bring chaos into your life, breaking you down and tearing relationships apart. My hope is that this book will be not only an extension of *Polysecure*, but also a new lens through which you can see and better understand the manifold challenges that can arise when transitioning from monogamy to nonmonogamy or attempting to make some kind of significant transition within a preexisting CNM relationship. Above all, may it be a helpful guide along your journey to becoming more polywise.

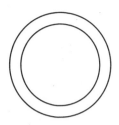

CHAPTER ONE

SHIFTING PARADIGMS

In my sophomore year of high school, I played Golde from the musical *Fiddler on the Roof*, a play set in an early 1900s Russian village. I was playing the part of a Jewish mother who, along with her husband, was highly determined to marry off her daughters to the right match. One of the songs I sang in the show was "Sunrise, Sunset," where my character reflects on the passing seasons, how quickly her children have grown and whether she's been able to pass on enough of her support and wisdom. You may recall the chorus, part of which goes:

> Sunrise, sunset
> Swiftly fly the years
> One season following another
> Laden with happiness and tears

As you can probably already surmise, there are plenty of patriarchal assumptions and mononormative expectations in this play that I could easily critique, but that's actually not my main point for this specific anecdote. Now, decades past my musical theater days, during the grind of a typical week, I sometimes hear myself singing the lyrics "sunrise, sunset, swiftly fly the years" when I am in the crunch hour of trying to get my son fed, ready and packed for school while also making myself look presentable for work and making sure the cat litter is clean. It's precisely in these moments where I feel the tension of being in the automated "wash, rinse, repeat" cycle of modern life that my mind can spin off with perplexity about how I live in a society where we have bound ourselves to the social constructs of consumerist capitalism, constant productivity and our purely fictitious yet ever-quickening relationship to time. While there is nothing inherently inevitable or objectively true about these fundamental tenets of contemporary North American civilization, the fact I am so thoroughly subject to their influence makes it seem as if they reflect the very fabric of the universe.

Recently, however, while hearing myself chant the chorus "sunrise, sunset," I had a completely different reflection, about how strange and yet completely commonplace it is that we still use the words *sunrise* and *sunset* to explain the daily activity of the sun. While modern astronomy has convincingly demonstrated that the sun neither rises nor sets, curiously, we still use these outdated terms to describe the Earth's rotation on its axis. On the surface, this is simply a song, a beautiful lament about the passing of time and the parental concern about whether or not we've done enough for our children. However, on a deeper level, the lyrics point to the tremendous difficulty implicit in changing the way we think about the world. Written in the early 1960s, this song came out over 400 years after Nicolaus Copernicus presented his revolutionary hypothesis, dethroning the Earth as the previous center of our universe. This Earth-centric paradigm, which posited the sun as simply one of the many celestial spheres revolving around our planet, completely dominated and shaped our perceptions and myths, even our language. Despite the fact that the empirical evidence via telescope, satellite and human space travel undeniably confirms the sun's centrality in our solar system, we still unthinkingly ask our smart devices questions like "what time is sunrise tomorrow?" instead of "when is daybreak" or "when is dawn?"

In a similar way, I find it interesting how many people (myself included) still reflexively say "bless you" when someone sneezes. The origins of this custom date back to a time when Christians actually believed a sneeze represented a moment of metaphysical vulnerability where evil spirits could enter your body and take control of your soul. Saying "God bless you" was like a protective talisman, offered more out of fear than social courtesy, which was meant to literally prevent potential demonic possession. And yet, while today you would probably find it hard to find someone who truly believes they are actually saving your soul by saying "bless you," the expectation to say it is so ingrained that our very moral integrity could fall into question if we don't. In fact, as a therapist, I have even been advised by other professionals that if *I* happen to sneeze during a session and my client doesn't say "bless you" to me in response, I could then reasonably suspect they have narcissistic or sociopathic tendencies, or simply lack sufficient emotional rapport to care about my wellbeing. I don't believe this, for the record. But it's fascinating how such a simple phrase carries so much weight.

Both of the previous examples about sunrises and sneezes are mundane, everyday occurrences that illustrate how deeply ingrained our ways of thinking and acting can become over time. Even though these particular examples carry relatively little impact on our lived experience, it's still curious to note how persistent they are, even in the face of ample evidence to refute their accuracy or truthfulness. I sometimes ask myself what it would actually take to get people to no longer use the word *sunrise* or forsake saying "bless you." Even more intriguing, perhaps, is the question, if it's this difficult to change fairly inconsequential customs and behaviors such as these, how much more challenging is it to change the way we fundamentally understand and experience love, romance, sex and partnership? Whether you are brand new to nonmonogamy or have already been practicing it in some form for many years, this is precisely the question you face when relating outside of the dominant, couple-centric paradigm of monogamy. You must figure out how to live out your nonmonogamous ideals despite the persistent influence of this monogamous paradigm, whether that influence shows up as deeply ingrained ideas within yourself or in someone with whom you are in partnership. Quite often, this is no small task!

What Is a Paradigm?

The term "paradigm" was popularized by Thomas Kuhn in his 1962 book *The Structure of Scientific Revolutions*, wherein he discusses how the various branches or disciplines of Western science—such as physics, biology, chemistry and geology—each have their own overarching theories, functioning to connect various ideas, pieces of information and experiences into a coherent whole. A paradigm is a particular view of the world that emerges to provide an overall framework for understanding different aspects of our reality. Interestingly, a geologist, biologist or chemist could each be examining the very same event or piece of data and yet have completely different hypotheses, interpretations and conclusions about what they are observing. Even within the same field of study, such as psychology, there can be differing paradigms, such as behaviorism, cognitive psychology, evolutionary psychology and social constructivism, all with vastly different answers to questions such as what makes us tick as human beings, or what mental health is and what the best means for achieving it are.

Since Kuhn's foundational work, the notion of paradigms has expanded beyond the sciences to everyday life, becoming a more general term that is now synonymous with our different *worldviews* or *lenses* through which we see and experience life. When trying to make sense of the world around us, we use paradigms to organize and consolidate the interpretations we make of things. They are the constructs and belief systems we use to make sense of the world and give our lives meaning. Something as commonplace as the birth of a human being or the growth of a tree can be interpreted as evidence for the existence of a God or the proof of evolution, depending on whether you are anchored in a religious or scientific paradigm. The different religious, economic, political and cultural paradigms that construct our society also frame our realities, guide our expectations, shape our wants and preferences, and even help us sort, organize and classify the information we receive through our physical senses.

One of my favorite examples of how our paradigms shape our actual perception and physiology concerns the sexualization of female breasts. In many cultures around the world, women's breasts are sexualized as erotic objects. Even though this phenomenon is purely a social construct, because of the physiological arousal that many experience in response to seeing, touching or thinking about breasts, the desire is believed to be innate and hardwired into us as humans, especially if you are a heterosexual man. This is absolutely the experience of many, regardless of their chromosomes, genitals or gender. In the presence of breasts—real, virtual or imagined—they experience physical pleasure, involuntary pupil dilation and increased blood flow to the genitals. To them, the appeal of breasts is experienced as their objective reality and truth, not some belief system they could just change at will. For such individuals, the physiological responses typically associated with pleasure that result from seeing or touching breasts confirms the impression that breasts, in and of themselves, are inherently arousing. This is the true power of our paradigms to shape our lived reality!

However, the sex appeal of women's breasts is not universal across all cultures, or throughout history. In previous times, the buttocks and the ankles were considered erotically irresistible, with breasts getting much less attention.* Also, certain Indigenous cultures, such as the Pirahã people of

---

* See, for example, Florence Williams, *Breasts: A Natural and Unnatural History*.

Brazil,* do not sexualize women's breasts at all, and even find humor in the colonizers' obsession with them. The reason that one culture or society can put breasts on a sexual pedestal and worship them as if they were inherently erotic while another can be utterly indifferent towards them is because of the differences between each culture's paradigm of physical attractiveness and sexuality. The culture's paradigm dictates what is arousing, and what isn't worth paying attention to sexually. Whatever the paradigm says is sexy becomes culturally acceptable and is more likely to trigger the physiological responses that then reinforce the "natural" desirability of the thing itself. So much so that any departure from the norm can earn you the label of being kinky, having a fetish or being sexually deviant. However, once you step outside of the dominant paradigm, this "naturalness" of our preferences can start to come into question.

As we can see from this example, our paradigms have the power to create not only our cognitive and emotional experiences, but our physical sensations and behavioral habits as well. They influence how we think, feel and act, often without us even realizing it. In the same way that a fish doesn't know it's swimming in water, our paradigms are often invisible to us, taken for granted and passed down from one generation to the next. Statements such as "that's just how things are done," "that's what's normal around here," or "everybody knows" are all signposts of the cultural belief systems that dictate what ways of being are considered acceptable and unacceptable. Sometimes our inherited traditions and taken-for-granted ways can be benign, such as holding the door for a stranger at the grocery store or shaking hands with someone you're meeting for the first time. However, many of our everyday assumptions and beliefs about how people are supposed to look and behave can be problematic or harmful. Many of the

----

*   See Daniel Everett, *Don't Sleep! There Are Snakes.*

beliefs that masquerade as "right," "natural" or "common sense" are actually paradigmatic beliefs rooted in racism, sexism, homophobia or polyphobia.

Reaching the Limits of Our Paradigms

Let's return to Thomas Kuhn for a moment. He believed that our paradigms—while helpful and necessary—could also become a trap, limiting our perspectives and eclipsing other viewpoints, evidence or experiences that fall outside of our paradigms' purview. This is similar to the now well-known phenomenon in psychology called confirmation bias, where our brains tend to only seek out, believe and remember information that confirms our current beliefs and then systematically ignore, disregard or write off any information that challenges or contradicts our fundamental worldview. Once a paradigm theory is established, those working within it can start doing what Kuhn calls the "normal science," which begins to account for most of what is considered acceptable and appropriate for any given scientist within their respective field of study. In the same way, because we live in a society where we are conditioned to internalize the monogamous paradigm as the default standard for relationships, it's incredibly difficult for us to think about things like dating, sex, marriage or having a family outside of the "normal" parameters of relationships set forth by monogamy.

But what happens when our paradigms are no longer sufficient to describe the fullness of our experience? What happens when we encounter repeated anomalies that cannot be easily explained by the dominant paradigm? What happens when the norms into which we've been acculturated are unable to explain what we personally feel, think or desire? When we are exposed to world events, scientific data, different identities or personal experiences, or have our own wants that fall outside of our current paradigm, it can be extremely unsettling. Paradigms are like the tectonic plates of meaning upon which our very identities are constructed, and when they are called into question, we can feel as though we are on the verge of an existential crisis. The framework we relied on in the past to make sense of ourselves or the world is no longer adequate. This leads to a turning point where we have to abandon the old paradigm and discover a new way of looking at the world. According to Kuhn, "when paradigms change, the world itself changes with them. It is rather as if the [scientific] community itself has been suddenly transported to another planet where familiar objects are seen in a different light and are joined by unfamiliar ones as well." Kuhn called this change from one way of thinking to another a "scientific revolution," and his description is particularly relevant when we think about the stark differences between monogamous and nonmonogamous paradigms.

As the old view is replaced by the new, the individual is irrevocably changed by their relationship to the new way of seeing the world. As US physician Oliver Wendell Holmes once said, "the human mind, once stretched to a new idea, never returns to its original dimensions." The reason for this is that the new model offers an expanded vision of the world; it seems better suited to reflect our own lived experiences and usually gives us a better or fuller description of the world based on the available evidence. For example, before the arrival of Einstein's Theory of Relativity and the subsequent quantum revolution of the 20th century, Newtonian theory dominated the world of Western physics, describing the universe in very mechanistic terms. However, when modern scientists discovered the subatomic world, the need for a new model to describe our increasingly complex universe became unavoidable. We simply could not rely on the old paradigm to understand our world anymore. Similarly, as more and more individuals recognize that their personal experiences of gender or sexuality do not fit neatly within the paradigm of a binary construction, the need has arisen for us to develop a new paradigm that conceives of these elements of human experience as existing on a spectrum.

Paradigm Shifts Are Different for Everyone

People come to nonmonogamy from many different starting points. For some, no matter how hard they tried, the monogamous paradigm never felt quite right, and their relational world only made sense when they discovered CNM. Others may have initially experienced monogamy like a comfortable pair of shoes that eventually wore thin and needed to be changed out for something that fit better. Some are drawn to CNM because they have struggled with the exclusivity of being with only one person, or they have felt philosophically misaligned with the tenets of monogamy and find more resonance with the principles and practices of CNM. Some find their way into CNM through kink or queer avenues—via their experience with a different paradigm altogether. Others, despite their faithfulness to their partner, have inwardly longed for more relational and sexual diversity and desire the opportunity to have new experiences. For some, leaving behind monogamy was a very conscious and deliberate decision, which clearly necessitated the search for a new paradigm to guide their journey. For still others, the idea of CNM would never have even crossed their minds unless it was from someone else, such as a close friend or curious partner, introducing it to them.

Just as the paths that lead people to nonmonogamy can be very different, so, too, are the processes of integrating a nonmonogamous paradigm. For example, some people experience nonmonogamy as if it were the lost blueprint of their romantic essence. Something in their soul just seems to recognize its wisdom, and they embody it with relatively little resistance or struggle. For others, however, the integration process can be much less elegant or easy. Some are drawn to the philosophy and principles of nonmonogamy but struggle with managing the challenges that arise in their relationships. Even though they resonate intellectually and emotionally with the tenets of nonmonogamy, their nervous system—conditioned by years of monogamous expectations—can struggle to accept the changes that come along with practicing it. In such cases, people can experience a kind of CNM paradigm jet lag where their nervous system needs time to rewire itself and catch up to the new reality. It's simply not enough to be on board with the *ideas* of nonmonogamy: we must also integrate the new worldview into our very ways of relating. This, for many, is easier said than done.

When looking back at some of the major paradigm shifts that I, myself, have made over the years, I am reminded that each big life change was either helped or hindered by a series of different factors and circumstances. When comparing some of those previous experiences, I am able to better understand the unique constellation of conditions that ultimately paved the way for my transition into new paradigms.

For instance, when I first read about Buddhism, when I was around 18 years old, it was very easy for me to cast aside the Catholic and Jewish beliefs that I grew up immersed in. I had an immediate resonance with the philosophical underpinnings of Buddhism that just felt intuitively in alignment with how I perceived the world to be. I was already aware of the fact that the Judeo-Christian worldview of my larger social environment was incongruent with many of my core political, moral and spiritual values, and thus, there simply wasn't much psychic residue from the dominant religious narrative for me to excavate or rid myself of. To make matters easier, I experienced zero resistance from anyone important in my life about changing my spiritual and philosophical beliefs. Numerous resources were also readily available on bookstore shelves on Eastern philosophy, meditation and mindfulness, which greatly facilitated my spiritual paradigm shift. I had the advantage of having plenty of retreats, spiritual teachers and local meditation groups to choose from, and my family and friends were mostly curious, even eager, to hear about the changes I was making. So, even though I was technically entering into a minority paradigm–in terms of the socio-spiritual context in which I lived–I experienced absolutely no marginalization.

Changing my diet in my mid-twenties after developing serious autoimmune issues of the gut was another story. I was diagnosed with a significant allergy to not only gluten but *all* grains as well. Even though I was raised eating gluten-dense foods for breakfast, lunch and dinner and was vegetarian for years, I was forced to make a complete one-eighty with my eating habits, from vegetarian to paleo, practically overnight. To this day, eating out in restaurants remains extremely challenging because I am constantly faced with the possibility I will be served foods that could cause serious immune reactions. This has also meant that seemingly normal activities such as buying food at a regular grocery store, eating out with colleagues at conferences, or attending social events are complicated—or simply not an option anymore. This has led me to seek a radically different paradigm of food, nutrition and health from the one I was raised in and which is still prevalent in the world at large.

My whole relationship to food has drastically changed: where previously I could take advantage of the conveniences of dining out or grabbing something on the go, I now have to cook almost all of my own meals every single day, consuming a significant amount of time that, quite frankly, I would prefer to spend doing other things. Even the typical dating options to meet over drinks or dinner are usually off the table for me due to my food restrictions. But as much as it's a pain in the ass to function within the parameters of this laborious alternative food paradigm, which has had an extremely isolating impact on my social life, I'm actually fully on board with it. Despite the challenges implicit in the new lifestyle, I'm healthier because of the changes I've made, and I have actually healed my gut as well as the associated mental health issues I had experienced as a result of my autoimmune condition.

When comparing my experiences of changing my spiritual and culinary paradigms—despite the fact that only one of these

paradigm shifts meant facing significant and difficult consequences externally—internally my experience of making both
of these changes felt relatively similar. The thing they both
share is alignment, a deep clarity that these paradigm shifts
were necessary and undeniable regardless of the possible
external implications that accompanied their implementation.
Inwardly, I felt no vacillation, no resistance. Thus it didn't
matter to me if the world agreed with my decision or not. It
was precisely this intrinsic congruence that made the changes
feel doable, even in moments of difficulty or inconvenience.

For some people, the transition to CNM is like mine with
Buddhism: it resonates with who they feel themselves to be;
their hearts and minds experience little to no resistance to
the shift; and they may even experience little social impact
from technically being in a minority. People who experience
their shift from monogamy to nonmonogamy in this way may
then also find it difficult to understand why the transition can
be so challenging for their partners. On the flip side, people
who don't experience their shift to CNM with this level of ease
and grace may judge themselves for the difficulties they face,
taking on the story that they should be able to make the change
without difficulty, struggle or resistance. For other people,
their paradigm shift to nonmonogamy looks more like my
experience with my diet, where the choice to make the shift
wasn't something they would have necessarily chosen on their
own but, because of life circumstances, was necessary to take
on, and they remained committed to seeing it through. Over
time, they recognized how nonmonogamy was actually more
in alignment with their personal values, and they realized they
wouldn't go back to monogamy even if they could, despite the
ostensible convenience and comfort it seems to offer.

But what about the paradigms that feel harder to get on
board with internally? For example, practically every time I
start shaving my legs in the shower, I am painfully reminded of
how patriarchy has influenced my perception of my own body,
making me judge my own legs as prettier when shaved than in

their natural, hairful state. Why, after so much conscious effort to deconstruct the expectations of capitalist beauty culture, and after so many books and courses on how to love my body no matter what it looks like, do I still struggle with my body image? From over-exercising to undereating, I have, at times, literally done myself harm in the name of being thin. Even though I conceptually know that beauty is subjective, socially constructed and ever-changing throughout history, I have nevertheless internalized the false belief that, as a white, cisgender woman, I am supposed to look a certain way. And if I don't, my attractiveness, value, lovability, worthiness and womanliness are all called into question. When the inner voice of the body critic kicks up, it's like a virus taking over my mind, getting me to think and behave in ways that are actually harmful to myself.

Over the past two decades, I have come a long way, but the shift into full body positivity is still very much a work in progress. Compared with other paradigmatic shifts I've made, this one feels glacial, and beyond my capacity to just hurry along. Thankfully, I am no longer imprisoned the same ways I used to be, and I can see the old paradigm for what it is and relate to it differently. However, it would be a lie to say I no longer feel or experience the very real and concrete impacts of those narratives on my sense of self. Despite my lucid recognition of its fallacy and all my best efforts to undo my attachment to the story that I need to look a certain way in order to be worthy, at times, I still fall under its spell. The spell of a paradigm I am actively resisting.

Similarly, for many of us the integration of consensual nonmonogamy into our relational lives is not a quick, easy or pain-free process. Whether pursuing CNM as an orientation, as an experiment, or for philosophical reasons, we can still experience significant resistance and difficulty as we detox from the deeply ingrained ideas of monogamy that continue to linger in our consciousnesses. Regardless of whether you are new to open relating or have been polyamorous for years, sometimes it can feel as though you're trying to let go of a paradigm that doesn't want to let go of you! When you add the moral judgments of a puritanical, monogamous culture or the negative opinions and potential rejection of friends and loved ones, it can become extremely challenging to fully embrace and embody consensual nonmonogamy in the ways you really want to.

New Paradigm as a Catalyst

New paradigms not only serve as the conceptual frameworks for new experiences; they also give us an important contrast against which we can better understand our own journey as individuals. When functioning within a certain paradigm, we are simply oblivious to many aspects of it. Often, we can recognize its shortcomings only by stepping outside of it. New paradigms act like gateways to things that were previously unavailable, and by experiencing the novel opportunities afforded by them, we can more clearly see the ways old paradigms limited our sense of what was possible. By recognizing what didn't work for us in a previous paradigm, we can get much more clarity about what we want for ourselves now and for our future. Therefore, as you deepen your relationship to CNM, you are simultaneously given the opportunity to see the potential for new, more fulfilling ways of relating, while also being forced to confront what hasn't worked up to this point.

In this sense, embracing a nonmonogamous paradigm can be a powerful catalyst for change that requires partners to both learn new things and address old, dysfunctional patterns of behavior. The stark contrast between a monogamous paradigm and a nonmonogamous one can expose a variety of issues that were either not a problem in the monogamous context or were there, but simply masked by the structure of monogamy. What worked to keep a relationship functional in monogamy is often insufficient to keep relationships healthy and functional in nonmonogamy. The greater degree of relational complexity means you have to increase your communication skills, emotional intelligence, STI awareness, relationship to time management and ability to handle conflict, among other things.

It is precisely this difference in complexity, along with the subsequent need to develop new skills to handle it, that represents both one of the most compelling gifts *and* challenges of CNM. As we experience the increased complexity of managing multiple intimate relationships at the same time, we are simultaneously brought face to face with new and exciting aspects of our relational selves, as well as painful and uncomfortable realizations about the places where we still have a lot to learn. In my work with clients, these difficult places most often have their roots in the lingering tenets of a monogamous paradigm, which typically only come to light in the context of nonmonogamous relationships.

Many individuals are already well aware of the dominant influence of monogamy and have been actively working to deconstruct it and disentangle themselves from it for quite some time. Those who practice nonhierarchical styles of CNM, including solo polyamory or relationship anarchy, are most likely very aware of the ways a couple-centric perspective can infiltrate the dynamics of their relationships. For them, the challenges that arise are often not a result of making a new paradigm shift per se, but rather, are the secondary effects of dating someone who is still in a process of monogamous detox (or whose partners are). In situations such as these, the direct impact on you may be more related to the need for holding space for one of your partners or metamours as they grapple with the withdrawal symptoms of a lifetime of monogamous social conditioning.

Support for Making the Nonmonogamous Paradigm Shift

The rest of this chapter focuses on some concepts, contemplations and exercises to support you in making the nonmonogamous paradigm shift. Some experiences will speak more to people who are newer to CNM, but what I have found is that these exercises can be relevant to people who have been practicing CNM for years but now find themselves in new CNM transitions. These can include changing the style of CNM that you or your partners are practicing, changing your configuration from a couple to a triad or a quad (or the reverse), introducing more commitment, prioritization, rules, decision-making power or nesting into a relationship, de-escalating a relationship, or even dating people who are relatively new to CNM. Chapter 2 offers even more ideas and practices to support you when troubleshooting larger resistance to the transition from monogamy to CNM.

Based on what has been discussed in this chapter, here are some questions to consider:

Paradigms
- What paradigms were you born into?
- What different paradigms are you situated in today?
- How have these different paradigms shaped your understanding of yourself?
- How have these different paradigms shaped your understanding of love, romance and sex?

Paradigm Shifts
- What paradigm shifts have you made in your life?
- What factors or conditions made these paradigm shifts easier or more difficult for you?
- Did you gain certain skills, capacities or perspectives in those paradigm shifts that you can apply to your CNM paradigm shift?
- What brought you to the paradigm of nonmonogamy?
- In your opinion, what are the benefits of the monogamous paradigm?
- What are the limits or costs of the monogamous paradigm?

- What do you see as the benefits of a nonmonogamous paradigm?
- What are the limits or costs of a nonmonogamous paradigm?

Paradigms as a Catalyst
- In either learning about or practicing a nonmonogamous paradigm, what has it catalyzed for you and
  your relationships?
- What things have become better for you, and what has
  become harder?
- If you opened up from a monogamous relationship, how
  has your partner's relative ease or difficulty with this shift
  impacted you? And your relationship?
- If you opened up from a monogamous relationship,
  how has your relative ease or difficulty with this shift
  impacted your partner? And your relationship?

Consenting to Consensual Nonmonogamy

As many people already know, *non*consensual nonmonogamy
has the power to break up families, destroy relationships and
ruin lives. Even though some relationships are absolutely able
to recover from affairs, it is also completely understandable
when this type of betrayal and broken trust are beyond repair.
While it may seem obvious to say that if you or your partner
are pursuing nonmonogamy, everyone needs to consent to it, I
actually come across a surprising number of situations where
full and explicit consent is missing among partners. In cases
like these, what I typically see is that one partner is excitedly
nudging a relationship into nonmonogamy, or a new style of
nonmonogamy, while another individual is resistant or still on
the fence about making the change. In this sense, the reluctant
partner has actually not given their full consent, and is potentially
being pressured—or coerced—into jumping from one paradigm to

another. Because of the enormity of the shift from a monogamous paradigm to a nonmonogamous one, I find it essential that people first connect with their own "yes," on their own terms, before committing to this process. Far too often, unilateral decisions are made for the relationship by an overeager partner who has taken a "maybe," a hesitant "yes," or tentative acquiescence as permission to start their explorations with other people. This kind of "consent" ends up creating a tremendous amount of emotional damage that must later get cleaned up.

I learned from Zach Budd, clinical social worker, sexual educator and consent advocate, about the idea of having a "hell yes!" as a primary prerequisite to true consent. As a response to the prevalence of rape culture, consent culture has arisen to assert and normalize the act of asking for consent. It is a deliberate attempt to recognize and empower the individual's unconditional right to say no to anything that feels out of alignment with what they want for themselves. With consent, the autonomous and sovereign ownership of our body is respected, which applies not only to sexual activity but to any kind of relational behavior. In the workshop I attended, Zach offered the acronym INVEST to capture his five pillars of consent: informed, voluntary, enthusiastic, specific and timed (as in limited to a defined time frame).

In particular, it was the *enthusiastic* part that stood out to me. In an interview I conducted with Zach for this book, he emphasized how consent activists believe the old standby of "no means no" is not sufficient to ensure true consent. This is partly because certain circumstances, such as being under the influence of substances, in subspace* or dissociated due to a trauma trigger, can alter our ability to give full consent with our words. Also, many people struggle with vocalizing a confident "no," even if they are clearly saying no with their

---

* *Subspace* refers to the trancelike state experienced by some people in a submissive or bottoming role during BDSM play.

body language or using different words to communicate their no. Therefore, consent culture raises the bar and brings more nuance to this by introducing the idea that anything short of, in Zach's words, a "hell yes!" is actually a no. If your answer to whether or not you want to do something with a partner is some variation of "I'm not sure," "maybe" or "I gotta think about it," then for right now, it's a no. In the same way, a hesitant "yes," "kind of" or "possibly" are all also no as well. Essentially, until someone can get to an enthusiastic "hell yes!" on their own, it's a no. The clarity in this advice is powerful because it emboldens people to give themselves permission to say no if they're not 100% on board with something.

The consent culture framework that Zach and others promote rightly cautions us to be aware of the ways we unwittingly give away our power and our voice in relationships and encourages us to take back the responsibility for setting clear boundaries with others in or out of the bedroom. Learning the importance of having a "hell yes!" before agreeing to anything not only greatly enhances our ability to truly enjoy ourselves but also means our partners can really trust that we want to be doing whatever it is we're doing. When I introduce this concept of a "hell yes!" to partners who are struggling with things like power imbalances, making clear boundaries or having issues around sexual satisfaction, the positive results are typically quite notable. So many of us have been taught to undermine our own sense of what we really need and want in a relationship and, unfortunately, have learned to make compromises or yield to our partners in ways that ultimately are not sustainable or healthy.

However, like any helpful or useful piece of advice, the idea of enthusiastic consent can also, unfortunately, get misused and weaponized. I've seen people use this idea of having an enthusiastic yes as a standard they hold over their partners' heads, expecting them to have an unconditional "hell yes!" to everything they want, no matter what. In some situations, hesitant partners are initially willing to try new or different aspects of nonmonogamy, but for various reasons are still not emotionally enthusiastic about it. Instead of being understanding or even grateful that their partner is at least doing their best to get on board with it, the eager person uses the idea of having an enthusiastic "hell yes!" against their partner and accuses them of being unsupportive, not having enough compersion or not being "poly enough." On the flip side, I've also seen cases where partners repeatedly dig in their heels and prevent the process of opening up from happening, or continuing, because they claim their partner shouldn't do anything for which they themselves are not saying "hell yes!" In such cases, the idea of a "hell yes!" is either being misused as a form of coercion or as an avoidance tactic. In either case, it is not appropriate or helpful to take a concept like the emphatic yes that was originally designed to be connective or supportive and use it as emotional leverage against a partner.

What, then, are we to do when not everyone is enthusiastically on board with CNM? What about all those folks who don't feel a "hell yes!" to nonmonogamy? Those who did not seek out nonmonogamy but are being asked or dragged into it by a partner and are more of a "maybe," "sort of" or "I'm not so sure"? What about those individuals who feel a thousand miles away from getting to a clear or effortless yes? Maybe they have a job that could be compromised if their nonmonogamous status were revealed, or have loved ones who would reject them and their decision. Maybe they have cultural or religious beliefs that make this paradigm shift harder to fully embrace. Or maybe they weren't the one to initiate nonmonogamy, but the fear of losing their partner meant they're reluctantly willing to give it a try.

This question of what to do when a partner has ambivalence regarding CNM is not just relevant to people at the beginning of their journey. I have had numerous clients, with years of experience with CNM, come to me with versions of this very same issue. For example, after years of living in the stability of a hierarchical, CNM primary relationship, one partner suddenly announced her desire to start practicing relationship anarchy, catching her nesting partner of 10 years completely off guard and sending him into an anxious downward spiral. Another individual who had been part of a relatively happy and secure triad was faced with his other two partners wanting to have a child together, which felt extremely overwhelming and threatening to his attachment with both of his partners. In other situations, I have seen individuals move new partners into shared living spaces where the original nesting partner(s) were less than thrilled about the new arrival. And I have also dealt with the fallout from people wanting to date individuals within the community or friend group of one of their partners. In each of these scenarios, the common thread is that someone makes—or wants to make—a decision that could dramatically alter the dynamic of a preexisting CNM relationship and one or more partners responds with resistance and trepidation.

Ideally, everyone involved in the decision to open a relationship or initiate changes in a preexisting CNM relationship would have a resounding and enthusiastic "hell yes!" However, in cases where one partner still has reservations about the choice, I have recognized the importance of that partner finding their "yes to consenting" or "yes for now." While I consistently coach my clients to embrace the concept of having an enthusiastic "hell yes!" in regards to sex and to the nonsexual acts of service they offer their partners, when it comes to embracing the shift to living nonmonogamously, the baseline requirement has some nuance to it. If a couple holds the expectation that all partners involved have to have a "hell yes!" in the face of going nonmonogamous, especially in the beginning, this can set them up for disappointment and failure. In this type of situation, what we need to move forward is enough openness to explore and see how things play out. This is also the case in preexisting CNM relationships where one or more partners are ambivalent about a potential change in their dynamic.

Generally speaking, when we truly want something, we're willing to endure the hardships that accompany it. However, there are also numerous times in our lives when, because of another commitment—be it to a partner, child, work or significant personal goal—we are willing to do things we're not 100% excited about or potentially wouldn't have decided to do on our own. We accept taking on the inconveniences and discomforts associated with the decision because we know it's important to the relationship or goal that we value. Perhaps there is no direct payoff for us, but we recognize the benefit the decision has for the relationship, and thus, for us, it's worth it. This is often the starting point for many partners who would not have chosen nonmonogamy on their own. They love their partner so much they're willing to try it, even in the face of uncertainty and apprehension. In cases like these, the important thing is that the choice be conscious, clear and uncoerced.

When we agree to either opening up our relationship or making a certain transition in a current CNM relationship, we have to be able to articulate *why* we wanted to take this journey in the first place. One of the most important things that can support you in moments of difficulty is your capacity to consciously reconnect with your reasons for wanting—or being willing—to explore CNM. If changing a paradigm is as arduous as I've described, you have to have a good answer to the question of why on earth you would want to take something like this on. You have to be very clear about *why* you want it, or are willing to explore it. This is the first step: making a conscious and well-thought-out examination of whether or not this is really something you feel on board with, and why. As many have already discovered, CNM can throw a lot of curveballs at you, and when the shit starts to hit the fan, it can be vital to remember exactly why you decided to jump into this process. In the hardest moments, you have to remember that you made a choice to be where you are and, as much as it may seem like it, you are not a victim of the circumstances.

Explicitly articulating the why of our decision to shift our paradigm to nonmonogamy or get on board with a significant change in a current CNM relationship is an important step to anchoring the right frame of mind that I mentioned earlier. It is also a vital part of embracing the commitment to this shift. This step is particularly useful for those who still haven't arrived at their "hell yes!" While the enthusiasm may still be lagging, you must at least have explicit consent to move forward. The willingness to explore CNM or make a big change in a preexisting relationship has to be mutual and clearly stated among partners before initiating the process. Personally, I like to revisit this exercise every so often, because I find that my why for practicing CNM changes over time. In the process of updating my reasons for wanting to continue practicing CNM, I feel a renewed commitment to my relationships and a deepening of the connection with my partners.

EXERCISE   Journaling on Your Own Why

Take the time to write out the different reasons why you are consenting to nonmonogamy. Some points to consider are:

- What benefits do you see it offering you? What benefits has it already offered you?
- What benefits will/does CNM offer your current or future partner(s)?
- What benefits will/does it bring to your relationship(s)?
- If you have been practicing CNM, has your why for doing CNM changed? If so, how?

After you get more clear on your reasons for practicing CNM, you can now focus more on the specifics of *what* exactly you are consenting to. Just because you're nonmonogamous doesn't mean you have to be up for everything under the sun that would be classified as nonmonogamous. For example, many people consent to their partners having other romantic and sexual partners, but this does not mean they have to also consent to seeing or hearing their partners have sex with other people. Other people feel the complete opposite, where they can enthusiastically consent to romance or sexual play as a group experience with their partners, but need more time before they have romantic or sexual experiences separate from their current partners.

Temporary CNM Vessels for CNM Transitions

In *The Polysecure Workbook* (2022), I describe how the radical changes that accompany trying CNM for the first time can initially be too much for some people. I also talked about how for those making big shifts in their current CNM relationships, such as going from a form of hierarchical polyamory to something like nonhierarchical polyamory or relationship anarchy, the transition can provoke a state of crisis and overwhelm. Challenging the tenets of a monogamous paradigm or confronting the lingering effects of couple centricity in your existing relationships can be extremely destabilizing. These kinds of changes can leave you grappling with elevated levels of attachment insecurity, which in turn, can make getting to your "hell yes!" seem very difficult. In cases like these, it's wise to have a way of giving your nervous system a chance to catch up and integrate the new experiences.

One practical strategy for giving your beleaguered nervous system a much-needed breather is by creating a temporary vessel in which you can slow down your relational explorations and take the time to get your feet back under you. A temporary vessel is an agreement between partners in which one or more people in a particular relationship or relationships intentionally stops pursuing new relationships for a limited period. Some of these vessels are more relevant and useful for couples who are new to being open and struggling with the transition to CNM, while others are more helpful to people who have already been practicing CNM for some time, but need a special container to manage and integrate new relational circumstances and arrangements. There are even vessels for individuals who are not currently in any romantic or intimate partnerships but want to make space for their own personal needs.

While it's reasonable to expect some level of discomfort when trying out new things, creating some type of temporary vessel can help you move forward without pushing beyond what your nervous system can legitimately handle. There are many times when CNM will require you to bend, but it should not cause you to break. Similar to the need for training wheels when first learning to ride a bike or using crutches after an injury, the process of creating a temporary vessel can help partners slow down and hopefully reduce some pain and suffering along the way. The concept of a temporary vessel can also be helpful for people who have just experienced some kind of major life event such as the death of a loved one, the birth of a child, a career change or a move to a new place. These kinds of experiences can create emotional upheaval and instability that make it necessary to simplify things and reduce relational complexity. For example, some partnerships will deliberately opt for a period of polyfidelity, where no new partners are added to the current CNM configuration due to an intensive period of grief or childrearing. Also, some solo poly people or people who are currently unpartnered may create a vessel for themselves, limiting their CNM explorations or interactions with partners during times when they need to focus on their health, education or a significant life transition. The important thing is that whatever vessel you create, it should be tailored to meet the needs of your particular relationship(s).

Here are some examples of different vessels that I've seen clients try. The first two in particular are more geared towards couples and offer practical ways of gradually dipping your toes into the uncertain waters of open relating by seeing how things go before plunging headfirst into fully committed relationships with other people. This gives couples the opportunity to have new experiences within the container of a highly structured framework that allows them to assess the impact of those experiences and decide whether to proceed with their explorations. The third vessel is for partners who for various reasons feel the need to create a bubble of exclusivity around their relationship for a time. The fourth vessel is particularly for people in preexisting nonmonogamous relationship structures. And finally, the last vessel can be applied to any relationship configuration, regardless of how many people there are.

- A staggered approach to dating others: One partner will start dating other people for a specific amount of time before their partner also begins seeing other people. Typically, what happens in these situations is that at the end of the allotted time frame, the original partners talk about how things have been for each other and then decide how to proceed.

- An experimental period of partial nonmonogamy: Partners pick a period of several months during which they agree to explore certain types of open experiences, whether romantic or purely sexual, that they engage in both together or separately, and that initially feel safe or less threatening. Examples of things that people do in this kind of vessel include attending play parties or other kinds of group-centered, sex-positive events, participating in CNM meetups, creating profiles and beginning to meet people on dating apps, and going to conferences and festivals that are geared towards CNM audiences. At the end of this period they reassess what worked and what didn't and then mutually figure out what additional experiences they want to include or explore.

Note that if you are going to try either of the aforementioned vessels, it's important to let the people you're exploring with know that you're either in a CNM trial period, or that you are not yet fully available for a committed relationship, so that expectations or hopes can be transparent and realistic. Also, if you are considering these options, please take the time to include in your discussions anyone who could be impacted by your decisions, so they can have genuine input into whatever process you are initiating.

- Phase of exclusivity: This refers to taking a period to be exclusive with just one partner, where neither of you are pursuing or relating to additional people in romantic or sexual ways—even through messaging or apps—in order to focus on what you need individually and together to heal and feel ready enough to move forward with dating others outside of the vessel. This could be applied equally to a couple feeling the need to return to the container of exclusivity as to people within a currently CNM partnership who have decided they need the temporary structure of this kind of vessel.

- Temporary polyfidelity: This vessel is meant to support partners who are involved in multiple relationships, i.e., situations involving more than two people, where everyone agrees to stop seeing new people or taking on new partners. All current relationships continue as they are, but the individuals in them are closed to any new partners, essentially making them polyfidelitous for a predetermined amount of time.

- Taking a pause: This is similar to the previously mentioned vessel of exclusivity in the sense that partners within a given dyad could decide to put a pause on seeking out any new relationships with other people; however, it offers more possibilities for maintaining certain aspects of other relationships, including newer connections, during the pause. For example, someone taking a pause might decide to put a hold on the more romantic or sexual dimensions of their newer relationships but still maintain the platonic, i.e., emotional or intellectual, elements of those connections. For others, taking a break or pause could mean intentionally taking some distance from certain relationships for a while, then later resuming these connections. A pause is unique in that the underlying intention is not to end any particular relationship, but merely to modify it or put it on hold while someone figures out what they need to take care of themselves and their relationships.

The vessels I have named here may or may not be right for you and your unique situation. Some things I suggest may not be possible for you, depending on how far along you are in your personal process and what your constellation of partnerships looks like at the moment. Additionally, vessels can be introduced at any point along your CNM journey, not just at the beginning. It is also important that people not make agreements they don't want to make or can't actually follow through on. Be honest about your needs and realistic with what you can offer, remembering that temporary vessels are a great way to support you in times of change and transition. Regardless of the vessel you choose, remember that its purpose is to create the space for answering what exactly you're saying yes and no to. Once you reach the end of a time set aside for a vessel, you can extend it for another amount of time, expand the parameters or conditions of the existing vessel, or simply release the vessel altogether.

I've found that partners who do well with creating a vessel and then are able to later expand beyond it typically have at least two of the following three supports in place:

- Weekly nonmonogamy check-ins together, such as the RADAR process outlined by the Multiamory podcast (multiamory.com/radar).
- Individual support from a professional to work on healing their respective attachment wounds, work through any jealousy or personal insecurities, and create more personal readiness for this process.
- Relationship coaching or therapy specifically for CNM and attachment repair.

What I have seen that does *not* work well when trying to create a vessel is when:

- People try to create a vessel to control their partners, stall the nonmonogamy process or control any potential metamours.
- People do not actually want to do CNM at all, and so no matter how many vessels you create to ease someone into the process, it's not going to work.
- Partners are not doing their individual inner work within the vessel to grow, heal, and gain the skills and capacities they need to expand beyond the vessel they created.

The last thing I want to say about vessels is that it's important to consider the feelings and experiences of everyone who could be affected by implementing a particular vessel. There are times when people create vessels without having to end preexisting relationships and other times when they do, and the latter often involves the painful process of ending relationships in which an emotional attachment has already formed. This can have a significant emotional impact on individuals who are left out of the decision-making process. If the latter is the case, make the effort to include these partners in an open and honest conversation about why you're making this particular decision. Be prepared to hold space for their emotions and sincerely acknowledge the impacts of these changes on their experience.

EXERCISE   CNM Vessel

Use the following questions and prompts to craft a vessel for yourself or for your relationships. If you are intending to create a vessel for one or more of your relationships, invite all the relevant partners to participate in this process. Take turns answering these questions, and don't rush the process. Vessels that are the most supportive and successful are usually ones that have had a few revisions along the way.

- When you read the above examples of possible vessels, which ones speak to you? Which ones don't? Why?

- If you could craft your own vessel, what would it look like and how long would it last?
- What do you think this would offer you and your relationship?
- What needs does this potential vessel meet for you?
- What are your intentions for the vessel? (State your intentions in positive language, focusing on what you want to experience, versus what you want to avoid.)
- What commitments can you make during this time to focus on your own inner work?
- What commitments can you make during this time to get support as partners?
- Who else would be affected by this vessel and how can you include and/or inform them about the vessel you are implementing?

After you and your partner or partners each share your preferred vessels, take the time to negotiate one that fits enough of what you all need and want, and then go try it out. I suggest trying it out for a shorter period, say for a week or two, to make sure that each of you feels like you can fully consent to the vessel you've created and that no one has said yes to things they don't actually want to do or may not be able to realistically follow through on. Don't forget to schedule your check-ins! After the initial two-week trial period, make any necessary changes or updates to your vessel, then agree to a longer time frame to implement it.

EXERCISE Your General Statements of Consent

Create one or two clear statements that articulate your consent to nonmonogamy. Make these statements reflective of your choice to do CNM, not anyone else's choice or reason. Even if you think you are only doing it because your partner wants to, you are still making an intentional choice to try out nonmonogamy because *you* want to stay with your partner. That's on you, not them. I would not recommend moving forward with CNM if you feel like you are being forced or manipulated into it, and, as further explored in the next chapter, you have every right to say that CNM is not for you. With that said, if you are going to move forward with it, I suggest finding the places within yourself that are consenting and willing to move forward, and make them clear to yourself and your partner.

A few examples of statements that reflect the varying expressions of consent are:

- "I really want to do this for myself!"
- "I really want to do this for us!"
- "I'm curious about this and willing to experiment."
- "I see the importance of this for my relationship, and I'm willing to give it a try."
- "Even though this may not have been my first choice, I am consenting to seeing if this can work before giving up on my current relationship."

Before moving on, I want to offer an important caveat. CNM requires a lot of transparency and trust. It can be an incredibly vulnerable and complex relational space to step into. If you are in a situation where your partner began exploring nonmonogamy without your consent (i.e., by cheating) and is now trying to recruit you, you absolutely have the right to say no and request that "affair repair" happen before moving forward into CNM. When one partner hasn't had the opportunity to say yes to opening the relationship before it happens, it is unreasonable to expect them to unquestioningly go along with it now. This is a significant violation of trust that must be addressed before any more discussions around opening up can safely continue. If a partner's hesitation around nonmonogamy stems from this kind of rupture, it must be treated differently than the situations I have just mentioned where no previous dishonesty has occurred, but one partner still feels reluctant or uncertain.

Paradigm Awareness and Deconstruction

Paradigm awareness is about making the unconscious conscious through a deliberate examination of the core elements of the paradigms that shape our way of seeing and experiencing the world. With paradigm awareness, we look not just at the vestiges of the old paradigm we are trying to shed but also at the tenets of the new one we are attempting to adopt. We bring to light and articulate the things we want to leave behind, as well as the new ways of thinking and behaving we want to integrate. It is also an opportunity to recognize the ways we have grown and changed—or continued to stay the same—over the years. For anyone facing challenges in their CNM journey, I strongly recommend undertaking the process of developing paradigm awareness and intentionally outlining the core elements of both the monogamous and nonmonogamous paradigms that influence your way of thinking and behaving in relationships.

When we first become curious about the ways we have internalized monogamous culture, it can be overwhelming because we are completely surrounded by it. We very quickly realize how thoroughly we are inundated with movies, shows, songs and social norms that constantly reinforce the monogamous ideal. While many of the beliefs and tenets of the monogamous paradigm are quite obvious, others are more subtle and harder to recognize. In order to shine a light on the more unconscious aspects of an internalized monogamous mindset, we have to examine all the taken-for-granted thoughts, behaviors and feelings associated with this worldview. Without criticizing, judging or placing blame on ourselves or anyone else, we deliberately cultivate the ability to notice all of the stories that pass through our mind about how relationships are supposed to be. As you do this practice of observing your paradigms, staying curious and open to whatever arises in your process will support you in disentangling the elements of the monogamous paradigm that continue to be problematic.

EXERCISE Monogamous Stories

The underlying values and ideas of any given paradigm are embedded in the stories we hear and tell. In the same way as we use fables as a convenient way to teach morals to children, so, too, as adults, do we rely on narratives to transmit and reinforce the values that underlie our paradigms. The following is an exercise to help you pick out and recognize which stories have shaped your monogamous worldview. You can do this as a journal exercise or use the questions as prompts for a conversation that you have with someone else.

- Growing up, what stories, anecdotes or gossip did you hear from the adults you knew about love, sex, romance, marriage and partnership?
- What did the presence or absence of these stories teach you about love, sex, romance, marriage and partnership?
- What specific lessons (whether explicit or implicit) did you learn about monogamy and nonmonogamy?
- Ask the same above questions regarding the stories you heard from movies, music, media, or friends growing up. Reflect on how these encouraged or discouraged a monogamous worldview.
- As an adult, what stories do your peers or social groups tell about love, sex, romance, marriage and partnership?
- How has this impacted your monogamous or nonmonogamous views?
- How has this impacted the choices you have made regarding, love, sex, romance, marriage and partnership?
- Next, write down the feelings that arise when you think about how these stories continue to affect your experience. Does this awareness make you mad, frustrated, or righteously indignant? Maybe you feel guilty or ashamed for continuing to find yourself in their gravitational pull.

Allow whatever comes up without making any special effort to change or do anything about it. For now, awareness is our only goal. The more energy you put into identifying the monogamous stories that still have a hold on you, the more you can start to weaken their grip. It becomes easier to start seeing them as merely stories as opposed to facts or statements about absolute reality.

EXERCISE   Creating Your Own Old and New Paradigm Chart

For this exercise, draw a line down the center of a page to create two columns. The left column will consist of the monogamous beliefs that you are deconstructing and the right side will be a list of the nonmonogamous beliefs that you are already living or currently constructing.

1.   On the left side, write out all of the monogamous beliefs you can think of. These don't have to all be ones you totally believe in, but they are the ones that nevertheless show up regularly in your field of awareness, hook you, and have probably had an impact on you and your relationships.

2.   Read through your list of monogamous beliefs. Reflect and tune in to how you feel when you read them. Do these beliefs resonate in your body? Do any feelings of shame, guilt or "should" arise? Do you relax or tense up as you read some or all of them? Do they feel like they lead you closer to or further from the partnerships or sexual expressions that you want?

3.   In the right column, write out the nonmonogamous beliefs that are a counter belief or a new updated equivalent belief from the monogamous one in the opposite column.

4.   Read through and reflect on your nonmonogamous beliefs, just as you did for the first column. Contemplate the same questions as in step two, and also pay attention to anything that's different about your experience during this second round of reflections.

Sample Paradigm Beliefs Chart

Monogamous Beliefs	Nonmonogamous Beliefs
Long-term monogamous relationships are the only "real" or legitimate relationships.	Romantic and intimate relationships can unfold in many ways. There is no one standard for love.
If you are truly in love with someone, you won't be interested in anyone else.	Love is not inherently exclusive, and can be genuinely felt and expressed in more than one relationship at a time.
You can get too close to other people; connecting with others outside of a relationship is dangerous.	Connection with others is expansive and relationship-enhancing. The more connected I feel, the more I have to offer all my partners.
My partner should be the only one who takes care of my needs for intimacy and connection, and vice versa.	It is impossible for one person to meet all of another person's needs, and having multiple, intimate connections can free us up from thinking that we have to be "everything" for each other.
The need or desire for space in a relationship means something is wrong.	Taking space for oneself and having separate experiences supports individual autonomy and can help maintain a romantic or sexual spark.
If a partner is attracted to someone else, it's because I'm not enough.	Attraction can be diverse and my or my partner's attraction to others has nothing to do with a deficiency in self or other.
Monogamy is just easier.	Some aspects of having only one partner are easier, and others are harder.

Deconstructing the Old to Make Room for the Preferred

To successfully integrate the paradigmatic beliefs with which we feel most aligned, we must create space for them by clearing out any opposing beliefs still lingering from the previous

paradigm. Because the beliefs from our old paradigms can
continue to exert a powerful influence over us, we need to
actively challenge them, reminding ourselves how they no
longer serve us. The purpose of the paradigm belief chart
is to help you further distinguish between the beliefs of the
past that you want to shed and the ones you want to integrate
into your life now. After creating your initial paradigm belief
chart, continue re-reading your monogamous belief column
to deepen your awareness of the monogamous beliefs you no
longer want to endorse or enact.

Many of these old beliefs are inherited from the culture
in which we were raised. Recognizing them as products of
our social environment versus reflections of ultimate truth
can loosen the sense that they are fixed or unchangeable.
The more we unpack the socially constructed nature of these
beliefs, the more agency we possess to choose whether or
not to uphold them. Developing this capacity to consciously
choose the beliefs we embody is at the heart of the practice
of deconstructing our old beliefs. When you encounter these
beliefs in the world, or they show up in your own inner voice as
self-judgment or criticism, challenge them by asking yourself
the following questions:

- Whose beliefs are these? Are these my beliefs or someone
  else's?
- What values or feelings are these beliefs an expression of?
- What impact do these beliefs have on me?
- What beliefs about love, partnership or sex do I want to
  align myself with?

As you continue to deconstruct the old beliefs that no longer serve you, you will also name the beliefs with which you do
resonate. As you do this, it is helpful to identify the values that
underlie your preferred beliefs. Directly connecting with the
values that are reflected in our beliefs bolsters our emotional
connection to them and strengthens our resolve to live accordingly. The more we consciously align with our preferred values,

the more sensitized we become to the moments when we fall out of that alignment. This creates a positive feedback loop where we start to pay more attention to the things we really want in life. I also recommend seeking alternative resources* that debunk some of the myths we have inherited about sex, gender and the history of monogamy. Exposing yourself to new or lesser-known science and more accurate portrayals of history can be a tremendous support in fortifying your paradigm shift.

Continuing to Internalize Your Nonmonogamous Paradigm Beliefs

After beginning the initial work of deconstructing the monogamous paradigm and identifying all the beliefs and values of CNM we want to embody, we then move on to the phase of internalization and integration. While the desire may be to rush ahead, we actually want to slow down a bit and take our time with this part of the process. We live in an increasingly impatient world where we can instantly download entirely new operating systems for our computers, talk to people on the other side of the earth in real time and even order anything we want online with the expectation it will arrive, at maximum, in two days! Who hasn't fantasized about the possibility of simply

---

* I suggest the following resources for a more in-depth exploration of common myths regarding sex, gender and monogamy: *The Myth of Monogamy* by David Barash and Judith Eve Lipton; *Sex at Dawn* by Christopher Ryan and Cacilda Jethá; *Race, Monogamy, and Other Lies They Told You* by Agustín Fuentes; *Untrue: Why Nearly Everything We Believe About Women, Lust, and Infidelity Is Wrong and How the New Science Can Set Us Free* by Wednesday Martin; *The Importance of Being Monogamous* by Sarah Carter; and *Marriage, a History: How Love Conquered Marriage* by Stephanie Coontz.

plugging a cable into the back of their heads like Neo from *The Matrix* and then proclaiming, "I know Kung Fu!"? I would love to be able to instantly learn to dance like a pro, complete a degree or speed read, or to learn another language in a matter of minutes, and yet, at least for now, some things still take time.

In shifting from one paradigm to another, there is no magic pill to bypass the steps it takes to learn new skills, rewire old patterns of emotional reactivity, embody new ways of being or change core beliefs about how relationships are supposed to be. As much as we may not like it, it just takes time, and we need to have patience. Integration only happens through repeated and sustained exposure to the ideas, principles, practices, habits, stories and experiences that make up any given paradigm. No one internalizes a new paradigm simply by reading something once or listening to a few podcasts about the subject of interest. Instead, we repeatedly gather new information, acquire knowledge, have conversations, go to conferences, attend meetups and workshops, and form new relationships. We need to immerse ourselves in the worldview we are trying to live in order for it to truly take hold in our consciousness. This consistent repetition reinforces the circuits in our brains associated with particular experiences, forming more neural connections for whatever it is we want to learn.

In neuroscience, the well-known Hebbian Theory* states that "neurons that fire together wire together," meaning our brain's neural pathways are reinforced through the same repeated actions or behaviors. The more we think, feel and encounter a certain concept or experience, the stronger the neural circuits associated with the particular stimulus becomes. This means as we expose ourselves to new material and experiences, we literally strengthen the neural pathways associated with the new information. Therefore, the key to internalizing and sustaining the changes we want to make is

---

*   See Donald Hebb, *The Organization of Behavior*.

to maintain the consistency of exposure necessary to develop these enhanced neural connections. By immersing ourselves in a nonmonogamous paradigm and the repetition of its beliefs, over time we begin to *feel* the world through the lens of the new paradigm.

Returning back to your paradigm beliefs chart, for the right hand side of the chart, rereading your more preferred paradigm beliefs is a great start. Some additional things you can do to reinforce the continued internalization of these beliefs are:

- Repeat your new beliefs often to yourself.
- Find evidence of your new beliefs in the stories of others.
- Find evidence in your own life, no matter how small, of your new beliefs.
- Visualize yourself in situations that validate your new beliefs.
- Act your new beliefs out in the world.
- Find friends and communities that share these beliefs.

Additional Supports for Making a Paradigm Shift

Aside from the above concepts and exercises, you can also use additional supports to help facilitate your paradigm shift. The following list suggests a few practices and modalities that are known to support people in changing their reactivity and subconscious or habitual thoughts and beliefs in order to leverage the conscious mind for more lasting change. Not all of the following items are for everyone, so please only consider the ones that feel right and supportive to you, as well as appropriate to your current medical or mental health conditions.

- **Meditation**: The practice of using a technique such as mindfulness or focusing the mind on a particular object, such as the breath, mantra, one's body or thoughts, in order to train the mind's attention and awareness in new ways.
- **Hypnotherapy or self-hypnosis**: Through the use of a practitioner or by oneself inducing a trance-like state

of consciousness in which a person is more responsive to
the suggestion of new thoughts, beliefs and behaviors.

- **Holotropic breathwork**: A method of breathwork
  created by Czech psychiatrist Stanislav Grof to induce
  altered states of consciousness for healing, growth and
  personal transformation.

- **Plant medicine journeys, microdosing, ketamine-
  assisted psychotherapy or MDMA-assisted psychotherapy**: The use of plant medicine, psychedelics
  or other mind-altering substances to work through
  traumas, grief, depression, anxiety and emotional
  stuckness, as well as to expand one's consciousness and
  life perspective. If you explore this route, it is extremely
  important that you work with practitioners who have the
  appropriate training, experience and safety protocols.

- **Emotional freedom technique (EFT) tapping**: A
  technique where people focus on a specific distressing
  situation, limiting thoughts or beliefs they would like
  to change while tapping with their fingers on certain
  acupressure points in order to change their emotional
  reaction and intensity.

- **Eye movement desensitization and reprocessing
  (EMDR)**: A therapy designed to facilitate the processing
  and resolution of traumatic memories and other
  adverse life experiences. It is also used to work with
  reprogramming negative beliefs and emotional triggers
  or reactivity.

Taken together, the practices and techniques presented in
this chapter offer a framework with which you can thoughtfully
and gradually retrain your nervous system to more easily manage and integrate the challenges and complexities of CNM. While
each practice offers something unique and valuable on its own,
when done in combination, they form the foundation of a very
useful skill set that will serve you throughout your journey with
CNM. One of the most important things I want to emphasize is the

value of having some kind of structured approach guiding your process. What Dave and I each find with clients in our respective practices is that, more often than not, people struggling with their relationship to CNM are shooting in the dark without resources, techniques or a coherent line of action to guide or assist them. Applying the practices offered in this section will remedy that feeling of being completely lost or overwhelmed and give much-needed direction to those still grappling with internalizing or integrating a nonmonogamous paradigm.

§

In concluding this chapter on paradigms, I just want to reiterate the importance of slowing down and anchoring yourself in the capacity to take the long view. When making the transition into CNM or changing the style of CNM that you are practicing, urgency can be one of your greatest obstacles. New things take time to come to fruition. Even though everyone is different in terms of the particular stage and phase of their CNM journey, any new situations and circumstances that arise will always require skill and patience to successfully navigate. The process of making big paradigm shifts should be approached like a marathon and not a sprint. If you are overly focused on quickly having a particular experience or are desperate to "fix" a struggling relationship with CNM, chances are you are setting yourself up for a crash-and-burn situation. Integration is a deliberate and gradual process that happens in an organic way, over time. Remember, monogamous beliefs that have been internalized over the course of a lifetime do not simply vanish because you decide to think and act differently one day. We are talking about deeply rooted thought and behavioral patterns that have been, and continue to be, reinforced by mainstream culture. It can take tremendous perseverance to undo these kinds of patterns and integrate new ones.

The people who make the biggest strides are typically the ones who are willing to slow down and work together. They recognize the importance of maintaining a collaborative approach and give each other the space to adjust and integrate each new phase of the process. Conversely, the partnerships that struggle the most are precisely the ones where someone is reluctant or unsure about making a transition while others are totally hellbent on moving as fast as possible. Within the subtext of this imbalance of wants is typically the tension between the desire for safety versus the yearning for freedom. When partners are unable to recognize the importance of prioritizing the wellbeing of the relationship over immediate personal gratification, the transitions within CNM tend to be extremely painful and destructive. This is why it's critical for partners to think in terms of paradigms, recognizing they are embarking on a much larger process of rewriting their fundamental relationship narratives together. When they see and understand the situation this way, partners can have a much more patient and compassionate view of each other, recognizing that everyone involved is actively undoing a lifetime of monogamous social conditioning.

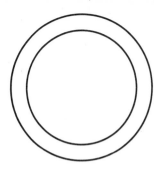

CHAPTER TWO

TROUBLESHOOTING UNCERTAINTY AND RESISTANCE TO CNM TRANSITIONS

I frequently encounter partnerships where one person is much more enthusiastic about CNM than the other. This may be a couple who are opening up their relationship, situations where a CNM individual or group begin dating someone who is new to nonmonogamy, or CNM partners navigating a change in their relationship structure, style or way of practicing CNM. While one or more partners are totally fired up and ready to get going, the other is resistant, unclear or uncertain about whether they can make the CNM changes that are being asked for, or even do CNM at all. Some people exhibit reluctance about a suggested CNM transition right from the start. Others may initially seem to be on board, but either repeatedly stall the actual start of the process, experience unmanageable emotions every time the topic is brought up, or both. Others are able to take some early, tentative steps towards the CNM transition, but then because of the overwhelm and intensity of their experiences, end up questioning whether it's even possible for them. Commonly, the reluctant or uncertain partner will do their best to try to accept their partner's nonmonogamous explorations with composure and dignity, even adopting a "fake it till you make it" approach (which sometimes can work). However, as the built-up tension of their emotional contortionism starts to take its toll, the relationship can start to experience significant blow-ups or meltdowns, and the reluctant partner may even bring up the possibility of calling the whole thing off.

One of the most frequently asked questions related to CNM resistance I hear is, how do you distinguish between the resistance that comes from trying anything hard or uncomfortable and the kind that actually indicates this is not a change you can or should make? When I am faced with a client who tells me they just don't know if they can do this, I offer them a series of assessments and exercises to support them in getting to their own clarity about whether or not they really want this for themselves, or are at least genuinely willing to give it a try. Part of what is so tricky to navigate is that when resistance to or uncertainty towards nonmonogamy is present, there's usually a lot of emotional reactivity that accompanies these feelings, and one's decision-making facilities can be compromised by all the emotional debris that gets stirred up.

Whether you choose monogamy or CNM, the decision should ideally be based on your own clarity: where you are connected with your authentic values, needs and desires versus the more reactive, resistant, judgmental, fearful or wounded parts of yourself. When these latter parts are present, they need care and attention—fast—and usually we need to deal with these parts before we are even able to access our own truth and sense of connection to what we truly want and believe is best for us. Whether you're going to say yes or no to CNM, I want your criteria to be grounded in a place of inner knowing and resonance versus fear, pressure or avoidance. My hope is that your answer will come from a clear, authentic place within you, and not a reactive one.

Over the years, I have learned that the degree of resistance or emotional reactivity exhibited by partners reluctant to practice CNM is not always an accurate indicator of whether CNM is a good fit for them. I say this because I have seen numerous instances when initially reluctant or reactive individuals identified and worked through some of the ideas presented in this chapter and later fully embraced a nonmonogamous lifestyle, or were at least able to accept or comfortably live with it. This chapter is intended to help anyone who might be struggling—or is in relationship with someone who is struggling—with resistance to making the paradigm shift into CNM, or some transition within their preexisting nonmonogamous relationship.

Permission to Be Monogamous? Granted...If That's What You Really Want

Before supporting you in the process of figuring out where your reluctance or hesitancy to CNM is coming from, it is important to level the playing field and acknowledge that both monogamy and nonmonogamy are valid relationship options. First and foremost, it is important to recognize that you absolutely have the right to be monogamous. Many people are confronted with a narrative that nonmonogamy is somehow inherently superior to monogamy, whether that message comes from proponents of nonmonogamy or from enthusiastic partners. I believe that both monogamy and nonmonogamy can be done with high levels of consciousness and intentionality, and when done in this spirit, either one can contribute to the growth and evolution of any relationship.

Wanting exclusivity with a partner does not mean you are somehow less evolved as a person, nor does having multiple partners guarantee that you are more conscious. The most important thing is that you have made a deliberate choice to be in the kind of relationship structure you are in, and you understand your own reasoning for making that choice. What is problematic is when individuals default to what others tell them is best, right or more "natural" instead of deciding for themselves what really works. This means that if, at the end of the day, someone truly feels themselves to be monogamous and wants to be in a monogamous relationship, it is ultimately in everyone's best interest for their partner to accept that person's choice and, in turn, make the choice that's right for them—even if it means losing or de-escalating the relationship.

While it might seem strange that someone could need permission to be monogamous in a culture where monogamy is dominant, I can't tell you how many people I've seen cry tears of relief after I've looked them in the eyes and reminded them they do not have to do nonmonogamy if they really don't want to. Just as monogamy is not for everyone, neither is CNM. Understandably, out of fear of losing their partner, some people try to contort themselves into being alright with nonmonogamy when in actuality, deep down, they know that it is something they absolutely don't want. Having to make a choice between the person you love and the relationship structure you need or want can tear you apart from the inside out. Additionally, the partner who eagerly wants CNM may be engaging in forms of persuasion, pressure, minimization or manipulation towards their more reluctant partner out of their own fear that their partner won't join them on this journey, and these strategies compromise their ability to hold space for a reluctant partner's valid inquiries into whether or not this is really what they want. All of this push and pull can create a lot of confusion for everyone involved, and lead to very challenging dynamics that can, at times, feel almost impossible to resolve.

If you are a more reluctant partner, my advice is to grant yourself the permission to be monogamous if that's what you really want. You should not be coaxed, bullied, guilted, dragged or threatened into nonmonogamy. Giving yourself permission to be monogamous does not mean that you will necessarily choose monogamy, but it means that you are allowing the space for your potential truth and not falling into the idea that there is something wrong with you if you do want monogamy. In long-term relationships, each partner may bring many different life changes to the table, and it is unrealistic to think that being a good partner means we must go along with anything and everything our partner initiates, especially when it comes at the cost of our own wellbeing or integrity.

Paradoxically, sometimes the permission to be monogamous actually opens up the space for you to feel safe enough to entertain CNM as an option. In this context, giving people who are struggling with nonmonogamy the permission to be monogamous can be like releasing the valve on a pressure cooker. Whether they eventually choose to go back to monogamy or not is not so much the point. What's important is merely having the momentary acceptance of this part of themselves and allowing all relationship structures to be on the table. In this space of unconditional acceptance for whatever relationship structure or style someone wants, you can better explore the possible hurdles or obstacles to trying CNM. Without the tension of having to deny various parts of themselves, they are often able to demonstrate an expanded capacity and willingness to consider new things. Before really giving up on a relationship where they have developed a deep connection and emotional attachment, most people will want to feel like they have exhausted all possibilities and given it their best shot before calling it quits.

Are You Experiencing CNM Paradigm Shock?

For some people, the difficulty they experience in CNM is related to the inevitable ups and downs that come with making any kind of significant paradigm shift, analogous to the kind of culture shock people go through when visiting other countries. People can experience "nonmonogamous paradigm shock" where they are initially disoriented, uncomfortable and uncertain about whether or not they can actually be non-monogamous. Just like the weary traveler, overcome by the newness of their host country, the newly nonmonogamous can feel homesick for the familiarity and comfort of monogamy, where they already know all the language, customs, expectations, gestures, signs and symbols of their paradigm of origin.

While certainly not enjoyable when you're in the midst of it, if you identify nonmonogamous paradigm shock as the source of your initial resistance, it can be easier to work through than some of the other issues mentioned in this chapter. With time and experience, you will become familiar with the terrain, and eventually it will be much easier to acclimate and adapt to the new paradigm. Please be gentle with yourself and your partners and allow the time and space necessary to ease into the new reality. The following are some tips for working through nonmonogamous paradigm shock.

- Know that acclimating to a new paradigm takes time, and usually only comes with repeated experiences with people and communities who are anchored in this paradigm.
- Learn as much as you can about the new and different customs and concepts of this paradigm.*
- Keep an open and curious mind.
- Remember that you don't ultimately have to do anything you don't want to.
- Don't compare yourself or your journey to others.
- Be prepared to make mistakes and learn from them.
- Make sure you're engaging in self care and stress management. The more you're able to engage with the

---

*   It is important to note that nonmonogamy is not a singular culture. The umbrella of nonmonogamy includes many subcultures in which people practice, gather and relate to each other in nonmonogamous ways.

new paradigm while maintaining personal space for resting and integrating your experiences, the faster you'll be able to adjust.

- When you feel "homesick," pause to acknowledge and allow it, without shame or embarrassment, but also without allowing that feeling to completely halt your forward momentum.
- Think of past situations when you experienced a change in your life circumstances that was not immediately an easy shift for you, such as work, school, going to another country, moving to a new place, etc., and recall how you got through that situation. Apply any skills or ideas you used in those particular situations towards supporting you now in this current transition.

Resistance to the Change

Part of the challenge of being human is that we are constantly subject to change and impermanence. Despite all our grandest efforts to create a world where we have maximum control over our lives and our environment, we still have to grapple with some degree of uncertainty. One of the places where change happens frequently is in the realm of interpersonal relationships. When we're confronted with big changes in our intimate relationships, often the only thing we have control over is how we respond. We can embrace the change and be open to the new, or we can resist and hold on to what was. The kicker is that we are programmed to get comfortable in our relationships. We get very used to the relative safety that attachment affords us, and we start to cling to the predictability implicit in the relationship structure we have constructed over time. It's understandable, then, why so many of us would feel resistance to welcoming in a set of circumstances that could threaten all that security we've created with our partners.

However, when a partner reveals they want to open up a relationship or change the current CNM circumstances that you have been in, the irreversible gears of change have already been set into motion. The relationship that existed before this declaration is now indelibly transformed and will forever be different moving forward. With that said, however, even though you weren't the architect of this change, you still have a lot of agency in terms of how you respond.

One option, of course, is to deny the change, shut down your partner's request, and hope they'll see the error of their ways and simply go back to business as usual. I've seen this happen plenty of times. Typically what happens in this scenario is one of two things, neither of which is good. Either the person who is initially interested in CNM or the one initiating the CNM change will move forward with their exploration on their own. In doing so, they may hurt their partner, end the relationship or begin cheating. Or they will repress their desire in order to appease their partner, in which case the desire goes underground, becomes toxic and eventually poisons the relationship.

Another option is to recognize the change they want is not for you and decide to leave the relationship—obviously not an easy choice to make, but a legitimate one nonetheless. Finally, you could accept the invitation to give your partner's suggestion a try and embark on the road of discovery together, deciding to embrace the uncertainty implied in this decision. The risk could bring you closer, or it could drive you apart. Whatever you decide to do, it's important to remember that even if we don't like the choices presented to us, it's entirely our decision how we respond and choose to move forward.

One of my clients initially reached out to me in distress because he and his wife were practicing polyamory and he was having a very difficult time with it. His anxiety was through the roof, and at first we identified the potential roots of his struggle as related to his insecure attachment history, issues of self-worth in partnership and his conservative, religious upbringing, which made polyamory seem sinful. As we made our way through these obstacles, he experienced notice-able shifts in his ability to function more securely with his partner, released his dependence on his wife for emotional self-regulation, and even came to accept polyamory, not as a sin or even denial of his religious beliefs, but rather as a legitimate expression of his religious values around love and relationships.

Yet even with all this progress, he still experienced signif-icant anxiety in response to his polyamorous experiences, so I guided him through a somatic process to identify any lingering anxiety and resistance, which eventually targeted the answer for him. It was change itself! He admitted that he just didn't like change, no matter what it was. It scared him, and it was uncomfortable. While he wanted him and his wife to move forward with CNM and embrace this new paradigm of rela-tionship, he didn't actually want the relationship with her to change at all. He playfully asked, "Can't we just do polyamory without anything having to actually change?" In a word, no.

What this client was really wanting was that transitioning to CNM would be simply like building a new addition to his house. He liked his house and didn't actually want to change its original structure—he just wanted to expand it a bit. He wanted a little more room to stretch out, to have more space to himself when things felt tight, maybe a nook he could call his own when he wasn't in the mood to hang out with the people he sees every day. He wanted something that added value to the existing structure without taking anything away from it. If only it were that simple! Unfortunately, transitioning to nonmonogamy is not just an add-on to the original relation-ship, where everything gets to stay just as it is, but with the perk of more partners. Instead, it is a complete overhaul of the relational foundation upon which your current relation-ship stands.

Making the transition to CNM means exposing and reex-amining the very concrete slabs, support beams, crawl spaces and even septic tank of your current relationship. Sometimes it can even mean an outright demolition of the current structure. Either way, it's a significant deconstruction of the monogamous way of relating that has existed up till now. As new people enter our lives, and the lives of our partners, they exponentially change our reality in ways that are completely unpredictable. For this to really work, we have to let go of the monogamous structures that have maintained our preexisting relationship and allow ourselves, and our partners, to be changed by the new relationships. Changing your relationship paradigm from monogamy to nonmonogamy means that you, your partner and, above all, your current relationship are going to change.

Naturally, when you're first opening up, you won't want to lose certain aspects of your relationship. Like special pieces of furniture or art from the old place that still have sentimental value, you'll want to bring elements of the current relationship along with you. You have a shared history, time, memories, rituals, routines and the uniqueness of a connection that is irreplaceable, and there's nothing wrong with holding onto or honoring these parts of the original relationship. But to successfully make the paradigm shift to nonmonogamy, we have to be willing and able to embrace the big, structural changes that inevitably come with opening up a relationship. If we are resistant to these changes, trying to keep things as they were, we will make the transition much more difficult, and we can actually begin to undermine, even damage, the very relationship we're so desperate to keep. The counterintuitive thing about resisting change is that the resistance itself often becomes the very force that hastens the outcome we originally wanted to avoid, often at the cost of a lot of unnecessary hardship or collateral damage along the way.

The concept highlighted in the analogy of the house not only applies to married couples opening up their relationship, but also to established CNM relationships. As new partnerships form with people in preexisting CNM relationships or polycules, those new partners, too, should not be expected to just fit right into the CNM structure that was there before they arrived. While it's important that new partners acknowledge and respect the unique configuration of relationships they are connecting up with, with all its particular rituals and routines, there also needs to be space for new people to influence the system, as well.

Returning to my client, the work we did together focused on updating his relationship to change. We looked at the numerous difficult and sudden changes of his past that had led to the core belief that *change,* in and of itself, was bad, dangerous and to be avoided at all costs. We did the paradigm exercise from chapter one to unpack his beliefs about change, and then figured out what new beliefs he wanted to embody. I later guided him through visualizations of the potential changes that felt particularly threatening and led him to imagine that, instead of fleeing those changes, he embraced them and allowed them to show him new possibilities. We also worked on the concept of surrender and the importance of developing more internal security and safety so that he could gracefully allow for his partner's experiences instead of trying to anxiously control her. As he reprogrammed his relationship to change, he was eventually able to identify himself not as a victim of life's circumstances or the choices of others, but rather as an active participant and co-creator of his own life.

The two points I want to leave you with from this discussion on change are:

1. Shifting our paradigms from monogamy to nonmonogamy usually means big changes for our current
   relationships. We cannot realistically expect that
   including new people in our lives will be as easy as
   putting a spare bedroom on an already existing house,
   or that our current relationships will stay essentially as
   they are. For nonmonogamy to work, it's important to
   allow your relationships to grow and change in the ways
   necessary to adapt to a new paradigm of relationship, sex

and love, and this may include significant growing pains along the way.

2. By its very nature, monogamy creates a buffer between couples and certain kinds of relational uncertainty and change. The exclusivity and predictability that monogamy provides offers many the luxury of not having to deal with the discomfort of radical and sometimes difficult changes in their relationships. This kind of conditioning can mean we're emotionally unprepared to handle the much more fluid dynamics of nonmonogamy. A big part of the process of integrating nonmonogamy into our lives means intentionally learning how to accept and embrace the changes that inevitably occur when we openly relate. Before making the leap into CNM, it's definitely a good idea to ask yourself about your relationship to change itself and to seek the skills and support to better navigate higher levels of uncertainty.

What If You Don't Believe CNM Is Really Possible?

Sometimes the hesitancy or resistance towards CNM comes from the belief that it's simply not possible, or that it may be possible for everyone else, but not for you. In such cases, our previous constructs and paradigms have put a ceiling on our imagination for what could be, and we are in disbelief that we could either find someone else who could find us attractive, or, on the flipside, we can't envision finding someone else as attractive or compatible as our current partner. The prevalence of this kind of scarcity mentality is interesting, considering we live on a planet with almost eight billion people. Nonetheless, I have seen over and over and over again how individuals of all different body types, genders, sexual orientations, kinkiness, vanilla-ness, neurodivergence, ablebodiedness, race, class, quirkiness, and obscure hobbies or musical tastes have found each other and been inextricably drawn to connect. Granted, it could take longer than you'd like to find them, or you may have to drive farther than you'd prefer to see them, but one thing CNM has shown me time and time again is that there is not just someone for everyone, but actually multiple someones for everyone. This is part of the true beauty and magic of non-monogamy: the possibility of finding other people in the world who share similar interests, values and ways of being, even when they seem so specific or unique to your experience, and having the freedom to make special connections with them.

The other common theme I encounter is the disbelief that a partner could have a deep connection or amazing sex with someone else and then still love and desire us in the same way as before. Similarly, others fear the possibility of falling in love with someone else and, as a result, losing interest in their current partner. While the previous examples had more to do with individual insecurities around attractiveness or doubts about finding likeminded people, I see all of these particular doubts and concerns as having their roots in the monogamous paradigm. Implicit in these fears is the idea that love is finite, meaning once you've found it, you're unlikely to find it again. (The old "lightning never strikes twice" story.) A similar notion is that giving love or affection to new partners means there is less for preexisting partners. Another idea related to this type of reasoning is that you can only have feelings for one person at a time. Therefore if you have feelings for another person then, by default, your feelings for me have to be diminished. Another persistent idea is that love is a contest between the "best" of all options. This creates the precarious sensation that the relationship is constantly at risk, because the possibility of finding someone prettier, sexier, smarter, more successful or simply "better" always looms on the horizon. This is where unpacking and deconstructing the beliefs from the monogamous paradigm around the idea of *specialness* is particularly important.

Initially, it could seem as though these kinds of monogamy-induced fears about our lovability and specialness are only the concern of the uninitiated. However, as many of my CNM-experienced clients will testify, these very same issues can show up for seasoned partners as well. Also, their prevalence is not limited to only particular demographics of people, such as cisgender heterosexuals. For instance, I have seen queer partners, with years of CNM experience under their belts, emotionally unravel when their primary partner begins a new relationship with someone who potentially seems younger, smarter, funnier, more successful or more attractive. I have also known self-proclaimed relationship anarchists who fell into fits of rageful jealousy because they felt like one of their partners was "more in love" with a different partner. In fact, I have seen some version of each of these monocentric narratives turn up in just about every kind of relationship style, structure or orientation you can imagine. Their pervasiveness and tenacity cannot be underestimated, and to really deal with them in an effective way, we must recognize and understand their monogamous origins.

It's fascinating to observe how this belief that love and specialness can only be shared between two people typically only applies to romantic love. For example, if you have more than one child, would you ever say the decision to have a second child was based on the feeling that the first one was somehow deficient or not enough? Did having the second child diminish your love for the first? I have yet to hear someone say yes to these questions—at least openly. The answer I typically hear to these questions is that people fully and unquestionably loved their first child, whom they saw as whole and complete, but also wanted to expand their family in general. The same logic can be applied to having multiple pets, siblings, friends, family members, and even favorite foods, musicians or sexual positions. Part of the re-identification process that we go through in the transition to nonmonogamy is the realization that, as humans, we are not singular or mono-amorous but rather capable of a multiplicity of loves, whether romantic, platonic or culinary.

And yet, even with all that said, many people still feel on a deep, fundamental level that the presence of more romantic partners in their relational field undeniably means a downgrade in terms of the love they will be able to give or receive. The fusion of the commercialization of romanticism with the monocentric idea of love as finite that we have in Western culture has created the deep-seated impression that romantic love is a limited resource to be coveted, clung to and protected. Even when we are adamantly opposed intellectually to this kind of approach to romantic love, our unconscious, collective programming jerks our nervous systems into alarm when we think about our access to it becoming "compromised." Left to their own devices, these powerful narratives about the scarcity of love will continue to run the show, and we will never truly believe that CNM is a legitimate or viable possibility for us.

Apart from actively dismantling our psyche's attachment to monogamous ideas of romantic love, quite honestly the most effective antidote to the belief that CNM is impossible is firsthand experience. Simply put, many people need to experience it to believe it. Until you've actually felt the rush of butterflies and hormones that comes from meeting someone new, had the chance to explore the connection—maybe even having sex with them—and then returned home to find you're still totally interested in and in love with your preexisting partner, you'll probably still grapple with some kind of doubt about the viability of CNM. Many times it is not until the reluctant partner has had positive dating experiences with other people that they are truly able to accept that CNM is actually possible for them, allowing them to also finally trust that their partner still wants to be with them after their partner has been with someone else.

Which Parts of You Are Struggling with CNM?

When I hear people describe being conflicted about CNM, vac-
illating between wanting to do it and absolutely despising it, I
ask, which parts of you don't want this? The question of which
"parts" of a person are actively resisting CNM comes from the
therapeutic modalities of inner parts work, such as Internal
Family Systems, narrative therapy and relational life therapy.
These unique systems of therapy acknowledge that we all have
different parts within us that can have very different wants,
needs, trauma histories, adaptive strategies, distinct personalities and, in this case, potential resistance to CNM. Our inner
parts can be younger, more childlike parts; they can be parts of
us that have been disowned or disallowed (i.e., sexual, creative,
sad or adventurous parts); or they can be very active everyday
parts that feel like our adult self, such as an inner critic part
that is trying to keep our behavior in check, or a perfectionist
part that is in the driver's seat while we are at work. Our parts
can run the gamut from healthy, helpful and highly adaptive to
unhealthy, unhelpful and highly maladaptive. Getting to know
our parts is a powerful way to heal, integrate and gain more
agency in how we respond to the challenges and joys of life.

Given the prevalence of relational trauma in both childhood and adulthood, it's totally understandable that you could
have wounded parts of yourself that are terrified of CNM or
stubbornly stamping their feet at the "injustice" of a partner's
CNM exploits, or that new transitions within your already
existing CNM relationships can activate your inner parts—be
it inner-child parts that want love and attention, awkward
adolescent parts that want to be accepted, or adult parts that
want to have as much agency or control as they can get.

The following are the steps I typically use when guiding
clients through the process of working with their different
inner parts. While this kind of work is probably most effective
when done with a trained professional, I want to give you the
framework of the practice so you can get a taste of the process

and, hopefully, begin to get a clearer sense of where your resistance is coming from. This section is one of my favorites because it offers a deeper level of inner work to support you in identifying and moving through any resistance.

Identifying the Parts That Are Reacting to CNM

The first step is to make a list of all the parts of you that could be strongly resisting or reacting to CNM. For some, it's possible that you already have a good sense of what those parts are, such as the part that has been rejected in previous relationships, or the part that saw your mom's deep wounding after discovering your father's infidelity. If nothing comes immediately to mind, you can also think about recent situations in which nonmonogamy was a trigger and you felt a contraction, reacted negatively or withdrew in a way that was either disproportionate to the situation or felt clearly related to a past experience. As you remember these experiences, which part, or different parts, can you identify?

You might be surprised by how many parts some people identify when doing this work. While some people can identify two or three, others have actually identified as many as eight different parts, all in active protest against nonmonogamy. I kid you not! The spectrum of possibilities in terms of what these parts look like is broad, just as the gamut of personal needs and wants they represent is also varied. A sampling of some of these parts could include a princess part that wants to be the only special one in their partner's life, a victim part that feels powerless and without choice in their relationship, a critical part that thinks nonmonogamy is bullshit and simply an escape for people that can't commit or are too needy, a competitive teenager part that feels like it has to fight off any potential competition for their partners' attention and affection, a child part that is afraid its emotional needs won't be met when a partner starts seeing other people, a hurt part that has experienced lies, deception and betrayal in previous relationships and is unwilling to let that happen again, and, of course, insecure parts that are afraid they won't be enough to keep the interest and love of their current partners if someone "better" comes along.

Taking the time to identify and name the parts of ourselves that are resistant to nonmonogamy is important not only because it gives us the opportunity to consciously recognize them, but also because it makes us aware of the needs and wants these parts are trying to advocate for. Without the tension of having to deny various parts of ourselves—and the needs and wants they represent—it is much easier to work towards moving beyond the resistance to CNM. Regardless of how irrational or exaggerated they may appear at times, these parts have something important to tell us about what we need and want in a relationship, and they tend to protest until we pause, turn towards them and listen.

Please note that I am not referring, here, to appropriate reactions that you might be having to overt mistreatment, inconsideration, dishonesty or disrespect from a partner. In such cases, it would not necessarily be a "part" of you that is creating a reaction disproportionate to what's happening or solely based on your past, but it would be a legitimate reaction to a relational experience that you are having right now. The next chapter covers experiences of relationship mistreatment or neglect that need to be addressed with your partners, which is not to be confused with the inner parts work that you are doing here to explore your own personal resistance or reactivity.

LOVE U and EASE Your Parts

After you've identified the different parts that are alive within you, you will work with them one at a time. The following steps will walk you through the process of setting the stage for dialoguing with these parts and, ultimately, changing your relationship with them. As you begin to work with them, really focus on loving and healing these parts of yourself. Recognize that, deep down, despite the difficulties they have presented you in moments, their true purpose has only been to advocate for your innermost needs and wants in partnership or life. In order to move beyond our resistance or reactivity to nonmonogamy, we must recruit them as allies in our process and stop treating them as adversaries. Have compassion and patience for them, just as you hopefully would with a child learning something new, and, if possible, thank them for the work they've done to keep your needs and wants from being forgotten. As you begin doing inner parts work, remember this is not just a one-and-done kind of thing. While some people do experience profound results after just one encounter with their parts, more often than not, the process must be taken on as an ongoing practice for real change to take root.

EXERCISE   LOVE U

The following steps make up the process I call the LOVE U parts work. This process is meant to be used when you are connecting with a part for the first time. In this first encounter, you want to get to know this part and relate to it in ways that will show it you are an ally and can be trusted. The intention is not to "fix" this part or make it go away, but instead turn towards it and give it the care and attention it needs to feel safe. During this first round, your goal is simply to make a connection and establish—or in some cases reestablish—a relationship with this part. After you've successfully connected with this particular part of you, you will then use the EASE parts exercise to address any resistance or reactivity this part is having to nonmonogamy.

Your External Environment

To get the most out of this practice, you will need to be in a space where you can have privacy and time for reflection. This is about creating an environment for yourself where you won't be distracted or interrupted. Remember, the more sincere you are and invested in the process, the more meaningful the results will be. Feel free to light candles, dim the lights, burn incense or play some soothing music to help you relax and get into a contemplative and focused state. For me, I prefer to just sit upright, but comfortably, in a quiet place, with a journal nearby for taking notes. Ultimately the way this all looks is up to you; the important thing is that you create a space that will best support and facilitate the LOVE U and EASE processes.

L	Locate
O	Origin story
V	Validate
E	Embrace
U	Update

Your Internal Environment

Take a few minutes to center yourself. Close your eyes and focus on your breath, relaxing into the present moment. You can imagine tree roots growing out of your body, grounding you into the earth, or you can imagine a waterfall above your head, washing away anything that might be distracting you from focusing your attention within. You can also use a mantra or prayer for a few moments, or any other method that you prefer to feel centered, grounded and resourced. What is important here is that you are connecting with the aspect of you that feels like your higher self. For some, it could be their Buddha nature, Christ consciousness, inner goddess or god, or prefrontal cortex, or even their adult responsive self. The terminology you use is up to you, but what I want is for you to consciously connect to a place within yourself where you can stay curious, engaged and open while dialoguing with whatever part you will be working with.

L: Locate the Part

Once you have gotten into the right inner and outer spaces for doing the LOVE U parts work and have decided on the specific part you're going to work with, you are then ready to *locate* and identify where this part shows up in your physical or psychological space. Is it somewhere inside of your body? Does it show up outside of or around you? Is it a voice you hear in your head? A feeling within your body? Once you locate this part, imagine that it is sitting in front of you at a comfortable enough distance for you to dialogue with it. This part may have a clear human-like form, it may look like a younger version of you, or it could even look a bit cartoonish or be completely abstract. It doesn't have to look like anything in particular. It's also perfectly fine if you experience this part as less visual and more intuitive, auditory or a felt sense. Everyone connects to their inner parts differently, and you may find that your parts are some unique combination of visual, intuitive, somatic or auditory elements. For some people, this can actually feel really strange or even silly, but what I've seen is that, with practice, this process can become more and more second nature and familiar. Many are often surprised by how much information they receive from these parts, even during the very first session. If the part you are working with is initially hesitant to appear or dialogue with you, you can reassure it that you are not trying to get rid of it or punish it in any way. Simply reassure it that you are just wanting to talk with it for a few minutes to know it better and, hopefully, give it what it needs.

O: Origin Story

Once you have the part located in front of you, begin to get to know it by asking about how it originally came to be (its *origin story*). In this round of LOVE U, you will hold off on asking about this part's feelings about nonmonogamy or your current CNM relationship challenges. For now, the intention is simply to get to know this part in a more general way. If you'd like, you can initially greet this part with a hello and speak to it aloud, or keep the dialogue internal—whichever you prefer is fine. You can also do this as a journaling exercise where you write out the part's answers. Some people who do this even like to experiment with using their dominant or less dominant hand when writing out this part's responses, which for some people helps them to better access the voice of their inner parts.

Here are some questions to help you draw out this part's origin story:

- How long has this part been with you, or how old is this part? Sometimes you will get a very specific age or number of years, while other times you might only get a range of ages. It's also possible the response will be that this part has always been with you. In this case, you can further inquire into the general time frame it came into being or when, specifically, it consciously emerged.

- What brought this part online? What life circumstance created this part as it is? Remember that you are listening to this part from your centered self, and by no means do you have to relive what this part went through or enter into any of the memories or emotions associated with its origin. Listen to this part as if it were a friend telling you their story. Be caring and curious, but also separate from it. If a part begins to overwhelm you in any way, you can ask it to slow down. You can play with making this part smaller in size or physically further away from you, so that you feel more comfortable continuing to relate to it. Another strategy that has been especially helpful to clients who tend to get easily overwhelmed by their parts is to imagine the part projected onto a movie screen or even the screen of their phone, so that they can watch it either from afar or safely contained in a manageable space. You can press pause at any time, and even imagine leaving the movie theater or hanging up on the video call when you're done.

- What would this part like to share with you about itself? Is there anything that this part would like to show or tell you about what it's been through? What does this part feel is important for you to know now?

- Based on what this part has shared with you about its own experiences, what did you learn about it, yourself, or anyone else that feels important to remember?

- What are some of the core beliefs or interpretations that this part is holding about itself, you or others?

- What role has this part been playing for you? What has this part been wanting for you, or what intentions does it have for you? While our parts can frequently act in disruptive ways, they are often holding a positive intention for us, such as wanting us to be safe, loved or valued. Their ways of enacting those positive intentions may not be positive at all, but this question is meant to clear through the confusion of their strategies and connect with their deeper, positive wish for you.

V: Validate

Once you have listened to this part's story and gotten a real sense of what its experiences have been and what its intentions are for you, you then want to *validate* it. Many times, our parts can initially seem irrational to us (and others), but when we take the time to really get to know them, many of the reactions that used to seem irrational actually make perfect sense in light of the circumstances that brought them into being. In this step, you are validating this part by acknowledging the challenges and difficulties it has endured on your behalf. With as much sincerity as you can muster, acknowledge how hard it's been for this part up until now. Let this part know that you see it and that you've heard it. Let this part know you truly recognize the hardships, pains, confusion and traumas it has been through. Recognize that, based on what this part has gone through, its feelings and beliefs make perfect sense. Validate that what it went through was not its fault and that it's not responsible for how it was treated by others. Also validate this part's positive intention for you. Again, even if this part has acted out that intention in distorted or harmful ways, acknowledge how you see that it has actually meant well and deep down wanted the best for you.

E: Embrace

Typically, after you validate and acknowledge the part's experience and intent for you, you will see a shift in its posture or energy. It may relax, expand, express gratitude or even take a different form. Now you want to take the next step in the LOVE U process, which is to *embrace* the part. Embrace is about going a level deeper with your validation towards the part by connecting with its feelings and needs. Ask this part what feelings it has and has been holding onto. Ask it about its needs and longings. As the listener, you are paying special attention to things like the need for love, connection, authenticity, autonomy, to matter, to be seen, to be understood or to be protected. If your part states that its need is for the absence of something, for someone else to do something specific, or for someone to be different in some way, you can inquire further by asking "what need would that fulfill if you were given that?" Once you are able to identify its core needs, embrace this part and offer it what it needs.

When embracing this part, you can literally imagine holding it, hugging it or offering to hold its hand. You can imagine love or light extending from your heart outward towards it. You can imagine that this part is being embraced by a loved one (alive or passed), an archetypal figure or an angelic being. You can imagine that you are being embraced by an aspect of nature such as a tree, rays of sunlight, ocean waves or the earth itself. If nothing occurs to you at the moment, you can also ask the part directly what it would like. Ask it how it would like to be embraced and supported by you. You may be surprised by what it tells you. This part of the process is what's known as inner reparenting or inner healing work, and there's no "right" way to do it, simply whatever works best for you and for this part. Trust the wisdom of what your nervous system needs to feel embraced.

U: Update

The final step in this process is to update the part you are working with so that it is truly inhabiting the present and functioning in a role that is current and supportive. Many times our parts are stuck in the past, unaware that we have become adults, or that we are no longer living in the original conditions that brought this part into being. It's very important that we make this part aware of our current circumstances so it understands it no longer needs to work so hard to protect our younger, more defenseless self. Some questions you can ask this part are:

- How old do you think I am?
- Do you know that I'm an adult, and we are no longer in those past situations?
- Are you stuck in a certain time or location?

Based on this part's answers, you can let the part know how old you are and remind it you have moved beyond the

situations that initially caused it hurt. If this part is still living in the past, you can imagine bringing it into the present
moment with you, just as you would fast-forward a movie
or use time-lapse photography to bring it up to speed. Some
people imagine airlifting this part out of the past and placing
it into the present, or they use a time machine to bring it into
the here and now, or they simply imagine the part in the room
with them, letting it know it is in the present and not in the
past. Regardless of the visualization you use, the process of
updating this part is an important step towards easing its
pain and reactivity. As this part comes to recognize it is no
longer subject to the circumstances that once triggered it, it
can finally let go of the strategies and defensive mechanisms
needed to protect you from harm.

Another important step in the process of updating your
part is letting it know you are now in charge and responsible for
creating healthy boundaries between the two of you. The fact
that these younger, wounded or more reactive parts show up
in our consciousness is not itself problematic, but we definitely
don't want them taking the wheel of our relationships. We
have to make it clear that our present-moment adult, responsive self is the only one allowed to make important decisions.
This part can be in the car with us, but *we* are the ones who
are actually in the driver's seat now. When these parts fully
recognize there is a responsible and responsive adult handling
business, they can relax and surrender the compulsive need to
intervene in matters of the heart.

Once this new relationship between you and this part has
been established, it's time to update its role and decide what
makes the most sense for both of you moving forward. I have
seen that some of these parts want to stay active in our psyche,
continuing to guide, protect or support us in some way. If this
is the case, educate your part about what is actually supportive
and protective for you now, versus what was needed when this
part initially came into being. You have the opportunity to
give it a role that is appropriate for its age and developmental

stage. After deciding what role you would like this part to play, communicate this change and discuss how you would like it to support you in ways that honor its original good intention. You can also coach it on how to speak to you in ways that are connective and healthy instead of critical, defensive, fearful or judgmental.

In some cases, after being updated, the part will simply want to be allowed to cohabitate with your system without having any kind of active role whatsoever. It may desire the opportunity to be the unfettered child it never got the chance to fully be. It could also just want to hang out playing, being creative, or helping you to stay connected to a sense of fun, wonder and the mystery of life. In still other cases, there may be parts that, after being put in their appropriate places, just want to be released. It could be that, after having the chance to put down the burden of constantly caring for us, all they want is a well-deserved rest. In situations like this, there isn't much to do other than thank this part for getting you to where you are now, and then bid it farewell.

§

After you complete the initial LOVE U process, hopefully you will feel that you have made some headway in getting to know your part, caring for it and redefining your relationship to it. Typically, these parts have been with us for years or even decades. The perspectives they hold, the beliefs they carry and the emotional reactivity they exhibit create strong patterns that are etched into our nervous system. It can take diligence and perseverance to bring these parts into the light of the present, embrace them fully and decide what role they will play in our lives, if any.

Since one of the primary intentions of the LOVE U process is to get to know a part's origin story, this is not something you will have to do more than once with the same part. But it's possible you'll need more than a single session to address everything that has been going on with a part. When doing follow up work with the same part, you'll want to use the EASE method.

The EASE parts work is a condensed version of the LOVE U process that is intended to reinforce and deepen the initial work you did with a part, minus the origin story. In a similar fashion as before, you will *externalize* the part you're working with; *ask* it about its struggles, feelings and needs; *soothe* it by validating and embracing it and, finally, *educate* it about the healthy expectations and boundaries you have for it.

For best results, I suggest doing the EASE practice daily until you really start to feel a fundamental shift in the way you experience the part you're working with. For some people, a full week of doing the EASE practice every day will be what's necessary to feel that shift, while for others it could take a month or more to start feeling changes. Personally, I have had some parts demonstrate lasting changes in as little as three EASE sessions, while others have needed several months of regular EASE work to really notice the difference. As you become more comfortable and skilled with the process, you will see a significant reduction in the time needed to EASE your parts, and eventually you will only use the method on an as-needed basis. The following is a step-by-step description of the EASE process.

EXERCISE   EASE

Once you have gone through the LOVE U process, give yourself some time before you begin the EASE process. Just as you did with the LOVE U exercise, you can set the tone for your process by making sure the external and internal conditions are conducive to focus and concentration. With time, you may find that you don't need as much attention put on the external environment to successfully engage with your inner world. Once you have centered and grounded yourself, you can follow the steps below.

E	Externalize
A	Ask
S	Soothe
E	Educate

E: Externalize Your Part

In the same way you located a part in the LOVE U process, you begin by finding the part you want to work with and *externalizing* it. Externalizing the part simply means imagining that it is outside of your body and located directly in front of you. The key here is to feel how this part is both an extension of your experience, but also not the totality of your being. I want you to intentionally create and feel the space that exists between you and this part.

A: Ask

After we externalize the part, we can *ask* it about what it's struggling with. We want to ask specifically about the feelings and needs it has in response to the current situation. This is the point where you can inquire about this part's experience of CNM. From a place of genuine curiosity, ask what it is about CNM, in particular, that this part is struggling with, afraid of, resistant to or hesitant about. Finally, ask about the feelings or needs that come up for this part in response to what's going on in relation to CNM.

S: Soothe

After you feel like you have an understanding of what this part's experience has been and a clear sense of what it is feeling and needing, you will *soothe* it by offering it validation and empathy. For some, this means offering it soothing words of encouragement, affirmation, acknowledgement or support. For others, the soothing comes in the form of purely nonverbal comfort, such as imagining sitting down next to it, holding it in a warm embrace, or gently caressing its back and shoulders. As you continue soothing it, really make an effort to imagine this part taking in and soaking up everything you are offering it. Take your time with this part of the process, until you genuinely feel there has been some positive shift or easing of this part's energy.

E: Educate

Now that your part has been soothed and set at ease, you can focus on *educating* it. Educating your part can look a few different ways. Often our parts need to be reminded of the updates we previously made with them in the LOVE U process. We may need to remind or reeducate them about living in the present, not the past, and remind them about how we want them to relate to us—that is, how they can speak to us using the language of feelings and needs, or by using language that is positive and supportive versus judgmental, fearful or critical.

Depending on the specific desires and needs of the part you are working with, the E for educate could also be an E for *emancipate*. If you are working with a part that doesn't want to necessarily have a new role in your life in an active way, but simply wants to let go of its responsibilities and just be an inner child part, you can remind it that it is emancipated from the roles it previously played and is now free to frolic.

The practice of EASEing your parts can be used in two ways. First, I recommend using it as an exercise to do when you are not in a triggered state. It's best to start getting used to the practice in a safe and spacious setting, without the overwhelm of strong emotions, where you can focus on healing the parts that continue to show resistance to making the transition to nonmonogamy and give them what they need. As you continue to develop a relationship with the practice, you can expand it to work with any part that needs attention regardless of whether or not it is related to issues of nonmonogamy.

Eventually, you will become so adept at working with the EASE process that you will be able to use it in moments of conflict. This is the second usage of the process, which entails using the same techniques you just learned, but in the context of an emotionally heightened state. In this way, EASEing your parts is like first aid for triggers, which will allow you to skillfully regulate your emotions and avoid escalating into full-blown reactivity. Successfully EASEing your activated part means that instead of spiraling into conflict and staying stuck in old patterns, you can actually move on to getting greater clarity regarding your needs and wants in the relationship, as well as what exactly is yours to change in the relationship dynamic and what is the work of your partners.

What I've found is that people who engage in this type of inner parts work are able to better sift through and disentangle the parts of themselves that still struggle with CNM from the ones that are actually on board with it. As they move forward and certain aspects of CNM feel challenging, instead of reacting from these parts, they are able to care for them and advocate for their needs, making the bumps in the road much less jarring. Additionally, this kind of inner work supports people in easing their high levels of reactivity to CNM and, even if they have decided they do *not* want to do CNM or at least certain aspects of it, allows them to stand more firmly in that clarity, but from a place of genuine self-awareness and wisdom as opposed to pure reactivity.

§

I hope this chapter, along with the exercises in the previous chapter on shifting your paradigm, was able to support you in either moving forward with opening up, being able to better navigate a CNM transition, or finding your clarity and acknowledging that nonmonogamy is not for you. While I do see many people who initially struggle with CNM eventually have a genuine change of heart through enough patience, process and experience, there are also others for whom, despite their Herculean efforts, it just doesn't work. Maybe they knew it all along and weren't ready to admit or accept the painful truth, maybe they really weren't sure initially and needed to give it a try before throwing in the towel, or maybe too much CNM-related trauma has transpired and they need a break or a pause. Either way if, at the end of the day, you arrive at the clarity that CNM is just not for you, or that the CNM changes you're being asked to make are not what you want, you have to be able to accept this clarity and come to terms with its consequences.

If you already know that you don't want to make these changes, but you don't want to lose your partner, I really understand this dilemma. You've tried and tried to make it work, but it just keeps getting worse. In the heat of the moment judgments are hurled, ultimatums are made, insults are exchanged, trust and safety are eroded...it's a painful mess. In extreme cases such as these, it probably means you need to face the fact that you and your partner are not compatible anymore. You consciously want different things. It's no longer about changing your mind or hoping the other partner will "snap out of it," "get it out of their system" or "come back to their senses": it's about starting the painful process of releasing your attachment to a relationship that can no longer give either of you what you want. It's time to surrender to what is.

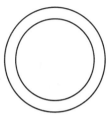

CHAPTER THREE
EXPOSING THE CRACKS IN THE FOUNDATION

For some people, open relating and CNM are catalysts for tremendous personal growth and expansion. As Dedeker Winston recalls in her book *The Smart Girl's Guide to Polyamory* of her personal journey into polyamory:

> All of the highs, lows and wrong turns have been an intense education about myself—what makes me tick, what sets me off, what turns me on and what truly brings me happiness. I have found the power to craft relationships that fulfill and energize, and I have discovered more love, security, affection, trust and stability than ever before.

Along with increased personal discovery, this journey can also initiate beautiful opportunities for partners to learn new things together, enhance their communication, deepen their intimacy and expand their eroticism. This potential to change our lives in such profound ways is a big reason why so many individuals and partners continue to explore and practice CNM.

But, as many already know, it also presents some significant challenges as well.

The further we step outside of the constructs of monogamy, the more we inevitably come to see our relationships through new eyes, and sometimes we may not like what we see. Whether you are brand new to CNM or have been living some form of it for years, the changes that come as you or your partners develop new relationships can radically alter your life in unpredictable ways. For many, the changes that CNM can bring act like a pressure cooker, heating things up and bringing to the surface all kinds of feelings, issues and dynamics that you were potentially never aware of, such as unprocessed trauma, unresolved ruptures, power imbalances, lingering resentments, poor communication habits, codependency or even deal-breaking incompatibilities. As CNM forces us to confront some of these exposed cracks in the foundation of our relationships, it can be helpful to remember they are not the result of personal shortcomings on our part, but often the remnants of relational dynamics that were most likely masked by the closed container of monogamy or the ostensible security of more hierarchical polyamory. The increased complexity of CNM can often put quite a spotlight on things that were previously invisible to us, or at least tolerable in a context of exclusivity or more domestic or entwined CNM partnerships.

Once exposed, it is important to figure out whether these cracks can be addressed and repaired, or whether they are signs of a relationship that is beyond saving. As we take a closer look at some of the more common cracks that can show up in relationships, you may identify one or more of these issues that show up in your own. Some of the relationship cracks that get exposed through CNM transitions, such as codependency and with unresolved conflict from the past, are addressed in later chapters. But for now, we'll focus on some other common cracks that Dave and I both see lots of partners grappling with, such as dysfunctional communication dynamics and relationship neglect, as well as discerning when the cracks in a relationship are too big to resolve.

Dysfunctional Communication Dynamics — I'm Gonna Wash Your Mouth Out with Soap!

My maternal grandmother was a true character. Everyone who knew her called her Grandma Marshmallow, because she would give marshmallows to all the neighborhood children. If you briefly met her, you'd think, "What a sweet old lady!" But to all of her immediate family, while she was at times very sweet and extremely generous, her persistent complaints, judgments and standards that few could ever meet also made her difficult to deal with. My grandmother had a fierce passion for social justice, and in her days of political activism, she was willing to fight and even risk her life for equal rights for all. In the day-to-day, her strong sense of what was right and wrong regularly showed up in how she grandparented me and my cousins.

As kids we loved to play tricks on her, putting marbles in her shoes or turning all the encyclopedias on her bookshelf upside down, just to get a rise out of her. One day all of us grandkids were hiding after putting her favorite frog statue in the freezer. She was frustrated and searching around to find and punish us, when one of us blurted out a curse. Well, that was a mistake, because Grandma quickly went from frustrated to fierce. We were three urban kids with permissive parents, so we probably didn't think cursing at Grandma would be that big of a deal, but we clearly underestimated our verbal offense, and our angry Grandma got a bar of soap and proceeded to chase us around her apartment, yelling "I'm gonna wash your mouth out with soap!" Lesson learned: don't curse in front of Grandma.

Through most of my adolescence and early twenties, I was frequently and reluctantly recruited into the fights between my mother and grandmother. My grandmother got jealous when my mom spent time with anyone but her, and her way of dealing with her desire for more time with my mom was to sling criticism and accusations about anybody my mom spent time with. No matter how much time and attention we gave my grandmother, it was never enough. In these continuous arguments, the comments that left my grandmother's mouth were at times so outrageous that it was actually comical to me, but understandably, my mother would get highly defensive and upset. Sometimes I just stayed out of it; other times I tried to join in with the same level of intensity to defend my mom and break it up. At still other times I would try to act as the voice of reason to defuse the situation, and many times I was even able to mediate between the two of them and support my grandmother in sharing her actual feelings and needs instead of her harsh judgments. But even if we made situational progress where my grandmother would calm down and actually apologize to my mom, a few days or weeks later she would start the same cycle all over again.

It was their codependent toxic tango, and it was so incredibly exhausting for me that I got to the point where I didn't want to spend time with the two of them together anymore. Finally, one day while the two of them were once again embroiled in the same dysfunctional banter, at my wits' end with no more skill or technique to throw at the situation, I just blurted out, "Grandma, do I need to wash your mouth out with soap?!" It stopped her right in her tracks. She paused and then innocently said, "But I'm not cursing?" and I replied, "You're technically not cursing, but what's coming out of your mouth is just as mean and maybe even worse than cursing." As a woman who had literally devoted her life to the pursuit of peace and justice, it wasn't until that moment in her 80s that she finally saw the discrepancy between the fight she had to enact in the world for women and people of color to attain equal rights and how that same energy of fight had turned her into the very villain with her family that she had no tolerance for out there in the world. With her defenses down, I followed up with, "Grandma, if you want to have peace and connection with Mom, then *you* have to speak with peace and connection to Mom." Something finally changed after that. Lesson learned.

From the story I just shared, it's probably no surprise how I came to be a mediator and a therapist. Some of the most powerful moments I experience in my work are with partners who, by slowing down together and receiving a few helpful prompts from me, are able to restore their connection after being stuck and disconnected for some time. When people already love and care about each other, the potential for growth and transformation is tremendous, and always a gift to witness. And when people love and care about each other, the potential to treat each other worse than anyone else is equally tremendous, and it is heartbreaking to witness. My least favorite moments as a therapist are the ones where, like with my mother and grandmother, I get enlisted into playing referee between partners or metamours who are dishing out one nasty, resentful, disrespectful allegation after another.

In the world of relationship therapy there are specialized trainings tailored just to working with high-conflict partnerships because, as a practitioner, it's one of the most challenging dynamics to deal with in the therapy room. Part of the challenge is that the intensity of the session can easily trigger our own flight/fight/freeze response or personal trauma history as we witness partners spew venom and attack each other. The pressure that nonmonogamy can put on a relationship has the power to make partners who were previously pleasant and kind become hostile and harsh, reacting in ways that neither of them has ever seen before. And while I've picked up many tips and tricks along the way to better handle these dynamics, sometimes it's just like it was with Grandma Marshmallow, where there is a temporary deescalation within the container of the therapy session, but after a few days or weeks, the pattern just continues all over again. Or, worst-case scenario, the techniques simply don't work at all.

As I continued to encounter more and more partners in my private practice who would express outright contempt and disdain for each other, I started leaving the sessions somewhat dysregulated and, honestly, dumbfounded by my clients' capacity to talk to each other in ways they would never dare speak to anyone else. The behaviors include harmful communication patterns such as interrupting one another while speaking, rolling their eyes, speaking for their partner without permission, telling their partner who they really are or aren't as a person, making negative assumptions about their partner's intentions, labeling, name-calling, blaming, criticizing, getting defensive, having reactive outbursts, being competitive, comparing partners to other people, and withholding care and affection as leverage to meet personal needs. Given that these partners were telling me some version of the story that this toxic way of relating was directly the result of their open relationship, I could recognize the patterns as symptoms of the CNM changes or new CNM paradigm stress they were under. However, in extreme cases, even with that recognition, I didn't always know how to help them. After finally reaching my wits' end, I threw in my therapeutic towel and began serving up my version of the "Grandma, do I need to wash your mouth out with soap?" intervention. Please know that I have never actually uttered *those* particular words in a session, but I do admit to coming pretty close in moments. Here are some of the highlights:

- Wow, you two! Are you aware of how you are talking to one another? I don't think you mean to, but this is really hurtful and damaging, even abusive language I'm hearing. Is that what you're wanting?
- I'm going to pause you all. By the way you're acting towards each other, I'm having trouble seeing that you even like each other. It actually seems like you despise each other. Is that the case?
- Are you wanting to pay me to watch you fight, or would you like to have a different kind of conversation that shifts this between you all?

- OK, let's pause. Do you talk to the grocery clerk this way, or your boss? There's a level of basic human kindness and respect that is missing here. I know you're both hurting, but without basic respect and kindness, forget about doing nonmonogamy together—or with anyone, for that matter—because there's no relationship at all.

Statements like these typically have the effect of getting people's attention and cutting through the interference caused by the unskillful communication of their unregulated nervous systems. In the opening that is created, I can reflect my firm belief that it is precisely this way of relating to each other that needs immediate attention before we talk about anything related to CNM. It's hard to talk tenderly about the hard stuff and come up with shared solutions in the absence of care and respect. No matter what has already transpired in the relationship, talking to each other in such destructive ways only adds more fuel to the fire and chisels away at the safety and trust needed to do CNM together. At this point, I typically ask three questions: 1. Do you believe you can change these unhelpful ways of communicating? 2. Has your behavior become abusive or out of your control, and does it require more intensive intervention? and 3. Are these patterns an indication that you are actually done with the relationship, or potentially should be?

In the book *The Seven Principles for Making Marriage Work*,* John Gottman and Nan Silver refer to these hurtful ways of treating our partners as the "Four Horsemen of the Apocalypse." This is the metaphor Gottman uses to describe the four predominant communication patterns he sees playing out in relationships that consistently struggle with conflict. Through decades of research, Gottman has developed the ability to predict the end of a relationship, with an over 90% accuracy rate, primarily based on whether or not these four

---

* See also gottman.com.

common patterns are present in the partners' communication. While individuals may know that the ways they communicate feel awful and unproductive, leaving them even more disconnected and less understood, they don't always recognize their part in the dynamic or see how destructive the pattern is, or they just can't control themselves.

As far as I know, Gottman's work has focused primarily on monogamous couples. If he has targeted the overwhelming likelihood that these kinds of communication patterns will tank a monogamous relationship, what can we expect in the case of an open relationship, where the triggers are guaranteed to be multiplied exponentially? While it is true that many of these problematic communication patterns can be changed through sincere and diligent practice, the consequence of not changing them is the end of the relationship. Many of the people coming to see me want to start their process by focusing on and healing the lingering pain of the ruptures that were caused by opening their relationship or the CNM transitions they are in. They consciously identify the questionable behaviors that were hurtful—intentionally or unintentionally—and want to do the work necessary to make repairs. However, doing deep repair work is contraindicated when such communication patterns are in play. Whenever Gottman's Four Horsemen are present in partners' communication dynamics, we have to begin with the basic, foundational work of creating safety and respect first. Before we can seriously take on repairing painful events from the past or sharing in ways that are vulnerable and intimate, there has to be at least a baseline of safety and healthy communication to move forward. The following chart is an outline of Gottman's Four Horsemen, along with antidotes for each way of relating.

CHART 3.1: (Facing page) Gottman's Four Horsemen and their antidotes. Adapted from *10 Principles for Doing Effective Couples Therapy* by Julie Gottman and John Gottman, 2015.

The Four Horsemen	Examples	Impact	Antidote	Examples	Impact
Criticism: Attacking the other person's character. Ascribing negative intentions to their words or actions.	"You didn't let me know that you were going to be late because you were too focused on getting laid. You only think about yourself and don't care about me." "You're always distracted on your phone and never pay attention to me."	The person receiving criticism can feel attacked, rejected, hurt and like who they are or what they do is never good enough.	Giving feedback that focuses on specific behaviors or a specific incident without assuming what the other person's intentions were. Talk about your own feelings using "I" statements and express a positive need. Invite your partner into the positive experience that you want with them versus just focusing on what you didn't like or don't want.	"It's really hard for me when you don't come home at the time we agreed to, especially without knowing what's going on. Next time could you send me a text if you know you're going to be out later than you said?" "I really love it when I get your undivided attention because it feels amazing to have you just focus on me for a bit. Would you be willing to have times when the phone is away and we just focus on each other?"	Safety can be restored when we experience that our partner no longer verbally attacks us, and trust is restored when we are able to take responsibility for our own experiences and needs.

The Four Horsemen	Examples	Impact	Antidote	Examples	Impact
Contempt: Taking a superior stance towards another. Acting as if your partner is beneath you in some way.	Eye-rolling, sarcasm, cynicism, mocking language, speaking with hostility, mimicking your partner's speech, ridiculing, patronizing.	The person on the receiving end can feel all of the previously named impacts from criticism, but also forms of humiliation, damaged self-worth and shame.	Treat your partner with respect. Even if you don't agree with them or like what they are doing, you can still speak to them with basic consideration. Build a culture of gratitude in your relationship, where appreciation is expressed daily.	"I understand that you've been busy lately, but could you please remember to load the dishwasher when I work late? I'd really appreciate it."	The overall wellbeing of the relationship depends on maintaining a baseline of care and respect and a culture of gratitude. Avoiding contempt, even when triggered or upset, is one of the most important ways to protect the health of your connection.
Defensiveness: Making excuses for our own behavior, playing the victim or turning what our partner is saying back onto them in a blameful way. This is often used as a response to feeling accused, judged or criticized.	Question: "Did you call Ron and Ralph to let them know that we're not coming tonight like you promised this morning?" Defensive response: "You know just how busy my schedule was today. Why didn't you just do it?"	Your partner will feel unheard and blamed for their attempt to get information from you. Over time, this creates a pattern where partners start to avoid bringing important things up because they fear having to deal with this defensiveness.	Accept responsibility for your part in the situation. Allow your partner's experience, even if it is different from yours. Take ownership for any of the ways you didn't follow through with an agreement and be willing to acknowledge the impact of your behaviors.	"No, I didn't. I'll call them now." "You know, I totally forgot. I should have asked you to do it this morning because I knew my day would be packed. That's my fault. I'll call them right now."	This kind of accountability promotes a lot of trust and respect. It lets your partner know that you value your commitments and can be trusted to repair broken agreements, which also creates a sense of reliability. It also makes partners feel safe to bring up important issues instead of keeping quiet and becoming avoidant.

The Four Horsemen	Examples	Impact	Antidote	Examples	Impact
Stonewalling: Withdrawing, shutting down or no longer responding to your partner after you've become triggered in a conversation or interaction. Often a specific response to contempt or overwhelm from experiencing one or more of the first three horsemen.	Silence. Walking away without saying that you need a break or that you'll be back. Hanging up when you're on the phone or intentionally not responding to texts. Giving your partner the silent treatment, tuning out or acting busy so that your partner won't interact with you. Statements like "just forget it," or "it's fine," (when it's clearly not), "Whatever!" or "OK, you win!"	Starts to foster an emotional climate of disconnection and lack of safety in the relationship. It creates uncertainty and sends the message you don't care about the other person's feelings. Also makes initiating repair even more difficult because there is no opening or way to approach.	Take the space you need, assert appropriate boundaries to avoid falling into the other horsemen and return to the conversation when you feel resourced again. Take a break, learn the signs and symptoms of when you are getting emotionally flooded and overwhelmed, so that you can pause or ask your partner to pause and slow down, giving you the chance to stay engaged, without having to cut and run. Lower your tolerance for receiving the fourth horseman. Speak up for yourself in a direct and respectful way if you feel like one of your boundaries is being crossed or you are being disrespected.	"To be honest, I'm feeling too angry to keep talking about this right now. Can we please take a break and come back to it in a bit? It'll be easier to work through this after I've calmed down." "I understand that you're upset right now, but what you're saying is hurtful, and feels like you're naming my experience for me instead of owning your own feelings about this situation."	Explicitly naming the fact that you're triggered and needing to take a break before things escalate into full-blown conflict goes a long way towards protecting the relationship from ruptures that can be hard to repair later. Demonstrating this kind of emotional regulation in the middle of a tense moment also lets your partner know that you are still safe. Clearly stating your boundaries without counterattacking allows you to have confidence in your ability to take care of yourself without needing to shut your partner completely out.

Sometimes the presence of one or more of the Four Horsemen is an indication, on some level, that partners don't actually like each other, or that they are over the relationship and just haven't been able to fully realize or admit it yet. In other cases, it is more of a sign that partners are in stress, stuck in trigger mode or in nonmonogamous paradigm shock with each other, and these patterns are simply the symptom of the accumulated tension. In still other situations, the Four Horsemen are, unfortunately, the only way partners have learned to communicate, and they simply don't have healthier models to follow. Or maybe they resort to these ways of communicating because their partner has been using the Four Horsemen on them. Whatever the case may be, it's important to figure out whether your use (or your partners' use) of the Four Horsemen is the primary issue in and of itself, or if it is a reflection of an "I don't actually like you anymore" situation. If you have been stuck in a dynamic with the Four Horsemen and speaking to your partner in ways that are disrespectful and unkind, I challenge you to consider the following questions to better determine whether the Four Horsemen are your primary issue or indicative of something even bigger.

- Do you like who your partner is and how they are in the world?
- Do you respect who your partner is and how they are in the world?
- Did you never really like them in the first place, or did your respect and appreciation for them diminish once the honeymoon hormones wore off or certain life stressors arose?
- Do you see your partner as fundamentally mean, cruel, selfish, narcissistic, manipulative, etc.? In other words, do you consider these things as personality traits versus occasional behaviors where your partner could learn better ways of emotionally coping or expressing themselves?
- Did you used to like or respect your partner, but one or both of you has changed through the years, and they are

no longer someone you would choose to be with if you
met them today?

- Is there too much resentment, betrayal, conflict, abuse
  or toxicity getting in the way of your relationship, and do
  you believe the situation is repairable?
- Do you have physical or sensory aversions to the way
  your partner looks, sounds, feels or smells?
- Are you actually done with this relationship and haven't
  been able to come to terms with this clarity yet?

If the presence of the Four Horsemen in your relationship
is more of an issue around communication and emotional regulation and represents the primary problem, there is still hope
that you and your partners can learn kinder and more respectful ways of talking to each other. However, if you answered yes
to one or more of the previous questions, and there is some
part of you harboring deep-seated disrespect, disdain, resentment, loathing or chronic irritation, then it's really important
to be honest about these feelings and assess whether or not the
possibility of working through the issues together is realistic or
even wanted. For some, it's quite possible these difficult feelings arose as a result of a traumatic event in the relationship or
is a response to years of accumulated stress, mistreatment and
negative relationship patterns. Maybe the dynamics were different in the beginning, but now the love has become clouded
by the influence of these unfortunate occurrences. Whatever
the case may be, it's critical to give yourself permission to be
done with the relationship and move on—if that's what's really
called for—or to at least create the space where you can work
on these issues together to start reducing the prevalence of
the toxicity.

Interestingly, I have seen partners who have literally
shocked me with the intensity of their poor communication,
leaving me completely convinced they were done for, only to
later be pleasantly surprised by the assurance they wanted
nothing more than to stay together. To their credit, they took

me pointing out how disrespectful and mean their treatment of each other was as a wake-up call and seriously reflected on how it was not their intention to be this way, realizing that they genuinely liked, adored and appreciated one another. The key is to suss out whether or not there is actually enough desire, energy and willingness to work things out and keep the relationship going. In order to get an accurate sense of this, you have to figure out whether the problems you face are a matter of changing the existing communication patterns between you and your partners or are more reflective of the potential end of your relationship. Whatever the case may be, you first have to address the presence of the Four Horsemen and determine whether they are a symptom of problematic communication patterns or a sign that your relationship either needs a break or has actually reached its end.

Relationship Neglect and Justice Jealousy

Another crack that I often see getting exposed in times when a relationship opens up or when new CNM partners connect with a polycule is relationship neglect. After years in the same relationship, we easily fall into grooves and get comfortable with the way things are. As we start to zone out and get caught up in the hamster wheel of daily life, our efforts to stoke the flames of romance or show appreciation for our partners can dwindle. And while it can be unrealistic to expect that we maintain the same level of focus, intensity and libido as we did at the beginning of the relationship, there is a difference between the inevitable decline of new relationship energy (NRE) and actually neglecting our partners.

Rarely do I see relationship neglect as something that a partner is intentionally doing. More often, it is the unintentional ways that partners fall into the trap of getting too comfortable, undervaluing each other, forgetting to show appreciation, becoming romantically apathetic, no longer trying, ignoring each other, making assumptions, projecting discontent, struggling with stress management, and even starting to get bored with each other that can be the issue. What may initially start as minor ways of taking your partner for granted, in time, becomes the increasing absence of certain types of important connection, intimacy and sex. Unfortunately, I've come to see relational neglect as a major obstacle in the path of partners moving forward with CNM, and if left unchecked, it can be a leading cause of the demise of the relationship.

While obviously taking a partner for granted needs to be addressed in any relationship, in the context of open relationships, it can be the absolute last straw that brings a partnership to the edge of collapse. When a faithful and loving partner sees their previously checked out, distracted or romantically apathetic counterpart suddenly be revived by their desire for someone new, it can shine a harsh and glaring light on what's been missing. This unbearable experience of seeing a partner swept up in NRE while feeling forgotten like yesterday's news produces a particularly painful kind of challenge that I refer to as *justice jealousy*.

I remember sitting with Dave in our car on one typically gray and rainy summer afternoon in Santa Cruz, California, regretting that I had forgotten my umbrella. As we waited for the rain to slow down a bit, we started to talk about a particular dynamic in our relationship. We were early for the dinner reservations I had made for us at a new health food restaurant that I knew Dave would like, so there was no rush. We hadn't had a date night in a while, so I was really looking forward to the evening. After dinner, I had arranged for us to see a movie, for which I had already bought the tickets and picked out Dave's favorite seats. Can you see where this is going? Even though I genuinely enjoyed creating date night experiences for us, I was becoming aware of how I wanted to be on the receiving end of date night planning for a change.

As we talked in the car, I shared with Dave that I was starting to feel the imbalance of always being the one to make the plans for our date nights. I acknowledged that it was something I didn't mind doing—and actually enjoyed—but it would mean a lot for him to, for once, step up and take that on too. I said I literally didn't care what the plan would be: a stroll on the boardwalk, a picnic in the park or playing Ms. Pac-Man at the arcade. It didn't need to be expensive, elaborate or even a traditional date in any way. I just wanted him to take the initiative and create an experience for me. I wanted more romance. I wanted to feel him turn towards me with interest and excitement. After saying my piece, Dave seemed to get it and agreed he would try.

Fast forward several years to us living in Boulder, Colorado, where we were now parents and polyamorous together. We were relatively new in our process of open relating, but Dave already had a particular woman in mind with whom he had a special connection. I was in complete support of their relationship, and when he mentioned they wanted to plan a getaway together to further explore their connection, I had no problem with it. A few days later, I was sitting in my office between client sessions when all of sudden, I got a text from Airbnb, providing me with the verification code *I* needed to complete the booking for *my* upcoming trip to Denver. A wave of fury moved through my body and an indignant "OH, HELL NO!" shot out of my mouth. Mind you, not because I didn't want them to have their adventure together, but because I knew that at that very moment, Dave was logged into *my* Airbnb account, trying to book *them* a trip that *I* was now going to be recruited into helping make happen. A few seconds later, without missing a beat, I received the text from Dave asking if I had gotten his precious verification code and if I could forward it to him. I was furious, and I was hurt.

To put my reaction into further context, we have to return to the conversation that took place in Santa Cruz a few years earlier. As I said, I was wanting Dave to initiate more romance in the relationship, and to be honest, it wasn't the first—or the last—time we would have the same conversation. As much as I knew Dave loved and valued me, the change I was hoping for didn't happen. I would get beautifully handwritten cards and specially cooked meals on holidays and birthdays—which I still get and adore—the bathroom would be regularly cleaned, and he would unconditionally support my career, but the work of tending to our romantic relationship most often fell on my shoulders. I eventually gave up, resigned to the fact that it wasn't personal to me or even our relationship, but instead just wasn't who he was, and so I just decided to focus on all the other ways he was an amazing partner. But then along comes another woman, and all of a sudden he's giving her the very thing I've been requesting all these years?! Suddenly *now* he has the skills and capability to create an experience *for her*, when I had just resigned myself to the idea he was fundamentally incapable of doing so. You better believe I was seething with justice jealousy!

Justice jealousy is different from the more typical types of jealousy where you feel possessive of your partner, insecure about your standing in the relationship or covetous of the other person's experiences. Instead, it is a direct response to an action taken by your partner that leaves you feeling like the victim of an injustice. It is typically a reaction to a situation like mine, where you've been asking your partner for a certain behavior, experience, change in the dynamic or expression of your preferred love language, seemingly to no avail because, try as you might, it keeps not happening. Then, as you start to accept you will probably never get it or assume your partner is simply not capable of such things, you suddenly see them giving that very thing to someone else. It's infuriating and feels very personal. It feels like a rejection, and it directly exposes the experience of being taken for granted and neglected in your relationship.

Dave here!

As painful and uncomfortable as it can be to acknowledge the way I hurt Jessica with this kind of dynamic, it's only right that I own up to it. Simply reading her account of the situation still makes me cringe with embarrassment as I reflect on the level of disconnect and unconsciousness that was in play. I even remember the reaction I had during some of those previous conversations with Jessica about her desire for more initiative on my part and how it felt like she was asking me to be someone else. I felt so much resistance, and it was extremely difficult to not take it as a personal criticism of who I fundamentally am instead of her asking for my behaviors to change and for me to grow in ways that would benefit both of us. I was never a good planner and got easily overwhelmed when having to make things happen, especially if it had to do with scheduling and making reservations online. I also see how my tendency to identify as a spontaneous person fed into the avoidance of logistical forethought and, frankly, I was grateful Jessica was someone who liked to plan and handle that side of things.

Thankfully, I've come a long way since then and have become much more assertive and engaged when it comes to initiating and planning romance. However, at that point in our relationship, I still didn't have the emotional maturity to realize how the imbalance in our dynamic was a symptom of some pretty toxic complacency on my part, as well as codependency between us. I didn't see how my avoidance of learning new behaviors in the relationship was actually indicative of taking Jessica for granted, because I assumed she would just keep taking care of it. I was asleep at the wheel and genuinely couldn't see how my laziness in the romance department was leaving Jessica feeling neglected and uncared for. Sadly, as I look back, I can now recognize how this glaring gap in my relational intelligence really laid the foundation for our romantic separation, which came a few years later. In all honesty, it wasn't until we opened our relationship and I saw other men shower her with affection and eagerly organize romantic adventures for her that I realized just how little I had shown up for her in that way. Seeing her light up as she received all this new attention was a brutal reflection of how checked out I had been all those years, and even though I scrambled to start showing some initiative in our relationship, at that point it was way too little, way too late.

Looking back, I can now see that I was living with the idea that Jessica and I would always be together, no matter what. My folks have been married for over 50 years, and my brother for over 20. I'm literally the first person in my immediate family to get divorced, as strange as that may seem these days. I had never even entertained the possibility we could split up, and I can see how my lack of experience with big relationship loss really played into a pretty significant blindness on my part. Some part of me, albeit mostly unconscious, really thought we would be together "till death do us part." Taking for granted that we would always be together meant, on some level, I didn't have to work as hard on the romance part of our relationship. It was only after I started dating again in the CNM context that I realized just how important this element of intimacy was. Having to watch my romantic circuits come online with other women after longing for it in our marriage became the perfect setup for Jessica's justice jealousy. This is one of the single most dangerous yet common pitfalls of monogamy or long-term domestic relationships, which I see play out over and over again with people in my private practice. The relative ease, predictability and familiarity of the daily routine, coupled with the closed container of exclusivity, creates the perfect set of circumstances for partners to start taking each other for granted.

To be perfectly honest, it's not that surprising. With the overwhelming array of logistics the average couple has to juggle these days, it's no wonder we start to let things slide, especially if it seems like everything on the surface is OK. And there's the rub. When it comes to intimacy, you simply cannot go on autopilot and assume anything, ever! You have to stay engaged, interested and curious, and not fall into the trap of thinking you have your partners all figured out. People change, as do their needs and wants, and we have to be tuned in enough to recognize those changes as they arise. Intimacy and romance are not like an investment portfolio you can simply outsource to someone else, stop paying attention to and expect easy returns from. It is a living, breathing, complex organism that is always in flux and in need of constant tending. While the particular features of romance and intimacy can—and should—look different for every relationship, the intention to be an active and mutually engaged participant is vital.

Relationship neglect and justice jealousy are not just issues for newly opened couples. Both these challenges frequently show up in long-term CNM relationships, or even relatively new ones, typically after someone even newer enters the picture. For example, one of my clients who practices nonhierarchical polyamory was very close to a partner with whom she did not live. Despite the fact they did not live together, their relationship evolved to a point where their lives intertwined in some very intimate ways: they hosted parties together, she helped care for his home, and they even talked a lot about making travel plans for the future. Since her partner kept pretty busy traveling for work, most of his other relationships were relatively casual. However, around two years into their relationship, he started to get more serious with another woman.

Initially, my client had a positive metamour relationship with this new woman and was supportive of their relationship, but she began to struggle as she noticed this new partner was getting prioritized over her. Many of the special experiences she had been promised were now being offered to her metamour first. He began to travel with his new partner, integrate her into his friend group and even offer her first choice of weekly date nights. My client was left feeling like she had been demoted to the status of domestic chore girl, where most of their time together was centered on either running errands for him or just hanging out at his house while he recovered from his more adventurous late-night dates with the new partner. As she began to get less and less time and attention from him, she initially judged herself for being "jealous," feeling bad about her inability to be a "good" poly partner and metamour. But later, as we unpacked her experience in our sessions, she came to realize that she was actually experiencing a form of relationship neglect, and this realization finally allowed her to embrace her justice jealousy.

The challenge of justice jealousy is one I frequently encounter when working with preexisting polyamorous vees, triads or quads where two or more partners predate the arrival of a new partner. It can be extremely triggering for the original partners, who have been around for all the good, the bad and the ugly, to watch as one of their dyad becomes enamored with someone new and suddenly transforms into an uncharacteristically cheerful, attentive, agreeable, fun, sexy, or just all-around amazing partner in the presence of this new person. For the original partners, it can feel as though you are being left the emotional scraps while this new person—who hasn't had to deal with all the bullshit of your partner's loveable but complex personality—gets to just enjoy the splendor of their enthusiasm and presence. While in general this can be a maddening experience, it is even more acute when you see it happening in your shared home or even bedroom.

On the other side of the coin, sometimes this kind of relationship neglect can actually happen right from the start of a relationship. Some new partners can feel overlooked or undervalued because they occupy a less primary position than the metamours who predate them. Because they are considered "secondary" or satellite partners, including typically not living in the same space, their wants and needs in the relationship can often be treated as less important. Also, partners who practice styles of CNM such as solo polyamory, or who are relationship anarchists, can experience their partners wrongfully assuming that their more independent and autonomous orientation means they need less attention, attunement, validation or belonging, often leaving the impression their relationship is less important than those that have some form of hierarchy or status privilege.

If you are in a situation where relationship neglect is at play, I suggest that you and your partners do your best to remedy this together by focusing on what you need to feel valued, attuned to and appreciated. Left unattended to, justice jealousy can quickly erode your connection and precipitate the end of your relationship. If your partner is unable or unwilling to address the ways they have been neglecting you, then you need to have an honest conversation and reassess whether you all still really want the same things. After being explicit about what you really want, maybe you'll find you can change the expectations you have for this relationship to make it fit the needs of your current situation—or you'll learn that it's time to walk away and find an arrangement that is better suited to you.

When a Companion Marriage Doesn't Work for You

Another situation that I see quite often, which can sometimes end up being problematic for at least one if not both partners in open relationships, is the phenomenon I call the *companion marriage*. Typically, a companion marriage is one where a couple is living in the same space, possibly raising a family together and sharing many aspects of domestic life that married couples normally do, but without the romance or sexual intimacy. In situations like this, it's possible for the individuals to genuinely enjoy each other's company and want to be around each other. They could have important shared interests, hobbies or projects, but the relationship is lacking some sense of romantic spark or sexual polarity. It's a relationship that has become more platonic than passionate.

In this dynamic, one or both partners will usually describe their partner as being more like a best friend or a close sibling than a lover. It's comfortable and safe, and partners often say they don't want to lose the familiarity and trust they have built together over the years. When couples find themselves in this situation and they *both* want it to continue as it is, opening up can be a fantastic way to maintain their life together while also having the opportunity to satisfy the desire for romantic or sexual experiences lacking in the current arrangement. As long as the companion marriage situation is completely mutual, it can be a great fit for CNM.

However, when a companion marriage consists of one partner not wanting romance or sex but the other one wanting them, the relationship itself is likely to become strained and, ultimately, unsustainable. Trying to incorporate CNM into a dynamic like this can often become a ticking time bomb, creating unbearable pain when a partner starts to see other people. Even though partners may lament the absence of sex or romance in a monogamous relationship, they will usually endure it because they know no one is really getting any, and there's typically enough good things in the relationship to warrant sticking it out. In monogamy, it's much easier to just chalk up a lack of sex to things like having a low sex drive, stress, or the old cliché that this is just what happens in long-term relationships. But when one partner still wants these things in their original relationship and the other partner doesn't, but is actively going out and getting those needs met somewhere else, it often becomes unmanageable and extremely difficult not to experience it as an outright rejection.

For fear of losing the original relationship, numerous individuals try to accept seeing their partners with whom they've lost sexual intimacy be with other people. They twist themselves into emotional contortionists in an attempt to deal with the pain of watching their partner get swept up in the intoxicating flurry of NRE, all the while having to swallow their own yearning to feel sexy, attractive and desired. In order to try and make the pain go away, people adamantly dismiss and minimize their own sexual needs, or use pseudo-spiritual narratives about the nobility of loving their partner unconditionally (regardless of their acute and unremitting anguish). They wait and hope against all odds that their partner will see the light and finally turn towards them once again. Or they may even try to date other people in order to get their own needs met, while underneath it all being completely uninterested in the new relationship because all they really want is to be with their original partner.

While there are various reasons why the phenomenon of companion marriage can happen, some of the more common are:

- You have incompatible views on what you want in a marriage or partnership, where some people are fine if marriage has little to no sex or romance, and some people are absolutely not. There's nothing wrong with either view of partnership, but they must be mutually shared for the partnership to work.
- You fell in love with who your partner was as a person, loving who they are, but you never really felt attracted to them in a romantic or primal kind of way.
- There initially was an attraction, but it's gone. You are no longer attracted to or in love with your partner, and no amount of therapy, toys, porn, tantra, role playing, audio programs, increased emotional intimacy or attachment repair has changed that.
- You have not successfully dealt with conflicts, so while things may be calm on the surface, one or both of you does not feel emotionally safe in the relationship. The lack of romance or sex could be a symptom of an avoidant relationship to having difficult but necessary conversations, or of one or both of you being stuck in a freeze defense response. (See chapter four.)

When the Cracks Are Too Big

Sometimes, it can be a tricky thing to figure out when it's time to leave a relationship. The fact that a relationship is going through a phase of intense conflict or faced with challenging life circumstances doesn't always mean it's time to throw in the towel. Every relationship has its ups and downs, and even the most loving or compatible partnerships can get tested. I definitely don't believe relationships should just be discarded when things get hard, and I acknowledge the importance of doing everything we can to make things work before walking away. So far in this chapter we have covered relationship "cracks" and challenges that theoretically can be remedied if all partners are willing and able: respect and kindness for each other can be embraced, unhealthy communication patterns can improve, past ruptures can be repaired, relationship neglect can be redressed, and in some cases, an imbalanced romantic or sexual desire in a companion marriage can even be restored, accepted as-is, or remedied with CNM.

Awareness of these issues creates an opportunity to improve them. However, unfortunately, in some situations the cracks in a relationship are just too big to be mended. Sometimes partners simply come to realize they have just grown too far apart over the years and now want very different things out of life and love. Or maybe one person very much wants to keep fighting for the relationship, but the other partner consistently doesn't show up and isn't willing to do their part. In some cases, a relationship is in such a high degree of conflict, dysfunction or toxicity that the only healthy thing to do is move on. How, then, do we really know when our relationship is simply going through a rough patch that needs more tending to, is in a critical condition that needs more urgent interventions, or is over and done with?

Some relationship patterns can muddy the waters and make it difficult to determine whether or not a relationship is worth saving. What I see a lot is that many partners who are struggling look to nonmonogamy as the potential solution to their problems without realizing opening up, introducing new partners or changing the CNM style they have been practicing can actually *hasten* the end instead of preventing it. While in some cases CNM could be helpful for relieving the tensions and challenges of a rocky relationship, in many cases, partners are grappling with situations where ending the relationship is probably best regardless of whether or not they are exploring CNM. In situations like these, the severity of the conflict and emotional difficulties isn't good for either person, and frankly, there isn't enough desire, capacity or goodwill on either part to really do what would be necessary to change things.

In some more extreme cases, partners are trying to initiate a CNM transition while in the midst of massive dysfunction, toxicity or crisis, and it's not that the crack is too big, but that it's an actual sinkhole. Thankfully, this category represents a relative minority when it comes to the people I work with seeking support for their CNM process. However, it's worth mentioning because many people out there still hope CNM will be the life-support system for a relationship better left unresuscitated. For some, the stigma of divorce or the fear of being alone can be so strong that they would rather try nonmonogamy than break up with someone who is mistreating them or with whom they are clearly incompatible. CNM should not be used as a way to avoid having to make a hard choice about leaving an unhealthy or abusive relationship. If anything, the decision to become nonmonogamous will just complicate your life in ways that will only make matters worse.

Additionally, people practicing CNM are not immune to abusive dynamics. Individuals who are already nonmonogamous can find themselves in dysfunctional situations with one or more of their partners like anyone else. Just because someone has multiple partners does not mean the abuse they experience in a particular relationship is any less severe than if they were monogamous. Just as the fear of being shamed or stigmatized can keep someone from revealing or seeking help for the abuse they experience in monogamous relationships, so too can it prevent CNM folks from speaking up. In fact, in some cases people in CNM relationships can be even more susceptible to the silence and isolation that can obscure abuse, because of the added stigmas and stereotypes that are often projected onto nonmonogamy. The fear of being judged, dismissed, or having their CNM lifestyle or identity blamed as the cause of their abuse can make the obstacles to telling the truth feel even more overwhelming.

In a situation where someone is enduring outright contempt, neglect or abuse, the only thing I can ethically recommend is either radical, therapeutic intervention where these issues are addressed and the abusive partner takes responsibility for their actions, or putting an end to the relationship.

Some clear examples of things that signal the need to end a relationship are:

- Your partner intimidates you through threatening looks or actions.
- Your partner makes threats to harm you or your children.
- Your partner has an active addiction for which they are not seeking treatment.
- Your partner exhibits extreme jealousy when you spend time away from them, or jealousy towards your friends.
- Your partner isolates you or discourages you from spending time with friends, family members or peers.
- Your partner is insulting, demeaning or shaming towards you, especially in front of other people, and is not willing to stop or address these behaviors.
- Your partner is preventing you from making your own decisions, including decisions about your own life, your work, schooling, other relationships, etc.
- Your partner controls your finances, and you are unable to have money for necessary expenses.
- Your partner pressures you to use drugs or alcohol or perform sexual acts you're not comfortable with or consenting to.

- Your partner damages or destroys your belongings.
- Your partner tries to convince you, your other partners, your metamours or someone else that you are crazy.
- Your partner does other things not mentioned above that leave you feeling physically, emotionally or mentally unsafe.

If you are experiencing any of the above situations, it is important that you prioritize your own physical, emotional and psychological wellbeing, as well as that of your children or other loved ones who may be in harm's way. If you are in a dynamic where you feel your safety is compromised, you need to get out of that situation. With that said, in some cases, healing and treatment for high-conflict relationships is actually possible, where everyone involved would enter into some form of therapy or recovery treatment. If partners are equally combative, explosive, mutually triggering and consistently bringing out the worst in each other, then an intensive period of individual therapy or even inpatient or outpatient treatment along with relationship counseling holds the possibility of really changing things. In cases like these, it's critical that everyone take responsibility for their part in the unhealthy dynamic, and time apart might be warranted. If you haven't given the relationship the opportunity to try some professional interventions then, at the very least, a reasonable hope remains that there could still be something left to salvage. But again, only if all parties are clear about the way they're contributing to the toxic dynamics and committed to getting help and changing. This is by far not an easy path, or one that is guaranteed to work.

Sometimes the responsibility for relationship challenges is not equally shared between all parties, and one person actually needs more help, as in the case of addiction or severe PTSD. In special cases like these, everyone involved will most likely need therapeutic support, but it's important to recognize that because of the longstanding effects of traumatic life circumstances, one partner can be particularly primed to struggle with conflict and attachment issues. There is absolutely no shame in naming the imbalance in a dynamic such as this, and in many cases, this can actually be the key to restoring balance in the relationship. When we can clearly identify what is ours to work on, we can start to take full responsibility for our part in a problematic dynamic. For some, it's vital that they take ownership for their personal issues such as addiction, uncontrollable anger, insecurities, reactivity, attachment wounds, etc., and for others, doing the inner work consists precisely of developing the self-worth necessary to no longer tolerate abusive or toxic behaviors from their partners.

§

After reading this chapter, I understand how the thought of having to face these kinds of challenges could seem daunting. And while they do represent many of the common issues that arise as partners navigate CNM, the point of looking at them is not to overwhelm you, but instead to make them explicit so you can either recognize them for what they are and develop the awareness to change them, or, ideally, circumvent them altogether. As I mentioned at the beginning of the chapter, CNM offers the promise of genuine, profound personal transformation and greater relational intimacy. The trick is to intentionally embrace all the difficult lessons that arise along the way in order to reap those benefits.

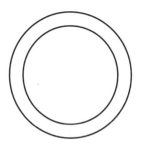

CHAPTER FOUR

MANAGING CONFLICT AND REPAIRING PAST RUPTURES

As mammals we are wired to connect. We evolved to cooperate and rely on one another, and in the absence of the presence, care, attunement and protection of each other, we experience pain, loss, loneliness and trauma. Tragically, because of emotional mis-attunement, misunderstandings and conflict, many of us who long to feel connected and close to our loved ones instead find ourselves struggling with distance and disconnection. The even bigger tragedy is that much of the relational discord we experience is actually avoidable, owing itself mostly to our lack of skill in how to handle it. Instead of using conflict as a genuine opportunity to develop greater intimacy and awareness with our partners, we fall into the trap of avoiding it or making it worse.

One of the biggest challenges I see in CNM relationships is conflict management. This includes the difficulty of handling not only the complex issues that arise in the moment, but also all the unresolved relationship ruptures from the past that continue to make the present even harder. For some partners, there can be months, years, even decades of hurt accumulated over the course of a relationship, and CNM has an uncanny way of bringing it all to the surface. Also, because of the added complexity of multiple relationships, you can often find yourself with limited time and energy to deal with all the rifts and schisms that need tending to. For example, let's say you and a partner have really been struggling with CNM recently, and next week your partner has a date scheduled with someone new. As the day approaches, you are plagued with painful memories of the first time your partner went out with someone new and broke a mutual agreement between you both to not have sex on the first date. Before the arrival of next week, you know you both desperately need to talk about this experience and get on the same page about expectations and agreements, but every time you try to broach the subject, the conversation devolves into an argument. The mountain of built-up, unresolved resentment related to your partner's past transgression has created a filter of pain that makes dealing with the issue at hand seem hopeless.

This is why it is vital to have a process of cleanup that allows you to address open wounds that continue to fester in your relationship and help undo the tangle of tension and confusion that can feel impossible to sift through. Before you can even hope to successfully connect with new partners, make solid agreements or negotiate major changes in the structure of your current relationships, you have to create space for working through the difficulties that affect your existing partnerships. This is where I defer to Dave and his process of Restorative Relationship Conversations. The rest of this chapter is in his voice. His offering is a much-needed tool for all the partners who continue to wrestle with unresolved conflicts stemming from painful incidents of the past. Many partners fear that it could take significant amounts of time and therapy to properly address their issues, and so they leave the hurt unattended. While I know that initially thinking about revisiting all the past ruptures of your relationship can seem daunting and even unrealistic, this is not something that can simply be left to work itself out. Thankfully, the restorative approach that Dave has integrated into his process allows partners to quickly get to the root of their issues while creating the necessary space to acknowledge and move through past ruptures in just a few sessions.

§

Dave here!

While monogamy may sometimes make it easier for us to get away with not dealing with our interpersonal conflict, CNM is not so forgiving. The inherently more complex dynamics of multiple relationships, combined with the fact that we are often faced with experiences for which a monogamous paradigm did not prepare us, means our exposure to potentially triggering situations is increased exponentially. For all the glory and magic that can come with CNM, for some it can also be a veritable minefield of emotional instability and relational turmoil. Unfortunately, because so many of us have grown up without proper models of conflict resolution, we often think of conflict as something inherently scary or threatening. Since no one ever taught us to handle it well, we have learned to fear and avoid it, usually making it worse in the process. This creates the feeling of being powerless in the face of our own reactivity or avoidance, which in turn makes our intentions to be supportive and gracious metamours or regulated and stable partners seem out of the question.

Shifting Conflict Paradigms

A big part of the challenge many of us face when dealing with conflict is that we are deeply conditioned to expect emotional discomfort and unpleasant outcomes. For example, what is your first thought when one of your partners stops you and, seemingly apropos of nothing, says, "Hey, can we talk?" Do you think to yourself, "Right on, we are about to have an exciting opportunity to deepen our connection and grow in our relational awareness!"? Or do you—like so many others—think something like "What's wrong now?" or "What did I do this time?" already primed to explain or defend yourself for some wrongdoing? Or maybe it's the other way around, and you are the one wanting to initiate an important conversation about your relationship, and instead of being met with open-minded curiosity, you instantly feel your partner's tension, knowing they are already on edge about what's to come. Either way, the fact that this is the default starting point for so many conversations makes safely addressing conflict extremely difficult.

Often what we think should be an easy conversation with our partners quickly devolves into someone getting defensive; you were simply trying to give them legitimate feedback about something you didn't like or set a boundary for yourself, and all they can hear is criticism and rejection. Or maybe you are the one on the receiving end, and all you can hear in the subtext of your partners' comments is how wrong, bad or inadequate you are as a partner, which sends you into a paralyzing shame spiral. Unfortunately, when conflict spins out of control like this, it is easy to blame ourselves or our partners for "not doing it right": for being too reactive or too sensitive, not really listening to us, lacking empathy, being avoidant, etc. And while it's definitely true that being able to genuinely listen to our partners, self-regulate our emotions and not get defensive are all necessary skills in moments of conflict (which we will cover later in this chapter), there is also an important sociocultural component to why conflict can be so hard, which many of us don't even realize influences our interpersonal relationships.

Before naming this larger issue, I want to first give a little context for how I started specializing in conflict resolution. My origin story begins in the field of restorative justice (RJ). Adapted from Indigenous practices of conflict resolution, RJ is a radical alternative to the broken and dehumanizing criminal justice system many of us have grown up with. Unlike the court system, which views acts of wrongdoing as crimes against the state or violations of the law, RJ sees them as ruptures in human relationships. Instead of punishing and stigmatizing individuals who have harmed others as "criminals" and separating them from society through incarceration, RJ offers them the chance to take accountability for their actions by sitting down with the people they've hurt and working together to find ways to repair the harm. RJ replaces the values of punishment and retribution with personal responsibility and relational repair. In RJ, the people directly impacted by a crime are offered a voice in the process, unlike the traditional justice system where "experts of the law," i.e., lawyers and judges, are the only ones who get to decide what should be done and who is to be found "guilty" or "innocent."

My initiation into this exciting paradigm of justice began when I was a bilingual case coordinator in a small but well-established nonprofit in northern Colorado. My passion for the work quickly led me to become an RJ circle facilitator and trainer. In these transformative processes, I had the privilege of guiding individuals through difficult conversations in which they had to find collaborative ways of working through their conflicts. I was continually inspired by the power of the restorative process to bring people together and give them the means to successfully navigate truly difficult situations without escalating them. I was also genuinely moved by the level of courageousness and vulnerability that it took—both on the part of harmed parties as well as responsible individuals—not only to openly share their experiences but also to really listen to and empathize with one another. In the course of any given RJ circle, I would bear witness to tremendous and heroic acts of forgiveness, which, in turn, allowed responsible individuals to move through and, ultimately, let go of the shame they carried. As a result of these profound experiences, I became convinced that the restorative approach had something incredibly important to teach us as a society about how to do conflict differently.

And yet, while the restorative approach offers new and refreshing ways of thinking about and handling conflict, its humanizing principles are still a long way from being accepted and integrated into mainstream culture. Unfortunately, much of the world is generally still very much anchored in a paradigm of crime and punishment, which continues to inform the ways we personally relate to conflict. From the way we parent our children to the way we talk to our partners in moments of tension, the concept of "being in trouble" and potentially punished as a result permeates many aspects of our interrelational experience. Making a mistake, whether at home, at school, at work or in public, can get you grounded, expelled, fired, fined or even arrested. Most of us are so conditioned to this that we simply accept having our rights and privileges taken away as a natural consequence of "messing up." Even though we may not like it, we accept it as the way things are, rarely questioning the validity, reasonableness or even efficacy of this strategy.

Similarly, many of us have also become desensitized to the ways that people who do wrong in our culture get labeled and stigmatized. In mainstream North American culture, the importance of being a "good" child or an "upstanding" citizen is emphasized, and when the rules are broken, one's very moral character can be called into question. This link between committing an infraction and then subsequently having a negative label attached to someone's identity contributes to a pronounced tendency to take on shame when confronted with conflict. The problem with all this is that people become conditioned to be hypervigilant to avoid messing up, or otherwise to get punished for it, and that punishment often includes the shame of a compromised self-image.

The flip side of this culture is when one feels wronged by someone because of something they either did or said, and then starts to feel justified in labeling that person unfavorably. The story the mind creates goes something like, "Because I have been wronged by you, I now get to judge and label you as a certain kind of person." The judgments and labels we use are typically reflective of the particular ways in which we feel hurt or wronged. For example, I was working with a vee relationship* where the two female metamours were really struggling to hear each other without quickly becoming triggered or reactive. The three of them were getting ready to go to the same festival and were feeling a lot of trepidation about being in the same space together. Neither of these women had had much contact previously, except for a similar multi-day event in which they both experienced an extremely painful conflict between them. Despite their mutual hesitancy, they really wanted to find a way to communicate with respect and care, but because of the past negative experience, they kept getting snared in the tangle of their reactivity.

One of the women had been working really hard on creating and upholding personal boundaries. It was something she and her therapist had decided was important to start focusing on, but she still had a somewhat fragile and tentative ability to put up boundaries in moments of heightened conflict. In one such moment during the original conflict between these women, she felt as though her metamour was intentionally crossing a line with her, and she became completely shut down and unresponsive. As a result, she started telling herself the story that this other woman was a domineering boundary pusher: that this was essentially who she was as a person. In our sessions together, every time she got triggered by her metamour, she would go on the offensive and start saying things like, "Why do you have to keep pushing my boundaries? You're not respecting me!" The tricky thing was that from everyone else's perspective (including my own),

---

* A relationship made up of three people in which one person is actively involved with two people simultaneously and functions as the "hinge" or "pivot" partner. In a vee, the other two people are not romantically or sexually involved with each other; when they are, the structure is called a triad.

the comments that provoked these combative responses were either neutral or actually meant to be supportive. The original hurtful action became mixed up with the idea of the other person, and she started to confuse her metamour's behavior with an actual characteristic of the metamour's personality. Now, every time she got triggered, she was prone to interpret her metamour's behavior or speech as simply more evidence confirming the label she had already created, regardless of the actual intentions.

Now we can see how certain elements of this woman's social conditioning had created a paradigm of conflict that, in many ways, only made it worse. She had inherited and internalized the values and vocabulary of a punitive justice system that perpetuates the idea that conflict is an inherently adversarial process, where someone invariably wins or loses. She was conditioned to compulsively determine who was "right" or "wrong" in conflict, with the underlying assumption that the "wrongdoer" deserved punishment or sanction. For those anchored in this worldview, often accompanying this determination of guilt is a feeling of being justified in labeling the other person as morally defective in some way, especially when we feel personally wronged by them.

This way of dealing with conflict positions us as disputants in a contest between competing interests where we are often pitted against people we genuinely care about. When framed like that, is it really any wonder why we reflexively fear and avoid conflict? Without first recognizing and acknowledging the tremendous influence this predominant cultural narrative about conflict has on one's psyche, it can be next to impossible to actually change the way you approach conflict. Thus, in the same way the premise of this book is about the importance of working at the level of paradigm to more successfully navigate CNM, in conflict, we also need to make a similar paradigm shift: from an adversarial approach to a collaborative or restorative one. And in the case of CNM, where there are even more players at the table, this shift becomes even more relevant.

So in order to handle conflict differently, we first have to start thinking about it differently. We have to redefine it, change the way we understand it, and even retrain our nervous system to respond to it without automatically going into a fight/flight/freeze/appease defense response. Instead of conflict being something we fear or avoid, we can openly and willingly engage with it. Instead of always expecting pain, discomfort and negative outcomes, we can learn that conflict can actually be a path to deeper understanding, more emotional trust and intimacy, and stronger connections with our partners. To do this we have to embrace a paradigm of conflict that fosters a spirit of genuine collaboration and relationality. Such a paradigm invites partners into a creative process that explicitly aims to address and repair conflict in ways that feel meaningful, satisfying and, above all, safe to everyone involved.

The restorative approach offers us just such a paradigm. The emphasis it puts on human relationships and connection encourages exactly the kind of attitude we want to have when stepping into difficult conversations. Instead of being primed to enter a heated contest between opposing sides, a restorative paradigm helps us to clarify our intentions and prioritize working together to create resolution and repair. It sees conflict as a collaborative process that offers everyone involved the chance to meet their needs, rather than as a zero-sum game where someone is inevitably the loser. It is a powerful reframe that makes disagreements stop feeling like threats to our relationships and more like invitations to strengthen our connection with partners. By embracing the relational posture offered by the restorative paradigm, we can start to genuinely change the way we feel about our interpersonal conflicts *and* the way we show up for them.

Punitive Paradigm	Restorative Paradigm
Reason-based focus	Relational-based focus
Purpose is to determine right from wrong and then assign blame to wrongdoer.	Purpose is to determine who has been hurt and how, then repair the hurt.
The wrongdoer is considered morally compromised and subject to negative labels; shame or damaged self-image is often a consequence of these labels.	Individuals responsible for harm are seen as complex human beings, capable of making mistakes and worthy of the chance to acknowledge and repair the harm they cause.
Outcomes are meant to punish or sanction wrongdoer; this is considered the proper application of justice.	Outcomes are meant to restore the relational ruptures between individuals that occur in conflict.
Individuals are positioned against each other in an adversarial posture, with the expectation of a "winner" and "loser."	Individuals are positioned as collaborators in a restorative posture, where everyone is considered a stakeholder in the repair of the relationship.
Primes us for emotional intensity and contentiousness, putting us on edge and making us apprehensive about engaging each other.	Creates an emotional environment of mutual respect and safety, allowing us to approach conflict with curiosity and an open heart.
Typically generates fear and avoidance, making it more likely that conflict lingers and goes unresolved.	Encourages empathy and vulnerability, functioning as an invitation to work together to change the conflictual patterns.

TABLE 4.1: Comparisons of punitive and restorative paradigms.

Working with the Pain of the Past

Dealing with the hurt from the past—be it from yesterday or five years ago—can be hard no matter what kind of relationship you are in. Most of us, unfortunately, did not grow up learning how to skillfully address conflict as it happens, in real time, and instead, have either learned to simply put it off, hoping it will eventually just fade away, or to get reactive and contentious. Neither of these responses helps the situation. In addition to the problematic influence of the dominant paradigm of conflict that I mentioned in the previous section, there are also several key obstacles that make it hard for us to successfully work through the hurt that accumulates in our relationships. Just as it is important to make a conscious and deliberate shift towards a new paradigm of conflict, it is also necessary to recognize these other challenges that make working with the past so difficult. Without first recognizing them as potential contributors to our own resistance and fear around talking about things that feel hurtful, they can continue to create gaps in our awareness that perpetually leave us feeling incapable of really moving forward in our relationships. In this section, I want to first name these additional obstacles, so that we can identify them in our own relationships, and then offer some practical, restorative strategies for overcoming them.

I have arranged these five obstacles into two different categories. The first two represent obstacles that keep us from even initiating a conversation about the past in the first place. They act as powerful deterrents to bringing things up in the moment, reinforcing the resistance and hesitation we often feel when even considering talking about something hard. The last three obstacles are ones that tend to ignite reactivity and conflict once we are already in the midst of a challenging conversation. They reflect both the ways we have been conditioned to exacerbate conflict with internalized ideas that are inherently problematic and the places in our own self-awareness where we still need to grow in order to reduce our reactivity.

Putting It Off

In day-to-day life, even if unknowingly, we can easily fall into the trap of assuming our partners will keep putting up with the ways we don't tend to the emotional wounds that accumulate in our relationships. These can be anything from minor misunderstandings or unacknowledged insults to criticism or judgment, intense emotional outbursts, or all the way up to full-blown ruptures of trust and safety. I have seen partners who, for years, minimize or dismiss their own experiences of frustration, disconnection or anger because, frankly, some part of them figures they can. Instead of actually working on the underlying issues causing their tension, they focus on their careers, kids, hobbies, friends or other relationships, simply resigning themselves to living with the discomfort. When considering just how relentless the onslaught of daily responsibilities and commitments can be, it makes total sense why the last thing we want to do is spend our precious remaining free time on dealing with things that make us uncomfortable.

The challenge of having limited bandwidth for processing relational hurt can be even more pronounced in the context of CNM. Having to track and deal with the dynamics of multiple relationships at once can make this kind of emotional housekeeping seem like just one more thing on an already full plate. It can also be the case that, with certain partners, we already feel like we're not getting the time we want and, when issues come up, we are hesitant to broach difficult topics because we don't want to spend what little time we do have with them processing potential conflict. This resistance can create a very common narrative about how "it's never the right time to talk about it." I see this particular story play out regularly in CNM relationships where people fall into a pattern of perpetually avoiding bringing up topics they suspect one of their partners will not respond well to. The opposite of preventing conflict, this kind of avoidance only compounds an already difficult situation by making the person who has been kept out of the loop feel lied to and betrayed when things finally do come to a head.

I remember one situation in particular where a woman in a vee with two men was afraid to talk about challenging things with one of her partners because she felt like he was always overloaded with his own problems. This particular partner also struggled pretty consistently with his own jealousy towards his metamour and, in the past, had gotten upset when his partner revealed details about her other relationship. Overtime, this created a dynamic where the woman would avoid bringing up anything that felt potentially triggering for this partner, and would even gloss over painful situations in their relationship because she "didn't want to rock the boat." Eventually, when the resentment accumulated from all this toxic, bottled-up energy finally exploded in the context of a disagreement between the two of them, the man was dumbfounded when she announced she was intending to leave the relationship because she could no longer take it. Without having had the opportunity to work through any of the underlying issues that went unaddressed for so long, the man was totally blindsided by a breakup that seemed to come completely out of nowhere.

When you couple the reality of our limited personal resources in terms of how much time we realistically have to devote to our various commitments and relationships with the fact that most of us have very little sense of how to effectively navigate conflict, finding the motivation to carve out time for difficult conversations can sometimes feel next to impossible. As human beings, we are typically inclined to prioritize what makes us feel good or is emotionally gratifying, and to put off for the indefinite future what feels hard, heavy or unmanageable. The fear of unwanted outcomes and emotional pain is compounded by our lack of a clear, practical strategy for maneuvering our hurt and upset, which leaves us feeling generally resistant to or incapable of addressing issues as they arise. However, when this obstacle is at play, we need to make the time to talk to our partners. The truth is, many of us say we don't have enough time to deal with the hard things that come up in our relationships, but when we meet someone who piques our interest or we get invited to a concert we really want to go to, all of sudden, like magic, we somehow find the time to make it happen.

Even though it can mean you will need to confront some emotional discomfort, it's extremely important for the health of your relationships to work on issues as they arise. Here are some initial suggestions to help you prioritize working on any lingering hurt in your relationships:

- Let your partner know you want to talk—sooner rather than later—and schedule a time to do so.
- Schedule regular check-ins for more difficult conversations so that resentment doesn't build up in the relationship.
- Take the long view and be brave. It's better to have an awkward or uncomfortable conversation sooner, when the issue is much smaller, than to wait until it has become full-on hurt or harm.

"Just Let It Go"

Another big challenge that many of us face is a particular narrative about what we should do with our emotional hurt. For example, growing up in my Christian household, I was often expected to just forgive my brother for things he did to me, without actually having my own hurt acknowledged first. Looking back, I can now see how my stressed and overworked parents were simply using the religious concept of forgiveness as a convenient means of bypassing the more complicated and time-consuming work of processing the conflict in an equitable way. Essentially, they just needed me and my brother to stop fighting as quickly and painlessly as possible. As a parent myself, I totally get it, and even have compassion for them. However, I can also see how my experience was actually indicative of a much larger cultural attitude about dealing with emotional hurt in general. Aside from the well-worn cliché of "forgive and forget," we are also taught to internalize the virtue of "letting things go" or "not holding onto the past."

This idea that we should stop holding onto the things that trouble us shows up in interesting ways in CNM relationships. Partners who are responsible for causing emotional hurt can easily fall into the trap of deflecting personal accountability by resorting to this narrative and insinuating that their partners are not being "poly enough" or are somehow "less evolved" intellectually or emotionally because they won't let go of the past and move on or are not displaying enough compersion. I have seen this repeat itself quite a bit in situations where someone is eager for a particular experience, such as having sex with a new partner, initiating their first group sex encounter, spending a night out or escalating the commitment in a relationship, and then decides to move forward without first making sure their partners are OK with (or even know about) what's happening. Afterwards, instead of holding space for their partners' upset and taking ownership for undermining trust in the relationship, they try and turn the tables on the conversation by suggesting their partners' unwillingness to let go of the issue means they are not really committed to the values of CNM or that they want to control their partner and limit their freedom.

When successful, this kind of redirection can leave the people who originally felt hurt to take on the blame for their own distress. It can also lead them to believe there is something fundamentally wrong with them as people, or that they are somehow incompatible with CNM because they are unable to accept their partners' behavior. It is a particularly toxic dynamic that can really erode the connection between partners as well as leave people with the impression that CNM is simply not for them because they are not evolved enough to let go of their hangups.

The idea that we should simply let things go also feeds into a common misuse of the concept that each of us, as individuals, are wholly responsible for our own feelings. While I believe that in principle, we are all responsible for the way we respond to our own feelings and internal experiences, this does not mean that particular words and actions cannot be hurtful, or that our partners are absolved from the need to acknowledge the impact of their behavior on us when we feel hurt. For example, eschewing our personal accountability for breaking a mutual agreement to not sleep with someone new on the first date by suggesting our partner's hurt is a product of their own attachment issues rather than an actual broken commitment is unethical and highly problematic. It creates an acute sense that the relationship is not safe by undermining the foundations of trust. In order to maintain a legitimately secure attachment in any relationship, we have to explicitly recognize that our behavior can have negative consequences on other people, even when we had no intention of harming them.

While perhaps in some circumstances the advice to let go of what troubles us can have the intention to relieve us of any undue internal burden, this is definitely not the case when it is the very person who has hurt us who is admonishing us to let go. Hearing your partner say something like "You're overreacting," "Well, you do the same thing," "It's in the past now, just get over it," or "Haven't we already talked about this? Why can't you just let it go?" essentially conveys the message that your hurt is not welcome and it's basically your fault you still feel this way. When framed like this, the person who has been harmed is actually now the one responsible for resolving the conflict by abnegating their own experience and absolving the person who hurt them without first receiving some kind of acknowledgement and repair. This kind of thinly veiled victim blaming is problematic precisely because it creates a dynamic where resentment and anger are likely to accumulate until they eventually poison the relationship beyond repair.

For as much as we would like to believe we can, we cannot simply let go of emotional hurt. It gets recorded in our minds, stored as negative feelings in our body, and replayed in our interactions with partners every time we find ourselves in situations similar to the one in which the original hurt took place. Emotional wounds big and small need to be taken seriously in order to maintain the health and wellbeing of a relationship. Just like physical wounds, when left unattended, they can start to fester and eventually become infected. When a partner is telling us that something we did or said negatively affected them, we need to stop and take it seriously. Dismissing their experience by telling them they're overreacting, being too sensitive or holding onto things that don't matter sends the message that we don't actually care about them or their feelings, and we start to lay the foundation for a type of distance and disconnection that can be very difficult to undo down the road.

When you feel like there are still things from the past that you just can't let go of, honor that! Name it as a form of personal wisdom: a deep, inner recognition that, on some level, you still haven't received the acknowledgement, understanding or apology you need to actually move on and genuinely let go. Take the time to write down any of the circumstances or situations from the past that still cause you pain, which keep getting you to tell problematic stories about yourself or your partners. Ask yourself what is needed for this to truly be resolved, or at least moving in the direction of repair. If a partner *has* actually apologized to you in a way that feels sincere and asked what you need from them in order to address the harm, then ask yourself, on a deep level, what within you still needs tending to in order to really move on?

The intention of recognizing and naming hurts from the past is to truly move towards repair and resolution and should never be used as a weapon, or a way to get the upper hand in conflict. If you find yourself—or a partner—repeatedly bringing up past grievances without making sincere attempts to name and work with the needs or wants that underlie those hurts, then you need to explore the impetus behind this pattern. It is never acceptable to continue leveraging the past as a form of emotional blackmail, control or abuse. If you are unable or unwilling to give a partner the chance to work on repairing past ruptures, then be honest and transparent about this fact. In some cases, the nature of the transgression may feel too big or damaging to repair, or it has happened too many times, and you no longer have the desire or bandwidth to work on resolution. Or maybe you are just not in a place where you can work on these things right now, and you temporarily need space before you can engage in a restorative process. Whether it's a question of time or of repair no longer being an option, it's important to communicate openly with your partners about the possibilities—or lack thereof—of working on past hurts together.

"I'm Not the Villain Here"

Another very common obstacle is when we try to talk about painful situations from the past and get caught in the trap of trying to figure out whose story of what happened is more "true" or "accurate." Like lawyers in a courtroom, we get sucked into contentious arguments, becoming more and more disconnected as we try to convince each other of what "really happened." We state the facts and present our evidence as we build our case in an attempt to secure the moral high ground. We cast ourselves as the righteous protagonist in the story of our conflict and justify our actions as reasonable and even necessary acts of self-defense against the hurtful and self-interested deeds of our antagonistic partners. When mired in

this kind of dynamic, we go back and forth, incessantly interrupting one another, getting progressively more and more
frustrated as we feverishly try to tip the scales of relational
justice in our favor.

Those of us who live under the specter of a paradigm
steeped in the principles of a punitive criminal justice system
are conditioned to do everything in our power to avoid being
put into the role of the perpetrator. When confronted by
someone who accuses us of mishandling a situation, we will
emotionally "lawyer up" and compulsively start building a case
for our own innocence. In such a society, being "in the wrong"
carries with it the weight of potentially being punished or
facing some form of righteous retribution. Given this template
for conflict, the need to be on the "right" side of an argument
can be overwhelming. While completely understandable given
the nature of the typical adversarial approach to conflict, this
unfortunate pattern is one of the hardest things for people to
stop doing when they get triggered or feel threatened when
revisiting the painful past.

Resisting the urge to make ourselves right and our partners wrong in the retellings of our own conflict stories requires
not only a lot of presence of mind but also a new intention for
talking about the past. Instead of setting out to determine who
messed up by debating the empirical facts of a past situation,
we need to remember that understanding each other's experience will do much more to dissolve tension and reposition
us as allies than figuring out who was right or wrong. While
"being right" in a discussion may initially feel gratifying on
some level, like the short lived rush of a dopamine high, it can
also come at a great cost in terms of connection and emotional
security. The antidote here is to not focus so much on the facts
or who is right, but to really hear each other's experience and
interpretations of what happened, even if they're radically different from our own. Ultimately, our goal is to create a space
for mutual empathy by trying to understand the emotional

impact of the situation on each other and how each of us has been uniquely affected.

When slipping into the "I know what's really going on here" mindset, we lose our connection to the process and our partners, and this disconnection can be felt immediately. What is most problematic about thinking in terms of rightness or truth is that you lose your ability to stay genuinely curious and open to other people's experiences. When that happens, the conversation is no longer about hearing other people, it's just about them conceding to your point of view and admitting they were wrong. As caring partners and supportive metamours, we want to recognize when the temptation to succumb to an oppositional posture arises in us and consciously choose a more relational and restorative stance.

With all that said, I do want to acknowledge that gaslighting is real and that, unfortunately, sometimes people do intentionally change or distort the details of the past to paint themselves or the situation in a more favorable light. It is a tactic that is all too common, and it has devastating consequences on relationships. When we find ourselves describing the same event in radically different ways from our partners, it can be extremely disconcerting, and focusing on details or verifying our understanding of empirical information can be helpful. However, this kind of inquiry should only be reserved for clarification purposes, and not be the central intention of the conversation. Ultimately, a restorative process is no guarantee against someone who is intentionally trying to confuse or mislead; it is only effective to the degree people are sincerely wanting to do conflict differently and to be open and honest about their experiences.

Conflict without Consent and Taking on More than We Can Chew

Let's say you're just getting home from a stressful day at work and feeling exhausted, and all you want to do is put down your stuff, change your clothes and get some much-needed food into your system before you completely fall into the throes of a blood-sugar crash. Unfortunately for you, the partner with whom you are currently living just happens to be having intense feelings about the fact you invited a new lover to their birthday party, and they want to talk about it right now. Since they won't let up, you reluctantly indulge them, and not surprisingly, the conversation starts to quickly go sideways. Or let's imagine you are out on a date with a partner, trying to enjoy your time together, but you're having trouble relaxing into the moment because you're feeling a lot of resentment about their recent getaway to the mountains with a different partner. You swore to yourself that during the date, you weren't going to mention your lingering jealousy about never having this kind of romantic vacation together but, regrettably, you just can't help yourself, and you launch into an impromptu tirade about the injustice of it all. Predictably, your special evening doesn't end as you'd hoped.

Conversations where there is the intention to process challenging content should not be treated like regular conversations. Not only do we need to approach them with a heightened sense of care and attention, we also need to be prepared to have them in the first place. Trying to launch into a conversation about past hurts without getting some kind of prior consent from a partner is like playing emotional Russian roulette: you get what you get when you pull the trigger. If the odds are in your favor, maybe the other person will actually be in a place where they can hold space for you, and there will be less chance of things getting out of hand. However, if you catch them in a bad moment and just start dumping your process on them, well, best of luck to you! Consent is critical not just in matters of the bedroom, but also in the context of talking about certain topics together. Before engaging in a conversation that is likely to produce emotional sparks, make sure everyone involved is really in a place to have that kind of conversation. If not, take a rain check and schedule another time to circle back around.

While it may feel awkward or unfamiliar at first, we want to create as much structure around difficult conversations as possible. Too often we just start talking about the past willy-nilly and then very quickly find ourselves in a Category 5 hurricane. There's no focus, order, coherence or, most importantly, safety. Another very common problem is that there are often too many separate issues that get brought up in the course of the conversation, and things get super messy. Before you start processing past relationship ruptures or hurts with partners, you want to get very clear about what exactly you are going to process. The more specific you can be about the details of the conversation, the better. The first thing you want to do is name what you want to work on together. If there is more than one issue to talk about, it's generally a good idea to focus on one thing at a time. Trying to deal with multiple issues in the same conversation can often generate a level of complexity that makes it too hard to really work through anything properly. If you and your partners have separate hurts to process, decide ahead of time which thing you are going to focus on first, agreeing to set aside time at a later date for another conversation. Narrowing your focus in this way will greatly enhance your chances of success.

In short, we can learn how to build more safety into our process of dealing with the past. It can help to be extremely deliberate and actually have a conversation about the conversation before we have it. As partners, try to be on the same page as much as possible about what you are going to talk about and explicitly agree to focus on a particular situation. Honor that working through the past is already hard enough, and put as many safeguards in place as you can to help stack the deck in your favor. Getting consent to talk about challenging issues and zeroing in on which ones you're going to talk about is one of the best ways to avoid finding yourself in the middle of a hot, unwanted mess.

The Storm of Your Triggers

In my experience, there are two levels of conflict: the *storm* and the *content*. The storm is where all the physical, emotional and mental intensity associated with our triggers is generated and, unfortunately, is where most people get stuck. More often than not, when our nervous system gets activated, it doesn't take long before those of our partners get activated too, and vice versa. If we're not aware of what is happening, we can quickly find ourselves in an extremely challenging situation where the emotional intensity of the conversation creates so much interference that we never actually get to the level of content. Ideally, the level of content is where we want to be, because this is where we really get to touch the underlying issues of our conflict. It is the space where we can speak from our personal values and genuinely negotiate our needs and wants in the relationship. However, without the ability to successfully weather the storm of our triggers, we never get the chance to dive deeper into the content of our disagreements, and instead stay stuck in the swirl of emotional intensity until we finally explode or capsize.

Sometimes merely the *possibility* of dealing with the past feels threatening, because you have never learned how to process the intense emotions that can arise. Maybe you (or your partners) express feelings like anger, rage, grief, frustration or sorrow in ways that are harmful or destructive. Or maybe one of you feels incapable of holding space for the big emotions that come up without becoming defensive or collapsing into shame. Sometimes, when we have a personal history of trauma, the intensity of our partners' emotions can feel too threatening to engage safely, leaving everyone else feeling like there's no space for their experience. Either way, the inability to handle the emotional intensity of conflict keeps you stuck in a devastating cycle of avoidance, hurt and resentment.

So what happens when you are in the midst of a conversation and you get triggered? What happens when a partner irritates you in some way or says something that really upsets or offends you, and you just can't shake it off? How do you manage your own internal experience so that you can continue to communicate without contributing to the escalation of the encounter? Managing our triggers and learning how to successfully regulate our nervous system in the face of conflict is one of the single most important skills that we can use to de-escalate tense situations, and yet sadly, many of us still struggle to do it well. I have found that deliberately anticipating and preparing ourselves for the possibility of experiencing these triggers can be an important practice to develop in order to keep us grounded and present during the trickier moments of our disagreements.

Reclaiming our power from triggers starts with the recognition that we are not helpless in the face of them, but actually have a great deal of agency to choose how we respond. Once we know this, our work is to become very familiar with our triggers, recognize when we are in a triggered state, and then apply the necessary techniques to bring our nervous systems back into equilibrium. While we don't always have the luxury of changing the event that is triggering us, we can interrupt the trigger and choose a different, preferable course of action. The pattern of reactivity can be halted and re-routed at any point in the process once we become aware that we are under the influence of a trigger. Awareness of the trigger is our decision point where the possibility of redirecting our behavior opens up new possibilities to choose differently, allowing us to creatively respond instead of simply reacting to the triggering situation.

Because we are all different in terms of what triggers us, the process of learning to recognize and manage our triggers is very personal and specific to us as individuals. Therefore we must get really familiar with the ins and outs of our own triggers and learn to identify the particular ways they affect us. This means becoming sensitized not only to what the things that trigger us are—antagonistic remarks, certain tones of voice, facial expressions, physical gestures, specific behaviors, etc.—but also the very distinct reactions we experience in response to these triggers, such as unpleasant bodily sensations, negative emotions, or intense thoughts or stories about what is happening. Our opportunity with this work is to become masters of self-observation. Ideally, we want to be able to track the entire sequence of events, from the external action or situation that provokes us right down to the cascade of physical, emotional and mental reactions that emerge as a result. This kind of trigger awareness allows us to actively track our nervous systems' progression through their various stages of activation. Intentionally strengthening this kind of awareness will enable us to better notice when we are either about to be triggered or already in reactivity. The faster we can recognize that we are under the influence of a trigger, the more quickly we will be able to interrupt its momentum or consciously step away from the conversation and create the space to reestablish our emotional equilibrium before reengaging.

So what is your current level of awareness in terms of your own personal triggers and your responses to those triggers? What are the self-regulation skills you already have at your disposal for managing your triggers and bringing your nervous system back into a state of emotional equilibrium? For example, when you are able to recognize that you are triggered, are you able to calmly name the fact that you are triggered, rationally explain why the situation is triggering for you and then negotiate how to move forward with the conversation without escalating any further? If not, what do you think are the main challenges to doing so, and what do you need to focus on in terms of skills to be able to respond differently to your triggers?

EXERCISE   Trigger Awareness

Learning to identify our triggers and the particular reactions
that accompany them can help us increase our self-awareness
during moments of conflict. Use the following prompts to
track and deepen your familiarity with your own process of
slipping into emotional dysregulation.

1. What are the common triggers that consistently throw
    you off balance during moments of conflict with others
    (antagonistic remarks, certain tones of voice, facial
    expressions, physical gestures, intense emotions, specific
    behaviors, etc.)?

2. When confronted with these kinds of triggering
    situations, at what point on your own personal scale of
    nervous system activation do you start to recognize that
    you are triggered?

1	2	3	4	5	6	7	8	9	10

← Totally regulated   Completely dysregulated →

3. What are the somatic components that accompany your
    triggered state?
    » Body sensations (pounding heart, tight
      chest, closed throat, tears, upset stomach,
      shortness of breath, sweating, etc.)?
    » Emotions (sadness, anger, fear, anxiety,
      overwhelm, rage, frustration, etc.)?
    » What stories come up? (Examples: "I
      always have to do everything"; "He doesn't
      respect me"; "What's wrong with her";
      "They are so controlling"; "I'll never get
      my needs met in this relationship.")

4. What are your typical external reactions (yelling, getting
    quiet, talking fast, getting choked up, hitting, withdraw-
    ing, exploding, getting short, ignoring, etc.)?

Addressing Conflicts with Restorative Relationship Conversations

Up to this point, we have seen how the first step in changing our relationship to conflict is recognizing the need to change our underlying paradigm of conflict and the way we approach it in general. By moving away from an adversarial stance and adopting a restorative posture, we can enter into potentially challenging conversations with an open mind and heart, as well as a nervous system primed, not for confrontation and injury, but for deeper understanding and connection. Along with clarifying this pivotal paradigmatic shift, I have so far identified five common obstacles to working with the pain that still lingers in our intimate relationships, and I have explored some initial ideas to overcome them. Now, continuing our exploration of the restorative approach, we want to take a step forward towards the practical application of this methodology.

In order to really address the pain points in your relationships without becoming overwhelmed by your triggers, you and your partners need to be able to hold space for each other and genuinely listen to one another's experiences without a fear of making things worse. To successfully do this, there are two key parts to focus on: a clear process to guide your challenging conversations, and communication skills to cleanly express your feelings and avoid unintentionally triggering your partners. While the second component, communication skills, is beyond the scope of this chapter, I do want to offer you an effective model that you can use to structure your process. Aside from helping us make this important shift from a punitive paradigm to a more restorative one, restorative practice also emphasizes the importance of creating a protected space in which conflict can be safely processed. When you know what to expect and have clear rules of engagement to follow, you are much less prone to getting reactive, and much more likely to really hear your partners.

Setting the Stage for Restorative Relationship Conversations

In the course of actual sessions with clients, there are often multiple interventions, techniques and modalities that I use to help people successfully navigate their conflicts, but I want to at least offer you something here that can prove useful in moments of difficulty. Although the process is greatly enhanced by having a trained professional facilitating the conversation, it is possible to have success without always having a third party present. The outline of the Restorative Relationship Conversations process that you will find on the following pages can support you in creating a safe container for working through your conflict, however, there are a couple of things you want to bring to the table before attempting to use this method.

Checking in with Your Parts

Before engaging in a potentially triggering conversation, it can be helpful to check in and see if there are any internal parts of yourself that might be primed to resist or undermine such a process. Are there parts of you that want to maintain the conflict, prove the other person wrong, be accusatory or deny any responsibility for the situation? Maybe there are parts of you that are afraid to step into the vulnerability of a restorative process because they feel it's not safe to do so with your partners. Whenever they're present, it's very important to identify these parts and get clear about what exactly they are trying to tell us. I recommend using the process of working with your parts that is outlined in chapter two so they do not end up sabotaging or keeping you stuck in unproductive conversations. If they have valid reasons for not wanting to participate in a restorative dialogue, listen to them and figure out whether or not you can address their concerns before moving forward. However, if they are simply resisting or standing in the way of your process, let these parts know they are welcome to "watch" the Restorative Relationship Conversations that you are going to have with your partners, but be clear they are not allowed to participate.

Setting Our Intentions and Taking on a Restorative Posture

As invested and caring partners in a relationship, we want to be as conscious as possible of the intentions that inform the way we show up to potentially challenging conversations. This is because our intentions are one of the biggest factors determining how these conversations play out, and the importance of naming them before entering the deep and choppy waters of conflict cannot be overemphasized. Our intentions are extremely powerful because they direct our minds and energy towards specific outcomes, and if we don't consciously set them before having a tense conversation, we are much more susceptible to whatever comes out of us in the heat of the moment, which, unfortunately, is often reactive. Therefore, we want to do everything we can to make sure our best selves come to the table and this means being very aware of the energy that we are bringing into the process. This is why I ask that partners explicitly state their intentions for every Restorative Relationship Conversation before we begin.

For some, the process of naming and setting intentions before a conversation is new and unfamiliar. At first, they can experience difficulty coming up with specific intentions, and they need help generating ideas. The types of intentions we want to have for a Restorative Relationship Conversation are the ones that foster a sense of sincerity and collaboration. An example could be the intention to stay genuinely interested in your partner's experience. We need to remain curious about their perspective, thoughts, feelings, emotions and motivations as they relate to situations in which there was conflict. As I pointed out before, we do not want to fall into the trap of debating the "facts" or "truth" of the past, but rather create the space to really hear what the impact of the situation was on everyone involved. This requires the intention to stay present and open as we receive our partners' words—even when they are saying things that we don't agree with or that are difficult to hear. Another supportive intention is to hear our partners' feedback about how our behavior has impacted them, without becoming reactive or defensive, or collapsing into shame. It requires a great deal of fortitude and inner strength to hold the intensity of our partners' emotions without falling into the trap of feeling responsible for those emotions, which is why we need to be prepared to hold that kind of space. We also want to set the intention of not taking what we hear as criticism or attacks on our character. Our partners have to be able to share with us how we've affected them with our behavior without us hijacking their process with our own issues and insecurities.

The other power that intentions have is their capacity to generate what kind of attitude or posture we take towards a particular process: open or closed, receptive or blocked, collaborative or contentious. When ruptures in relationships happen, the primary means of restoring the connection is through empathy and understanding, and acknowledgement is the key to communicating these intentions. I have noticed that for some partners, there can be a certain resistance to offering acknowledgement for how their behavior has had an impact before explaining themselves or their own position first. Often the underlying assumption that fosters this resistance is the mistaken belief that acknowledgement in and of itself is an admission of guilt, of being a perpetrator or otherwise being in the wrong. Consciously or unconsciously, if we are holding the intention to be right in an argument, we are going to be fixed in a posture that sets us up for worse conflict.

The challenge then is how to actually get people to enter into the space where they feel safe enough to acknowledge the impact of their behavior. How do we face the discomfort of humbling ourselves and acknowledging the hurt we've caused, even when we had no intention of doing harm? The fear of retribution or the worsening of conflict can keep people from even stepping into the process in the first place, and thus it takes a great deal of courage to do such work. However, we must see that validating someone else's experience does not invalidate our own, and that acknowledgement is actually a very empowering and connective act. Therefore, we want to hold the intention of being willing to acknowledge our partner's experience and approach them with an open and relational posture before diving into our Restorative Relationship Conversations.

The Restorative Relationship Conversation Process

Now that we have set the stage we are ready to take a look at the steps of the process. The following is a description of the essential components of a typical Restorative Relationship Conversation:

Assigning roles: By having clearly defined roles for everyone, you know what to expect during the conversation and can lean into the structure of the process for increased emotional safety. The two roles that each person will play are the speaker and the listener. Before starting the conversation, it is important to figure out who will first be the speaker and who will first be the listener(s). Assigning the roles ahead of time will reduce the likelihood of problems during the actual conversation. Sometimes choosing who goes first can be difficult because each of you feels like you are holding your own pent-up anger, resentment, frustration, hurt or sadness. In situations like these, it can feel like a stretch to initially concede the speaker role. This is why it's important to remember that everyone will get a chance to speak and share their experience, but for the sake of the process, there does need to be the willingness and flexibility to let someone step into the speaker role first.

It is important to understand what the specific expectations are for each role. As listener we:

- Do not respond or interrupt (except to clarify something that was unclear).
- Give our full attention, remain open and stay curious.
- Reflect back only what we've heard.
- Acknowledge the impact of our behavior.

As speaker we:

- Inform others about the impact of their behavior without attacking, shaming or blaming.
- Speak from our own perspective, making "I" statements as much as possible.
- Never say what other's intentions or feelings are.
- Take full ownership of our emotional experience.

Reflecting back what you heard: After the speaker has had the chance to name the impacts of the conflict on their experience, it is the task of the listener(s) to reflect back what they heard the other person say. While reflecting back the speaker's experience, it is absolutely vital you avoid the temptation to justify our own actions, dismiss any part of their experience, offer explanations for events that occurred in the past, make personal observations, analyze the speaker or try to solve anything. Simply having someone accurately reflect back to us what we have shared is one of the most important steps to begin releasing stuck feelings and loosening the grip of the conflict dynamic. Knowing we have really been heard without having to deflect or manage other people's experience is extremely powerful, validating and healing. The following are examples of some useful phrases to help you form your reflective statements:

- "What I'm hearing you say is that you feel..."

- "It sounds like when I said/did _____, you felt really _____."
- "You're saying this is really hard for you because..."
- "For you, this situation was_____."

Acknowledging the hurt. After the speaker has confirmed they feel heard in their experience, it is up to the listener(s) to then offer an acknowledgement of the ways the speaker has been affected by the situation. Acknowledging the impact means empathizing with the speaker and recognizing that your words or actions caused harm, even if you had no intention of doing so. Here are a few phrases of acknowledgement to help get you started:

- "I hear how difficult this situation has been for you, and I acknowledge how I've contributed to that difficulty."
- "What you're saying makes a lot of sense to me, and I can see why you feel the way you do in this situation."
- "I recognize why this has been so hard for you, and I'm sorry."
- "I'm sorry to hear how much of an impact my words/actions have had on you."
- "I understand why you feel the way you do."

Taking turns: During the Restorative Relationship Conversation, everyone gets the chance to play the role of both speaker and listener. Knowing ahead of time that you will get the chance to both speak and listen greatly reduces the anxiousness or impatience you can feel during the process. Make sure to wait until the first speaker has had the chance to confirm they feel fully heard and acknowledged before switching roles.

Making agreements: Repairing the trust in the relationship can be achieved by making agreements to do things differently. Together you come up with specific agreements about how to repair the harm and what things need to be different in order to move forward with the relationship. This is an important opportunity for you and your partners to work together to create the changes that are needed in your unique relational dynamic, and it's helpful to make those agreements as practical and doable as possible. These agreements can focus on specific communication issues, such as the way you talk to each other in moments of tension, as well as agreements about relational patterns in general. The following is a list of potential agreements for intimate partners to give you some ideas:*

- We agree to not belittle our partners or threaten the relationship in moments of conflict.
- We agree it is not necessary to share all of the same interests, tastes or experiences.
- We agree that we are each responsible for establishing and upholding our own personal boundaries and limits, which can change over time.
- We will make every effort to understand each other's behavior, given the context of our unique personal history and experiences, and will suspend judgmental attitudes and avoid making negative assumptions about our partners' or metamours' intentions.
- When faced with triggering comments or behaviors, we agree to first try to interpret them in a loving and generous way.
- We recognize there will inevitably be times when each of us will lose sight of these agreements, and when this happens, we agree to lovingly come back to them and keep working towards cultivating a space where each of us feels heard, respected and understood.

---

*   These six relationship agreements are adapted from the 2003 DBT workbook by Scott A. Spradlin called *Don't Let Your Emotions Run Your Life: How Dialectical Behavior Therapy Can Put You in Control.*

Applying the Restorative Relationship Conversation Process

Use the following outline of the Restorative Relationship Conversations process to work through regrettable incidents, past fights or lingering emotional hurts that still feel present in your relationships. Carefully follow the sequence of guidelines to help you talk about the incident without falling back into unproductive conflict.

Set a time to do this process: When needing to process a potentially challenging issue with your partner, always ask them about their willingness to have a conversation about the conflict before launching into your feelings about the situation. If the other person is not in a space to have the conversation at the moment, ask to schedule a time to meet with them that works for both of you. Plan to meet in a space that offers privacy, where there will be no interruptions or distractions.

Intentions and posture: Set the intention to stay curious, open and receptive to each other. Assume a relational posture that recognizes that each of your particular perspectives and experiences is valid, even if those perspectives are based on misunderstandings or incomplete information. This means you won't focus on the facts of what happened or who said what, but instead will seek to genuinely hear and understand each other's experience.

§

After agreeing on a specific incident or past conflict to focus on during the Restorative Relationship Conversation, decide who will play the role of the speaker first. Afterwards, follow the steps in the next table.

SPEAKER   **LISTENER**

1 **Describe your own experience** of what happened. Use "I" statements and avoid commenting on other people's feelings or interpreting the reasons and intentions behind their actions. Try to present your position without blame or criticism.

As the speaker shares their experience, stay connected to the intention to listen to them with an open heart and mind. Continually reconnect with the intention to listen fully with interest, empathy and sincerity. This is an extremely active process that requires you to resist distraction and really attune to the other people involved. Track your own internal reactions as they arise. Be aware of the thoughts, feelings, judgments, memories or stories that arise within you when listening to the speaker. Silently acknowledge their presence, but then quickly return your full attention to the speaker.

Summarize what the speaker just shared. You don't need to recite their words verbatim; you just want to capture the essence of what their experience was, along with the feelings and needs that accompanied their perception of what happened. Do not add any of your own commentary, explanations, analysis or perceptions. It is imperative that the other person feels heard before moving on to more content. When you're done summarizing, ask the speaker if you got it right, or if they want to change or reiterate something that you may have missed. Postpone sharing your own experience until you switch roles after step 7.

SPEAKER

LISTENER

 After the listener reflects back what they heard you say, **pause for a moment and check in with yourself** to see if you feel understood by them. If yes, go on to step 4. If no, repeat anything you think is important that the listener may have missed or that you really want them to understand. It's important that you not move on until you really feel understood. It's OK if you need to go back and forth a few times. Be patient and manage any defensiveness or inner frustration that you may feel if they didn't fully get it the first time. Once you feel like they "got it," go to step 3.

If the speaker does not feel fully understood, ask "What do I need to know to understand your experience or perspective better?" Listen to what they said and then summarize what you heard, checking in as to whether you got it or if there is anything else you missed, or anything else they need to say.

Go back and forth as much as the speaker needs to until they feel like you really got it. Stay open and manage any defensiveness or inner frustration that may arise if you didn't get it the first time. Once the speaker feels understood, move to step 3.

SPEAKER   **LISTENER**

❸ Receive the acknowledgement from the listener.

> Once the speaker feels like you understand
> their experience, now it is time to **acknowledge
> their experience** by saying something like, "*It
> makes sense to me why you see it this way,*"
> "*I see why you would have felt the way you
> did,*" or "*I understand why this was so hard
> for you,*" etc. Acknowledging your partner's
> experience does not mean that you have to
> agree with it 100%. It also doesn't mean that
> your own experience is invalid by validating
> theirs. It means that you are connecting with
> what they went through as if you were listening
> to a friend who just went through a painful
> situation and you're empathizing with them.
> *Avoid explaining how this makes you
> feel or launching into an apology.

❹ Thank your partner for acknowledging
you and then share any positive impact
or feelings that you're experiencing as
a result of them taking the time to see
you and understand your perspective.

> **Take responsibility:** Share with your partner
> what you see as your contribution to the
> incident. Without making excuses for your
> behaviors, share what you specifically regret,
> what you wish to apologize for and what you
> see that you could have done differently.

SPEAKER   **LISTENER**

5 **Accept your partner's apology,** or let them know what you still need in order to really accept their attempt to be accountable.

6 **Take responsibility:** Share with your partner what you see as your contribution to the incident. Without making excuses for your behaviors, share what you specifically regret, what you wish to apologize for and what you see that you could have done differently.

· ·

SPEAKER & LISTENER

7 **Switch and repeat** steps one through seven with the other participants.

8 **Take turns sharing** what you each think are the important takeaways and lessons learned from this situation. Decide whether any of these insights could be useful for crafting agreements about how to do things differently in the future.

9 **Make agreements:** Finally, talk about anything that's needed to repair what happened, and how to do it better next time. Share if there is anything that any of you needs from each other to be able to put this behind you and move on. Take turns sharing one to three things that you agree to do differently the next time something like this happens again. Then share one to three things that the other participants could do to make it better next time. If you need to, write these agreements down so that you all can refer to them and keep them fresh in your minds.

TABLE 4.2: Nine steps for a better conversation.

§

Many of us who were raised under the influence of a criminal justice system based on punishment and retribution have internalized a way of relating to conflict that, instead of turning us towards our partners for mutual support and collaboration, actually pits us against each other as adversaries. Tragically, this punitive paradigm has conditioned us to approach our interpersonal conflict in a way that is likely to make it worse, robbing us of the opportunity to use it as a means of deepening our intimacy and connection with loved ones. Part of this unfortunate legacy is that many of us have grown up with very few skills and resources to successfully manage our disagreements, which can make our relationship to CNM, where conflict is often abundant, feel even more difficult. And while changing our relationship to conflict doesn't happen overnight, the first step is to recognize there are better ways to approach it.

The principles of the restorative paradigm offer an exciting and practical alternative to what many are used to vis-à-vis conflict resolution. By shifting our focus away from a need to figure out who was in the wrong towards an intention to acknowledge and address harm, we take an important step in the direction of a more relational way of working with conflict. Coupled with this powerful shift, the restorative approach also gives us a structured process with which we can safely manage challenging conversations. As we bring more and more precision and clarity to our particular conflict dynamics, we are able to navigate them with more skill and confidence, allowing us to really get to the needs and wants that underlie most of our disagreements. My hope for all those people out there continuing to struggle with interpersonal strife is that this brief introduction to the restorative paradigm and the Restorative Relationship Conversations model serves as a helpful resource for recalibrating your orientation to conflict and provides you with a sense of legitimate hope that things can truly be different!

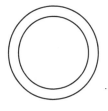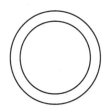

CHAPTER FIVE
CODEPENDENCY AND DIFFERENTIATION

After Dave and I opened our marriage, my first polyamorous love was Sam. To my initial surprise, Sam and I could not have been more alike. We were the same Enneagram number and Myers-Briggs personality type, our astrology was well aligned, we spoke each other's love languages, and we even had similar Erotic Blueprint styles.* With Sam, I felt seen and fed in ways I hadn't experienced before and, for all intents and purposes,

---

* The Enneagram is a system of personality typing that describes nine personality types based on a particular core belief about how the world works. Myers-Briggs is a personality inventory based on Carl Jung's theory of personality types. Astrology is the study of the influence that distant cosmic objects have on human lives. Love languages is a concept created by Dr. Gary Chapman, who identifies five different ways of expressing and receiving love. Sexologist Jaiya Ma created the Erotic Blueprint framework, which includes the five styles of language (energetic, sensual, sexual, kinky and shapeshifter) in which people express their eroticism.

it seemed like a relationship recipe for success. Even though there was a high level of compatibility between the two of us, Sam was my first lesson in the importance of being differentiated from our *other* partners in CNM because there are more than just two in the tango. While the quality of a connection and compatibility between two people is important, CNM is not just about two people: it is also about the network of intersecting relationships in which those two individuals move. This means any potential enmeshment and codependency that we have with a partner can significantly hinder our ability to have a substantial relationship with anyone else.

When Dave and I opened up, I became increasingly aware of my own enmeshed tendencies (more on this story later in the chapter), and I realized that if I was going to have space in my heart and life for another relationship, I needed to address my codependent overfunctioning and caretaking for Dave. As Sam and I began to date and build our own relationship, I quickly saw how important it was that I have the freedom to call and text him when I wanted, plan dates and generally have more personal space for transitioning between partners as I integrated all the new changes into my life. I also began to notice the subtle ways my identity was unknowingly fused with my marriage, as evidenced by things as mundane as the fact all of my online passwords were some combination of Dave and my names and birthdays. In monogamy, having my passwords reflect my *only* romantic relationship just made sense, and seemed like a sweet way to pay homage to our relationship, but in polyamory, it actually started to feel too hierarchical, and a sign that my personal identity was too enmeshed with Dave's.

On Sam's end, he was in a marriage where he played the role of the emotional, logistical and physical caretaker. Initially, I admired how caring and committed he was to his wife, but as time went on, I became concerned about how much of their dynamic was highly codependent, and what that actually meant for him and me. Before making plans with me, he would first defer to the comfort level of his wife. I saw him struggle to assert his desires to have time with me and create the kind of relationship we wanted, and it was unclear how much actual autonomy he had in general, let alone in relationships outside of his marriage. In our case, neither Sam nor I were even looking to become co-primaries, or to domestically entwine our lives together. I lived with Dave, and we were raising our son together—which was my top priority—and Sam was running a business with his wife that consumed a great deal of their time and energy. So being secondary partners seemed like the perfect arrangement for all of us. However, over time the possibility of even being a secondary partner in Sam's world started to feel difficult to negotiate.

When I first began to question him as to whether he was independent enough from his wife to actually have space for me, I unwittingly initiated the beginning of the end of my relationship with him. The question of his codependency seemed to be a massive eye opener for him, and after admitting that their enmeshment did make it difficult for him to be CNM, he later retreated from our relationship because of how overwhelming it felt to even begin addressing their issues. While this wasn't the only challenge we had had, I do see the end of our relationship as mostly a result of the collateral damage incurred from the monogamous, romantic ideal that frequently gets people within couples to forgo their own autonomy and become a partial person for the sake of their coupled identity.

As nonmonogamous partners come to me to try and make sense of why they're having such a hard time with being open, they often express confusion about why their relational freedom can feel so difficult to enact. For some, taking time away from one partner to be with other people brings up their own guilt about spending time apart, having separate experiences and even enjoying certain things about their new partners that are not present in their other relationships. In an attempt to compensate for this kind of guilt, they often do some version of over-caretaking or walking on eggshells before or after they go on a date, trying to alleviate the guilt, much like when a wife in a more traditional gender role cooks and then freezes all the meals for the week so her husband won't have to feel the impact of her taking a trip by herself.

Other people express frustration because they feel like they have done everything their partner asks of them in terms of offering quality time, attention and reassurances—ironically showing up with even more relational attunement now than before—and yet still have to deal with their partner's fear of abandonment every time they are with someone else. Some people are deeply hurt, even offended, when a partner starts to create healthy boundaries or admits to wanting more space in the relationship. Additionally, many a drama can ensue as new partners ask for more time, attention, overnights or unbarriered sex. If people practicing CNM enter certain nonmonogamous communities that promote behaviors like asserting one's boundaries, being more autonomous, or being less couple-centric or hierarchical, people are often baffled and frustrated by how enacting these things, which seem so healthy, creates so much strife with their partners. "If autonomy and separation are supposed to be so good, creating more passion and desire like so many relationship experts claim, then why is it making my relationships so much worse, instead of better?" In a word, it's all about *differentiation*.

Differentiation is an important developmental step in any relationship, whether monogamous or nonmonogamous, where partners learn to clearly define themselves and their boundaries as individuals while at the same time maintaining closeness and intimacy. This initially sounds great on paper and seems like it would definitely benefit most relationships, but it is actually much easier said than done. As the Polyamory School points out in their article "The Most Skipped Step When Opening a Relationship," differentiation between partners is a critical yet often overlooked prerequisite for successfully opening up. In the beginning of their article the authors humorously describe a couple's painstaking process of getting ready to open their relationship, including things like having lengthy conversations about what polyamory will mean for them, reading numerous books on the subject, listening to all the relevant podcasts, diligently crafting dating profiles, and making shared lists of boundaries and agreements, only to find themselves knee-deep in crisis as soon as they start to see other people.

In their rhetorical answer to the question of "What the hell just happened to our relationship?" the authors offer a valuable insight into one of the most unrecognized consequences of the current monogamous paradigm: "What you didn't realize when you were living in the cocoon of a monogamous relationship is how much a monogamous relationship is a favorable breeding ground for codependence." Codependency and enmeshment are typical dynamics that show up when partners have not yet managed to differentiate themselves from each other, and they are issues that are far more common than one might think. It is specifically this lack of differentiation that represents a significant roadblock for many open relationships, which, to me, is not a criticism of the partners per se, but more of a lesser-known consequence of the mono-romantic ideal that most of us have grown up internalizing.

Defining Codependency and Enmeshment

Before we look at how many of the current ideals espoused by our predominantly monogamous culture can actually interfere with our ability to differentiate from our partners, let's get on the same page about some of the terms we'll be using. In the same way that words like *narcissism* or *gaslighting* have achieved mainstream usage in the last few years, each having different shades of meaning depending on its usage in either clinical or everyday settings, so too have the terms *codependency* and *enmeshment* made their way into the popular lexicon, holding different meanings for different people. Enmeshment is a psychological concept introduced by the Argentine child psychiatrist Salvador Minuchin to describe families where the parents' over-involvement and blurred personal boundaries interfere with the healthy development of a child's psychological autonomy. In the context of adult relationships, enmeshment refers to the lack of clarity around personal boundaries and to merged identities between partners.

The uses of the concept of codependency are more varied, with some professionals referring to it as a personality trait, a disorder, or even a disease, as in the case of Co-Dependents Anonymous (a 12-step program for people looking to overcome the codependency of their childhood and develop functional and healthy relationships as adults). For the sake of this discussion, I want to avoid the weaponization of these terms or the pathologizing of individuals by describing them as "codependent" or totalizing their partnerships as "enmeshed relationships." I do not see codependency or enmeshment as essential descriptions of a person's way of being, or as personality flaws that people are born with. Instead, I see them as patterns of behavior that are typically learned in early childhood relationships—often dysfunctional and traumatic ones—or as expectations we internalize through our exposure to the monogamous ideals that are predominant in our culture. For this reason, I see codependency and enmeshment as habits that can be unlearned. While the unlearning process may not necessarily be quick or easy, it's definitely possible to change these patterns with persistent practice.

Broadly defined, enmeshment and codependency describe certain patterns of behavior that interfere with the development and expression of an individual's healthy sense of personal autonomy. We can clearly see them in action with people who have personal boundaries that are too permeable and who struggle to function independently in the context of their relationships. Enmeshment and codependency can limit the healthy interdependence of partners, creating imbalances where individuals either over- or underfunction in relation to their loved ones. These dynamics can be quite obvious in a relationship, such as when someone has trouble making their own decisions without deferring to a partner, when someone finds themselves repeatedly rescuing or bailing out a partner from chaotic or dangerous situations, or when someone continually makes excuses for a partner's unhealthy, abusive or addictive behaviors. Sometimes codependency and enmeshment can play out in more subtle, covert or ordinary ways, such as when all of one's personal profile photos include a partner, only ordering a dessert at a restaurant if a partner does too, not thinking or feeling for oneself, or continuously putting one's own needs aside for a partner.

Some more examples of enmeshment and codependency are:

- Your feelings, mood and happiness are contingent on what state your partners are in.
- You have difficulty identifying your own feelings and needs, or you have trouble distinguishing between your own feelings and someone else's.
- You enter an aroused emotional state if your partners are upset, anxious, angry or disappointed.
- Your identity is defined by your partner or by your relationships.
- You desperately seek your partners' approval.
- Either you struggle making your own decisions, or you make all the decisions.
- You have trouble saying no.
- One partner is overfunctioning through doing the majority of the emotional, practical or logistical labor in the relationship, and other partners are underfunctioning.
- You are so over-involved in other people's business that you are not paying attention to your own self-care or life responsibilities.
- Boundaries between you and your partners are unclear or even discouraged.
- You feel your partners' emotions and take them on as your own.

- You put your needs last and subordinate your desires to your partners' wishes.
- Your sense of self-worth and self-esteem is based on being in your relationships.
- You value the opinion or approval of others more than your own.
- You fear abandonment, or you fear that you can't function without your partners.
- You have an exaggerated sense of responsibility for the actions of others.
- You participate in excessive caretaking, rescuing, controlling and preoccupation with others.
- You expect your partners to caretake or rescue you from your own emotions, hardships or problems.

As you can see from the above list, these relational patterns do not just reflect the way we relate to others, but also how we relate to ourselves. Are we able to know our own truth and reality as separate from someone else's truth? Can we identify our own feelings and needs without first referring to a partner, a relationship or an external authority? Are we able to connect to our own self-value, self-esteem and self-worth regardless of what's happening in our intimate relationships? Can we regulate our own emotional states or solve our own problems instead of always expecting our partners to do it for us? In her book *Facing Codependence*, Pia Mellody states that codependency is reflected in two key areas of a person's life: in relationship with the self and in relationship with others, and says that the work of changing our codependent tendencies in relationship with others most often lies in our capacity to strengthen our own sense of self.

In this sense, the work we do to break the chains of codependency is the same work necessary to create a healthy differentiation of self, where we develop the ongoing ability to identify and openly express important aspects of ourselves such as thoughts, feelings, wants and desires. In order to relate to our partners in ways that feel truly fulfilling, we must know ourselves enough and be able to identify what is going on in our internal world. As we mature in our own self awareness, the process of *differentiation of the other* means we develop the capacity to clearly communicate that internal world to our partner(s), set boundaries with them, as well as respect the boundaries of our partners.

Romance or Codependency?

Another important part of deconstructing codependency is recognizing the particular ideas and narratives that endorse it. When I think about most of the love songs that I grew up with, I'm left wondering if it was truly love, or codependency they were singing about. Similarly, when I scroll through most of the romcoms or dramas available to stream these days, I'm left wondering if they are really promoting romance, or simply the idea that we are all inherently incomplete without a partner. When pursuing love, we are often encouraged by the people, culture and institutions around us to be in an exclusive relationship where we pour most of our time, energy and focus into being a couple and, eventually, a family. This well-worn relationship trajectory has been aptly named the relationship escalator, which, in the book *Stepping Off the Relationship Escalator*, author Amy Gahran refers to as the progressive and default set of social customs dictating the proper, suitable and legitimate forms of conduct in romantic relationships. It is the series of highly predictable steps that serves as the default template for conventional relationships for the majority of couples in our society: you first date, then get serious, move in together, get married, have kids, grow old together and retire to Florida.

While this model can indeed work for many people and provide them with healthy and satisfying relationships, the mono-romantic ideal does not stop with just promoting healthy levels of prioritization of your partner or family, but instead typically includes the idea that you and your partner should merge identities, that it's dangerous or problematic to spend time apart or have separate interests, that you have certain ownership of or rights to each other's time or sexuality, or that part of being a good partner means sacrificing selfhood in the name of the relationship. In such cases, the values of togetherness, investment and commitment step too far outside of their healthy expression, turning into engulfment, obligation, entitlement and the loss of self. The common monogamous, romantic notions of *I'm nothing without you, you complete me, we're half of a whole,* or *I can't live without you,* while very dramatic in their affect and even tempting in the sense of security they ostensibly promise, can actually be forms of unhealthy enmeshment or codependency that many of us confuse with love and romance. The notion we are left with is that the consummation of a truly transcendent love only comes when we completely fuse our life with someone else's, perpetuating the arrested development of healthy differentiation by promoting aspects of codependency and passing them off as the highest expression of love.

I do want to make a distinction here between the *temporary* loss of self that can happen through peak states of consciousness, or what mystics have identified as the oceanic feeling of being one with everything, versus the *chronic* loss of self that we are referring to as codependency and enmeshment. These momentarily elevated states of human consciousness can be generated through meditation, high intensity sports, heightened sexual experiences, psychoactive substances, breathwork, kink play, dance, playing music, being in nature, contemplating great works of art or even having a deep conversation with someone else, and they are most often accompanied by feelings of expansiveness, being more alive, connecting to the whole of life or simply being imbued with a sense of deep joy or contentment. These experiences typically leave us with a paradoxical transcendence of self as well as a more fortified sense of self than before, and they are not at all the same loss of self that I am referring to when I talk about codependency or enmeshment, where someone is struggling to know themselves, recognize and speak up for their own needs and wants, or maintain healthy boundaries between their emotional experience and that of their partners.

Similarly, I want to recognize the value and beauty of the emotional, spiritual or erotic desire for union that, as human beings, we seek. As social mammals, we have a strong urge to bond with others, and in particular, the erotic drive to experience sexual intimacy with someone else can be extremely powerful and completely worthwhile. The temporary loss of self that can happen in the context of passion should also not be reduced to mere codependency or enmeshment. Nor should the rush of hormones and the subsequent tunnel vision that accompanies NRE be confused with the patterns of behavior that we have been associating with codependency up to this point. The trick is to recognize the difference between a fleeting but beautiful and mutually shared experience versus an ongoing dynamic of unhealthy behavior that leaves individuals feeling insecure and incapable of taking full responsibility for their emotional experience. So while we ultimately want to embrace and celebrate the elements of romanticism that support healthy emotional bonds between partners—the experiences that allow us to momentarily let go of our egoic preoccupation with self and deeply connect with someone else—we want to do so in a way that allows us to remember there is a big difference between "I love you and I love being with you" and "I don't know who I am without you and I can't live without you."

Codependency or a Developmental Stage of Relationship?

As we continue to explore the relationship between romance and codependency, I want to take a look at the work of Ellyn Bader and Peter Pearson called the Developmental Model of Couples Therapy. Based on the stages of early childhood development, Bader and Pearson's model suggests that adult monogamous romantic relationships go through a series of developmental stages in a way that mimics the psychological growth of young children. By using these stages as a lens for examining the issues coming up in a relationship, we can better understand whether or not the people involved are moving through one of the stages, or are perhaps stagnating in one of them. In the same way that learning how to walk can be both frustrating and necessary for the developing child, romantically involved people learning to differentiate from one another can experience tremendous discomfort in that process, even though it represents a critical step in their relationship. Although nonmonogamous or non-escalator relationships may not track through all the same stages, or may move through them with a different order or pacing—which I discuss later in this chapter—seeing adult relationships as a journey that unfolds through a series of identifiable stages can help contextualize the challenges partners face in their process towards more integration. In particular, it can be a helpful way for us to deepen our understanding of codependency and enmeshment and see these challenges more as symptoms of struggling to move through certain relationship phases instead of as something purely negative or pathological.

According to Bader and Pearson's model, the first stage that romantic relationships typically enter is called *symbiosis*, which represents what many of us think of as the "honeymoon" phase. This includes things like getting to know someone for the first time—or in a new way if you already knew each other—falling in love and, to varying degrees, merging boundaries with them. In symbiosis, separateness falls away, and Bader jokes that people can actually experience a temporary feeling of psychosis during this time. It is similar to the initial bonding phase that happens between parent and child characterized by intensive eye gazing, lovey-dovey talk and the child's literal lack of awareness of where their own body ends and their parent's begins. For adults it is during this stage that a sense of "we" is created and an identity as a couple is first formed. Symbiosis typically feels really good and is most often accompanied by a flood of intensely positive emotions and even highly addictive hormones. The importance of this stage is directly related to the creation of the necessary emotional bond that will allow a relationship to deal with the challenges that inevitably arise down the road. Interestingly, it is precisely the elements of this initial stage of symbiosis that are most often associated with modern North American popular ideals of romance and love, and when they begin to fade or diminish in intensity, many assume it means there is something wrong with the connection.

After the initial rush of enthusiasm and passion subsides and the all-consuming focus of symbiosis starts to wane, the nudge to begin the next phase of *differentiation* is set in motion. During this stage, the individual self begins to re-emerge from symbiosis and is faced with figuring out how to be in a relationship with another, fully separate individual.

The process of differentiation is characterized by partners being able to actively define their own thoughts, feelings, needs and desires to each other and then acknowledge, respect and negotiate the differences between them. It's not that those differences weren't there in the stage of symbiosis; rather they were often downplayed or eclipsed by the cocktail of hormones generated by all the free-flowing affection and physical connection at the beginning of the relationship. According to Bader, a central task of this developmental stage is to lay the groundwork for resolving the higher levels of conflict that inevitably arise in long-term relationships. Because we may not always like all the same things, approach life the same way or agree on everything, we have to develop the capacity to recognize and accept these differences in ways that honor the connection instead of creating tension or discord. When couples are able to allow and respect their differences, they are actually creating the foundation for deeper levels of intimacy and greater degrees of interdependence despite the potential temporary discomfort or challenges of doing so.

When the stage of differentiation happens and partners are able to integrate their respective differences, they continue on to the third stage called *practicing/individuation*. While partners are still very much invested in the relationship, practicing is about recentering oneself in the "I" again. It is usually a time when people put more energy into their career, friendships, parenting, continuing education or other important endeavors that take place outside of the relationship. In symbiosis, a partner's sense of self is directly related to their romantic relationship, whereas in the phase of practicing, people develop their self-esteem in other areas of their lives. Practicing is the stage of individuation, reconnecting with yourself and who you are in the world beyond the container of the relationship. In this phase, couples will typically ebb and flow between periods of closeness and connection and doing more things on their own.

The final two stages are *rapprochement/reconnecting* and *synergy/mutual interdependence*. In rapprochement/ reconnecting partners begin to return back to the relationship, but will go back and forth between moving away and returning to each other.

Often, a couple's sex life will deepen during this phase, and a newer version of "we" begins to form that includes the "I" of each partner instead of eclipsing it. In the final stage of synergy/mutual interdependence, partners experience higher levels of intimacy, recognizing how a couple can be stronger together than each member is alone. This stage is where the "we" of the relationship and the "I" of self is integrated, and the "we" of the relationship is nourished by the individuality of each partner. As Bader says, this is where one plus one truly is greater than two, and partners are often working on passion projects or their legacy together.

Most partners who come to therapy seeking support with issues related to the various stages just mentioned are either stuck in symbiosis or experiencing conflict related to the transition into the differentiation stage. As previously stated, the bonding stage of symbiosis is very important for the long-term survival of the relationship, but it is certainly not meant to be permanent. As partners begin to leave symbiosis and start to differentiate, conflict often increases because they are now addressing things they have never dealt with before. Without the knowledge or capacity to manage these challenges skillfully, the process of differentiation can be very difficult and taxing on the relationship. As partners really start to confront their differences for the first time, anxiety can soar and uncertainty can arise, making the relationship seem at risk of falling apart.

Unfortunately, for many the phase of differentiation often feels more like disintegration than evolution, and the involuntary impulse to alleviate the discomfort leads couples to regress back into the familiarity of symbiosis where things seemed easier, closer and more comfortable. However, the return to symbiosis comes at a high cost. The intoxicating fusion of self and other that characterized the original bonding experience now becomes a state of relationship stasis, leaving partners as partial individuals harboring obscured desires and muted preferences. The initial pleasure of symbiosis turns into stagnation of both the relationship and the individuals, creating the perfect breeding ground for codependency and enmeshment.

While obviously not every relationship is destined to fall into the trap of codependency, many partners do succumb to the dynamic just described. Part of what makes this reversion back to symbiosis so prevalent is the fact that the monogamous romantic ideal aggressively promoted in North America actually encourages the fusion of our personal identity into coupledom, suggesting that this fusion is the endgame of romantic love. Instead of being a beautiful but transient step along a much more integral journey, symbiosis is touted as the end-all and be-all of "true love." The tragic shortsightedness of this narrative leaves many partners left with the sensation that they, as individuals, are somehow not good at love, while failing to recognize that the all-encompassing intensity of symbiosis isn't meant to be sustained forever. Collectively, the impact of our over-fixation on symbiosis has created a culture where we're generally unaware of the importance of developing the skills that would facilitate our progression through the stages of relational growth. When you combine this hyperfocus on romanticized symbiosis with the fear and discomfort that arise during the differentiation stage, it can feel almost impossible to resist the gravitational pull of codependency.

The ways that people can get stuck in the early stages of symbiosis or differentiation can manifest in a variety of different dynamics. Bader makes a distinction between two patterns in particular, which she calls the hostile, angry couple and the conflict-avoidant couple. Both of them are characteristic of issues related to the first stage of symbiosis. The hostile, angry couple constantly bickers, nitpicks and argues, often frustrated by their respective differences as individuals. Tragically, instead of embracing their differences or dissimilarities in a way that would facilitate the transition into the stage of differentiation, they instead experience themselves as victims of each other's idiosyncrasies. Like two fish seemingly trapped together in the fisherman's net, both individuals have a sense of themselves being at the mercy of the relationship, each completely subject to the disagreeable qualities of their partner. They are caught in a perpetual competition of needs, acting as if only one of them can get their needs met at any given time, and are embroiled in a tension between feeling bound to the relationship and resentful for not having a way out of it. The result is a dynamic where each individual makes their discontent known to the other through a variety of contentious behaviors, each seemingly committed to the perpetuation of this withering pattern.

In a relationship where there is a pattern of conflict avoidance, differentiation is carefully avoided because it would simply be too threatening to face each other's differences. Typically, at the heart of this avoidant behavior are two things: an underlying fear that disagreements or divergent points of view will inevitably mean the end of the relationship, and the recognition—conscious or not—of a lack of know-how for managing these differences. Given this fear of losing the relationship and the gap in their relational skill set, couples will continually opt for the relative safety of symbiosis. On the surface, they may look like they get along really well, and they may actually take pride in the fact that they barely ever fight, but underneath this veneer of tranquility there is often some version of walking on eggshells, subsuming personal needs, over-caretaking, concealing tension or contorting oneself in unhealthy ways to keep the peace. Too afraid to venture into the uncharted waters of increased autonomy, partners resign themselves to the lukewarm familiarity of a dynamic where everyone implicitly agrees to not challenge each other. Unfortunately, over time this lack of healthy tension neutralizes the polarity in the relationship and creates a situation in which the partners generally feel unfulfilled.

Other patterns that are possible are situations where partners are actually functioning in different stages simultaneously. Instead of individuals being stuck in symbiosis together or facing the difficulties of trying to differentiate at the same time, they are actually going in opposite directions. This can be due to partners just being in different stages based on their own personal history and growth trajectory, but in some cases certain cultural, religious or gender norms can create the expectation that one partner is supposed to stay symbiotic while others are more free to differentiate. This commonly looks like a situation where one partner is still trying to maintain symbiosis while the other is attempting to initiate the differentiation process. In dynamics like this, the partner who is still anchored in symbiosis feels like their partner is on the verge of leaving them, because their newly emerging attempts to express their personal preferences and desires are seen as a move away from the relationship instead of as a healthy move to the subsequent relationship stage. Does one of these patterns sound familiar to anyone?

Opening Means Differentiated...or at Least It Should!

Even though the Developmental Model of Couples Therapy was intended to plot the course of monogamous relationships, the way it contextualizes differentiation as a critical step in *any* relationship helps shed light on why newly opened couples who haven't taken this step still struggle in their process. For starters, opening up from monogamy *is* an act of differentiation. Both partners are choosing experiences with other people, which by default means they will be exploring the gratification of needs, wants and connection outside of the context of the original relationship. Even if couples decide to only date new people together, the relationship that each partner has with those new individuals will have its own tone and flavor. The challenge this kind of differentiation represents is that it often creates a dynamic that may not have existed before in the monogamous relationship. Therefore, while in monogamy you can get away with sidestepping differentiation, in nonmonogamy, this simply isn't an option. This is because the inclusion of new partners forces individuals to develop not only enough autonomy to know themselves in terms of their own personal wants, desires, needs and boundaries, but also the ability to express and assert those preferences to their partners—sometimes for the very first time in their relationship!

For partners still anchored in the stage of symbiosis, the inevitable differentiation that comes along with opening the relationship is often not only a big transformational catalyst, but also a literal shock. Symbiosis has a way of masking our enmeshed or codependent patterns, and initiating new relationships outside of the cocoon of the original relationship forces those patterns to the surface—sometimes brutally so. As we have said, one of the major benefits of the nonmonogamous paradigm is the way it requires you to develop new elements of your relational consciousness, but if you're not prepared to face all the ways you have been enmeshed, it can be painful to recognize these things for the first time. It's perfectly understandable that many of us still linger in the cozy confines of symbiosis, given the importance our culture has put on this particular stage. However, it is precisely this stunted transition to differentiation that so many couples seeking to open up need to understand as they are diving headfirst into new relationships.

Ideally, people practicing CNM would be at least in the practicing/individuation stage of this model, where they are functioning more independently from their partners and can come and go from each other with more ease and grace. The couples that I have observed who were already in this stage and opened up their relationships may still have had some bumpy turbulence in their transitions, but comparatively it is much smoother than when partners have yet to differentiate, and it seems to take much less time for them to find their CNM groove. Another factor is that under more monogamous circumstances, each of these stages can take years to move through, but in CNM, people have to either move through them at light speed, or move through them from different starting points or in different ways, which can unintentionally lead to challenges along the way.

If you are seeing yourself and your relationship in what has been discussed thus far, my first recommendation is to begin recognizing and deconstructing your couple identity. Couples are often eager to start their journey into nonmonogamy, but quickly get into trouble because they haven't yet identified all the ways their deeply ingrained sense of being one half of a monogamous pair still determines their sense of what's right or fair in the relationship. Wrapped up in the idea of being a monogamous couple are a whole bunch of unspoken assumptions and expectations that can represent significant obstacles to transitioning into healthy differentiation and doing CNM well. For example, what would the possibility of spending a birthday or a significant holiday apart from your partner mean to you? More specifically, what would it mean if your partner wanted to spend their birthday with another partner instead of you? Or if perhaps they wanted to spend New Year's Eve or Thanksgiving with someone else this year?

For many, it's a given that being a couple or primary partners means spending the majority of your free time together, and if you aren't doing that, either there are some special circumstances to warrant the change, or something is wrong with the relationship. But as other people make requests for our time and affection, we're forced to make choices that will inevitably challenge these kinds of taken-for-granted assumptions about how we're supposed to spend our time, and whom we spend it with. The more we open ourselves to other relationships, the more we're faced with the limits of our own freedom and availability, which for many exposes varying degrees of enmeshment or codependency. For example, do you have the freedom to tell a new partner that you can commit to seeing them once, maybe twice a week without your preexisting partner protesting or vetoing your desire? If not, how will you explain that to your new partner? What will that say about your relative level of differentiation, or lack thereof?

Some of the differentiation challenges that partners experience in the opening up process are not necessarily codependency pitfalls, but just a byproduct of how you have lived your life as a couple or a team of two, especially if you live together, and even more so if you have children. When partners open up, they are then faced with the logistical realities of dating others and having to figure out who is using the shared car, who is watching the kids or which credit card you can use for your date. In monogamy, when I check in with my partner about these kinds of details, such as which account to withdraw from or who's going to call the babysitter, the gesture can feel like an act of genuine consideration and support. But within the paradigm of nonmonogamy, the very same logistical check-ins can begin to take on the tone of asking permission or tiptoeing. In the CNM context, most people want to get to a place where they have the freedom to do what they want to do without having to prep, plan and process everything with their partners just to go on a date. And just like a teenager resisting the influence of their parents, they can get frustrated, even resentful, about how much time and energy has to be ceded to the relationship, parenting or domestic life.

While I'm certainly not suggesting that all of the behaviors monogamous couples engage in are inherently unhealthy or problematic, the point is that we need to recognize when our allegiance to these behaviors undermines our ability to differentiate ourselves from our partners. This means we can't allow the assumptions grounded in our previous monogamous mindset to dictate the agreements we make as an open partnership. It's fine to keep or continue using any of the arrangements from the original partnership as long as they've been explicitly negotiated and discussed. The most important thing is to bring our expectations to the light of conscious awareness and then decide whether or not they actually still serve us in the context of our evolving relationship. Also, part of the work is to make sure we are intentionally shifting the gravitational center of our personal identity away from simply being one half of a couple to being an independent individual and interdependent partner, operating within the context of open relationships. While obviously easier said than done, this last part in particular is something I think all partners making the transition to nonmonogamy need to keep in the forefront of their minds. Without first examining and letting go of the identity forged within the monogamous paradigm, making the leap to a nonmonogamous one will be all the more difficult.

Differentiation and Codependency in Preexisting CNM Relationships

While in general I do see codependency and the need for higher levels of differentiation as an issue largely facing newly opened couples, it's also important to recognize that long-term CNM relationships have their fair share of difficulties with codependency as well. As I mentioned in the beginning of the chapter, as Dave and I were opening up our marriage, I had to face my over-caretaking tendencies with him, which impacted my availability to new partners, and I was also trying to navigate my partner Sam's enmeshment with his wife, as they too were new to opening up. However, the realities of codependency showing up in CNM relationships didn't just stop there. Personally, I have had several different periods of time where, for various reasons, I was polyfidelitous with partners, and honestly, every time I've opened up again, it's been challenging to confront the ways being closed with multiple partners unintentionally replicated some of the dynamics of undifferentiated, monogamous couples. Additionally, I find I have to work much harder at maintaining my own sense of self within my CNM nesting relationships, as living all together in the domestic soup can easily consume autonomy and exacerbate enmeshment.

Any intimate relationship can become less differentiated over time, and CNM transitions can expose all of the ways we've potentially become codependent or enmeshed with our partners. In CNM relationships, we can still get into a groove with particular partners where we become accustomed to a certain amount of time, attention and couple-ness. It's easy to get used to these rhythms, and over time, this can foster a unique sense of "us" or "we." This kind of connection often feels really good and generally promotes some form of sweet emotional attachment. This can all be fine, until a partner with whom we've created this kind of bond wants to date or play separately with someone else or starts to invest more time, attention or commitment into other relationships. Then we can quickly find ourselves face to face with a lot of codependent discomfort.

Another way codependency and lack of differentiation can show up in CNM relationships is in the context of quads, triads, polyamorous families or other groups where multiple partners have chosen to either live together or intertwine their domestic lives in significant ways. On the one hand, being highly involved and close with your partners can be a beautiful gift, but on the other, it can also lend itself to a certain kind of apprehension about speaking up or challenging codependent patterns within the network of relationships. The fear of destabilizing the entire group dynamic can create a situation in which people can be reluctant to bring up issues. As one woman in a long-term quad created from two previously married couples admitted, "It's been at least two years since I've been getting my needs met in the quad. My original husband is now closer to our other wife, and I just feel like I'm everyone's secondary. No one really focuses on me, but our entire life is about managing the quad and raising our kids together, so I'm terrified that if I even mention that I need something different or more, then I'll screw it all up."

Because there are multiple relationships at play in these configurations, the stakes of having conflict between individuals can feel significantly higher than in the context of a dyadic relationship. The pressure to keep the peace often fosters a dynamic where issues of enmeshment or codependency are simply left to fester until something eventually gives way. Similarly, another client in her mid 20s who created a triad with a man and a woman who had been together for 25 years confided that even though she lived with them and felt integrated into their lives, she couldn't really ask for the things she needed or wanted. When I questioned her about this, she said that every time she spoke up about imbalances in their relationships, it would "cause ripples" in the original dyad, and she was scapegoated as the source of the problems. Eventually, she gave up trying to voice her opinions and opted for silence, preferring to "not rock the boat."

Even when practicing a style of non-hierarchical CNM such as solo polyamory or relationship anarchy where your desire for more differentiation and less entwinement is more explicit and upfront, you can still be subject to the enmeshed or codependent tendencies of your partners. For example, you may have partners who want to be enmeshed with you, or you may find yourself dealing with codependent dynamics spilling over from another partner's more hierarchical or nesting CNM relationship, which ultimately infringes on the autonomy and freedom of your relationship with that particular partner. Additionally, you may also find that you are taken less seriously by certain partners because, despite the fact they practice some form of CNM, they still prioritize relationships where there are explicit elements of relational hierarchy or escalator-style markers of relational importance or "realness," especially those that imply some merger of domestic life.

Finally, looking back at Bader's model of couple development discussed earlier in this chapter, I've seen how some healthy CNM relationships do not necessarily go through all the developmental stages, and the stages can occur in a different order for people who are already CNM, particularly in the sense that partners often start out more differentiated before even entering the stage of symbiosis. If you are dating someone new but both of you already have other partners, you are typically not able to enter symbiosis in the same way monogamous singles would. New CNM partners usually cannot create a romantic life together from scratch, but have to adapt to, work around and hopefully influence the preexisting relationship structures that are already in place for each person.

In general, I think that CNM requires more individual differentiation, which can support new CNM partners in being more healthfully differentiated from the start, even allowing them to more skillfully circumnavigate the gravity of codependency. In this sense, you are much less inclined to bring the expectation that you will be each other's everything to a new relationship, and instead will answer the question, "What can we be to each other given our current life circumstances, our unique connection and our preexisting relationships?" Additionally, being more differentiated from the start of a relationship can facilitate strong bonds rooted in partners' better knowing of themselves, their relationship needs and their desires.

Chasing Symbiosis

The last two sections have explored the ways CNM can support differentiation; however, you may also find that the circumstances and arrangements of your current relationships can actually postpone, restrict or interfere with your ability to enter symbiosis with a new partner because you have limited availability, or because your other partners are not ready for you to have the kinds of experiences—such as sex, sleepovers or travel—that typically foster bonding. These kinds of circumstantial impediments to experiencing symbiosis can function as both an advantage and disadvantage. On the one hand, the intermittent availability created by CNM life circumstances can actually prolong the phase of symbiosis because you are forced to stagger your bonding experiences. This can create the sensation of having an extended honeymoon period, where it takes longer for either the intensity to wane or the inevitable bumps in the road to emerge in the relationship. On the other hand, not being able to immediately enter this phase with a new partner can provoke feelings of resentment towards longer-standing partners or metamours because it feels like you are being thwarted from something pleasurable and enticing, leaving you constantly yearning for more of what you're not getting with a particular partner. The desire to dive into symbiosis with another person can be incredibly strong, particularly when you haven't experienced it in a while. Similar to how intermittent winnings at a casino can create positive reinforcement and a euphoric response that can lead to a gambling addiction, sporadic, limited or irregular opportunities for connecting and bonding with a partner can create an addictive, obsessive or all-consuming hyperfocus on a partner who feels just slightly out of reach.

Another phenomenon that arises in CNM relationships is a situation in which the emergence of the differentiation phase in one relationship spurs the start of a new, separate relationship. As the excitement and hormones of NRE subside, some partners will actively seek out new connections in an effort to stave off the discomfort and unfamiliarity of differentiation while perpetuating the pleasure and stimulation of being in a new relationship. This pattern creates a vicious cycle where people can become "NRE junkies," compulsively chasing symbiosis over and over again with new people. This makes the differentiation phase genuinely threatening to other partners, because the partner who is prone to set their sights on greener pastures is very likely to withdraw emotionally, or simply abandon the relationship when differentiation starts to emerge. In response, partners can feel a continual pressure to revert back to the restrictive parameters of symbiosis in order to protect the relationship. If you notice this pattern within yourself, it's important to ask if you are actually wanting a new partner or simply wanting the feelings and exhilaration of NRE. Bringing new people into your life just to maintain a steady fix of NRE is not advisable or ethical, and it can be very damaging to everyone involved.

Finally, it's important to note that symbiosis-chasing is not specific to CNM relationships, but can happen in every relationship structure, and some CNM relationships, whether by choice or circumstance, may not experience a symbiosis phase as described by Bader and Pearson, or a honeymoon phase as typically portrayed in North American culture, and yet they can still be healthily bonded and enduring. As we come to recognize the importance of differentiation in our relationships, regardless of how long we have been CNM, we can start to step into the process more deliberately. As we embrace this challenge, we have to be aware of the two lines of development that are necessary to successfully initiate this stage: differentiation of self and differentiation of the other. These next two sections explore different ideas and exercises to support you in your differentiation process, individually and within a partnership.

From Enmeshment to Differentiation as an Individual

As already mentioned, differentiation of self requires the ability to identify and express important aspects of ourselves such as our thoughts, feelings, wants and desires. To do that, we have to have a certain level of self-awareness, which includes the ability to identify what is going on in our inner world. However, as some people step outside the fusion of symbiosis—and the potential codependency that can accompany it—they may encounter a self that doesn't yet know who it is, what it wants or what it needs, let alone being able to articulate those things to another person. Instead of making contact with a coherent and well-defined self with its own laundry list of clear wants and needs, a newly differentiating person may meet only a vague sense of self who has yet to identify their preferences. Some people can even experience a sense of emptiness that leaves them feeling lost and directionless. Or they may have painful or traumatic experiences from the past that left them with the message that being their own separate, autonomous self was unallowed, or even unsafe. In cases like these, it is important to allow yourself to move through a phase of getting to know yourself, or even inventing yourself for the very first time.

In order to get a better sense of what's really necessary to develop differentiation and healthy autonomy, it's important to have a clear sense of what skills and capacities we need to have. The following list is meant to give you a better sense of what each of us needs to pay attention to as we initiate our own journey into self-differentiation:

- Know or be able to figure out what your own thoughts, feelings, boundaries and opinions are.
- Share and affirm your truth, which includes your thoughts, feelings, boundaries and opinions, in ways that are respectful and noncombative.
- Allow and respect another person's truth (even if you disagree or don't like it).
- Ask for what you want.
- Take full responsibility for your own thoughts, feelings, behaviors and decisions, and ask the same from others.
- Recognize and accept that people have different emotions than you that you are not the cause of, and that they can make their own independent decisions.
- Acknowledge the impact of your decisions and actions on others when necessary, and expect that your partners will do the same.
- Assert and maintain the necessary boundaries when your partners act in ways that are hurtful to you.
- Empathize, listen and offer support to your partners when they're struggling, but still allow them the space to solve their own problems.
- Take space when necessary to preserve your own mental and emotional wellbeing, and allow others to do the same.

As you can probably see from this list, differentiation requires a certain amount of self-esteem, as well as personal skills around introspection, communication, emotional regulation and boundary-setting. In the book *Facing Codependence*, Pia Mellody distills codependency to the five challenging core symptoms of struggling with:

- Experiencing appropriate levels of self-esteem.
- Setting functional boundaries.
- Owning and expressing one's own reality.
- Taking care of one's adult needs and wants.
- Expressing one's reality moderately.

When I read Mellody's list of the five challenging core symptoms of codependency, I like to reread the list not just as a list of what is usually missing for people struggling with codependency, but to read it as the positive skills and capacities that people have gained when shifting out of codependency and moving towards differentiation. Try rereading the above list as the five core capacities of being healthfully differentiated. How to work on each of these five core capacities or skill sets can each take up an entire book, and I've noticed that they are not mutually exclusive abilities, but rather each one reinforces and enhances the other. For example, having appropriate levels of self-esteem can create the courage to set boundaries, own and express your own reality and take responsibility for your own self-care, just as taking the risk to own and express your own reality can be a form of self-care and boundary-setting, which can in turn bolster your self-esteem.*

---

* To further your cultivation of these abilities, I suggest additional resources such as *Set Boundaries, Find Peace* by Nedra Glover Tawwab, *How to Be An Adult* by David Richo, *Unfuck Your Boundaries* by Faith Harper, *Not Nice* by Aziz Gazipura, *Decolonizing Nonviolent Communication* by Meenadchi, *The Art of Everyday Assertiveness* by Patrick King and *Befriend Your Nervous System* by Deb Dana.

Becoming Your Own Source

As we continue to explore the dual process of disentangling ourselves from enmeshment and stepping into the differentiation of self, we want to expand the list of things that will help us along this path. One of my favorite concepts is what I refer to as "becoming your own source." In *Polysecure* (p. 198), I introduced the idea that when we relate from an insecure attachment style:

> [W]e can make our partners into the source of our hope, love, strength, ability to feel or regulate our own emotions, as well as the source of our meaning and purpose in life. Our partners can be the inspiration for these things, as well as the objects or focus of our love, but they should not be the source of it. You are the source of your happiness, love, courage, emotional regulation and purpose...

Whether because of attachment insecurity or enmeshed or codependent dynamics, there is often a lot of overlap between these two things. The urge to use our partners as our surrogate source can be tempting, especially when our self-esteem or self-worth isn't what it could be. Having a clear sense of our own value as a person and being able to consciously connect with that value is extremely important for giving us the fortitude we need to become our own source.

Ideally, as adults our sense of source would be anchored inside of us, radiating outward to our relationships and all other areas of life. However, as children, our self-esteem and self-worth are developed to the degree that the adults in our lives paid attention to us, validated our experiences, and expressed an appreciation and love for who we were as individuals. If this kind of emotional support was absent in childhood, we can end up struggling to experience a strong or coherent sense of self-worth. Growing up without having our intrinsic value reflected back to us from our parents or care-takers, we are left to perpetually turn outward in search of who we are, why we matter and what makes us worthy. This creates a self-esteem that is based on external circumstances, where we are always subject to the fickleness of conditions outside of our control. This kind of external dependency leaves us vulnerable to the actions, opinions, judgments and whims of the people or things we have made responsible for our importance. If we haven't recognized and addressed this misplaced source of our own existential worthiness, we will continue to stumble with the process of self-differentiation.

Another challenge that many of us face on the journey to differentiation is the powerful influence of colonial capitalist culture, which constantly reinforces the idea we need to look outside ourselves for our sense of worth and self-esteem. By conditioning us to believe that our value as people comes from what we do, how much we achieve, what possessions and credentials we have, and how "good" we look, we are taught from an early age that our value and wellbeing can only be gained through our compliance with the systems we are embedded in. These capitalist narratives and structures actively dissuade us from feeling content with what we already have and who we already are, and they can keep us from experiencing a sense of value and worth based on who we feel ourselves to be on the inside. Because of this, so much of the self-work of our adulthood is about establishing or reestablishing a positive sense of our own inner value, independent of our accomplishments or socioeconomic status.

Couples therapist Terry Real offers an important perspective on how unhealthy self-esteem is not just about having *low* self-esteem: it can also exist when we feel superior, arrogant or too egoistic. Real defines self-esteem as the "capacity to recognize your worth and value, despite your human flaws and weaknesses." I like to think of self-esteem as one of the essential elements that allows us to successfully move out of codependency and into differentiation, and ultimately to pivot between differentiation of self and differentiation of other. Terry Real supports this observation when he points out that healthy self-esteem is an internal sense of worth that pulls one neither into "better than" grandiosity nor "less than" shame. The trick is making an honest appraisal of your own sense of self-esteem and working on the ways in which there is room to strengthen or develop it further in service of your own differentiation of self. The testament of your progress would then be the capacity to strike the right balance between differentiation of self and other.

For anyone reading this who struggles with self-esteem issues and is potentially feeling overwhelmed by the task of working on their sense of self-worth, I want to offer my firm conviction that we are always capable of taking charge of our self-growth and making positive changes in our lives and relationships, even if it is slow, just one baby step at a time—or as one of my clients liked to joke, "One small yet emotionally massive adult step at a time." The key to making tangible strides in our process is to first recognize that we need to consciously shift our way of thinking about our fundamental sense of self. Just as the successful transition from monogamy to nonmonogamy requires an overhaul of our relational paradigm, healing our wounded self-image requires a similar shift. We can begin this work by deliberately shifting our focus away from the thoughts, judgments, comparisons and ideas of ourselves as somehow deficient, and instead direct our minds to the things we value most in this life. We can intentionally connect with what we value most about ourselves and begin to actively affirm our inherent worth as a person. If you've been operating most of your life with a predominantly negative self-perception, changing that overnight is probably not realistic. However, with consistent and dedicated practice, you can make legitimate strides towards a new, preferred way of seeing and feeling yourself in the world.

The following exercises are meant to be practical tools for changing the axis of your negative self-view and shifting it towards a new, more integrated self-image that incorporates the things you hold most dear in life. I suggest trying each of the exercises at least once and then decide which ones resonate with you or feel most useful to keep practicing. Once you have made your selection, I recommend committing to doing them at least once a day for several weeks, and then on an as-needed basis. I think you may be surprised by how different you can start to feel after devoting a relatively short amount of time to your practice.

EXERCISE   Calling Myself Back

In the course of any given day, we are constantly exchanging energy with other people, places, and situations. Through the myriad interactions we have with the outside world, be it virtually or in person, we are always broadcasting energy in the form of words, thoughts, feelings and actions. When you find yourself constantly exerting a lot of physical, emotional or mental energy, that energy doesn't always come back to you automatically. In fact, it could still be tied up in whatever conversation, meeting, project or task you were involved in previously. The mind has a way of lingering in the past, and this can leave us feeling drained, divided, distracted and underresourced. As you continue to think about troubling interactions, situations or daily responsibilities, you lose the capacity to be in the moment and fully recharge your personal batteries. This is why practicing energetic hygiene is always a good idea, especially during challenging or stressful times.

This phenomenon of energy drain is also particularly relevant to anyone dealing with the issues of codependency or enmeshment. If we still haven't learned how to maintain clear emotional or energetic boundaries between ourselves and our partners, there can be a lot of sticky dynamics where we are giving over too much of our energy to the other person, or taking on too much of their energy. This visualization exercise is very helpful for training individuals to consciously reclaim the parts of themselves that have been compromised or overextended in the context of an emotional attachment with someone else or in their day-to-day activities. As you do this exercise, you will be tuning in to the ways that your self-energy has been left in other times or places, or with other people. As you deepen your visualization, you will imagine that all of you is being called back to yourself—back into the present moment.

- Close your eyes and tune in to your inner experience for the course of several breaths to center yourself in the present moment.

- If it's helpful, you can imagine letting go of anything from the day that has already happened and putting aside anything that is to come, just focusing internally on this present moment. If you get distracted by any thoughts, images or feelings, just observe them, or imagine they are like clouds passing in the vast sky, and then come back to your inner focus.

- Now you are going to focus your awareness outward and take an inventory of the aspects of yourself that continue to remain outside of you, either in another time or location, or with another person. This could be a more general sense of your core energy, life force, or overall focus or attention that is too externally centered or outwardly preoccupied, or that even feels as though it has been left with others. You could also think of specific traits or qualities, such as your power, purpose, voice, sexuality, happiness or agency, that have been living too far outside of you.

- For example, someone might feel that their general sense of self is still wrapped up with another person, like they are living too much in the other person's skin and are too involved in their personal business. One client, after a significant heartbreak, was able to identify that his Lover archetype—the part of him that was romantic and willing to open his heart to another person—was still frozen in the experience of that heartbreak. Other people have identified the way their voices, opinions or points of view were never allowed as children, and thus these elements of themselves were still trapped in the past, hesitant to come forward and show up in the present. When I do this exercise for myself, I get a visual of cords or channels of my life force that are being funneled to another person or situation, or I sometimes see parts of myself that are swarming around outside of me, somewhere else. Other people might have more of a felt sense, like a tug that pulls them out of their own body and self-awareness. What you see and feel can vary in terms of how literal or abstract the experience is for you.

- Once you get a sense of what parts of yourself still remain outside of you, imagine that you have a powerful magnetic ability or gravitational pull that easily draws back all your self-energy, qualities or parts that have been residing somewhere else. As you imagine these aspects of yourself coming back into your own body, breathe and allow yourself to be filled up with the energy of these parts. Take as much time as you would like. Enjoy the sense of fullness and wholeness. State the intention that these wayward energies or parts of you can be fully reintegrated and remain within your own being.

Do this exercise as much as it feels helpful. Rarely is it ever a one-shot deal. If you have had a history of enmeshment or codependency, I suggest doing it daily for several months, probably several times a day or as you transition from one activity to another. Keeping the focus of our energy on other people or things outside of our own body can become a reflexive habit that depletes us and leaves us feeling underresourced. Therefore it is important to train ourselves to redirect the energy that habitually leaks out towards the external world and channel it back into our own being. Once you get the hang of it, you can do it in just a few minutes, even seconds, so it can be something you do multiple times a day or simply as needed. The purpose of the exercise is to ultimately retrain your system to be sensitized to any potential energy leaks and proactively reclaim that vital energy in service of your own wellbeing.

EXERCISE   Everything Out of the Room!

This exercise is meant to support you in accessing your own clarity in terms of your personal preferences, opinions, feelings, wants or needs. I guide people through this exercise when they are struggling with knowing what it is they want, think or feel about a particular issue, or are having a hard time discerning their own experience apart from other people's opinions and perspectives. This is especially helpful for individuals struggling to separate their own wants and needs from those of their partners.

- Do this exercise in a private space. Given the name of this exercise, most people do it in a room where they are alone with a door that is closed, but you can also do this in your parked car, or another enclosed space where you will have total privacy.
- Close your eyes and tune inward for several breaths to center yourself in the present moment.
- If it's helpful, you can imagine letting go of anything from the day that has already happened and putting aside anything that is to come, just focusing on your inner experience of the present moment. If you get distracted by any thoughts, images or feelings, just note them or imagine they are like passing clouds, letting them go without hooking onto them, and then come back to your inner focus.
- Now think of the issue, challenge or question you are wanting clarity on and feel all the aspects of it that are causing you static or seem to be eclipsing your ability to know what your own answers, feelings, hopes, wishes or

dreams are around this issue. This might be the thoughts and perspectives of specific people in your life, or it might be something like your own guilt or perfectionism getting in the way. Or it could be the larger cultural or societal narratives that are at play, influencing your sense of what's acceptable, right or even possible.

- Once you get a sense of everything that is interfering with your clarity, put it out of the room! Imagine that your loved ones, partners, friends, boss, employees, coworkers and children are all out of the room. Put concepts like what you're supposed to do or should do out of the room. Put the ideas and beliefs of monogamy, nonmonogamy, religion or political discourse out of the room. Place your own judgments, fears or guilt out of the room. Put anything and everything out of the room that doesn't feel like it's truly yours or that is interfering with your connection to your own clarity.

- Now just breathe and feel yourself alone for a few minutes. Feel yourself without all these other interfering influences. Feel the spaciousness and silence of being with yourself in the room. Enjoy this for a few moments.

- Now bring forward the question or situation that you are looking for your own answers or clarity to again. You can ask quietly or aloud, "What is my truth regarding this situation? What are my thoughts? My wants? My feelings? My needs? My hopes moving forward? My solutions to this problem?" Allow the answers to arise from within you.

- If anything you placed outside the room creeps back in, just keep reminding it to stay outside until you're done with the exercise.

- The answers you get from yourself might be instant and obvious, or they might be subtle and slow, needing some time and space to come forward. If your own answers feel difficult to connect with or slow to arise, be patient and remind yourself that this exercise is about connecting

more fully with yourself, and you don't have to immediately act on your insights or inner knowing.

- When you feel complete with this exercise, you can say
  thank you to everything that stayed out of the room, and
  you can decide what comes back in or not as you resume
  your day.

It's important to keep in mind that just because you're
using this exercise to come to your own clarity, it doesn't
mean you're disregarding the needs of others. This exercise is
not meant to create a dynamic in which you only take care of
your own needs to the exclusion of others. It's also not about
having to make a drastic life change—unless that's what you
want. It's about clearing away the obstacles to inviting your
personal clarity to the table so that you can better understand
yourself, take the steps you want to at the pace you want to,
and ultimately communicate that clarity to significant others.

Again, this type of exercise is specifically for people who
have trouble knowing their own needs and advocating for
those needs in the context of an intimate relationship. It is
for people who no longer want to feel stuck in a pattern of
people-pleasing or denying their own needs just to stay in
their partnerships. Of course, arriving at our own clarity can
come with the risk of realizing the relationship we're in might
not actually be working for us. As we begin to connect more
consciously with what matters most to us, our perspectives can
shift, and we can start to realize that certain relationships, or
aspects of those relationships, are actually out of alignment
with the kind of life we want for ourselves. When this is the
case, it's important to try to make the necessary changes that
are possible in a relationship.

EXERCISE   Becoming My Own Source

In this exercise, you are connecting to the source within you, be it the source of your own self-love, power, happiness or meaning in life. When you are in the habit of outsourcing these things to someone or something outside yourself, the following approach can be extremely useful for refocusing your attention on yourself and remembering that you are ultimately the source of whatever you need. Becoming your own source does *not* mean that you no longer have relationship needs or no longer find meaning, purpose or happiness through your relationships. Nor does it mean that your partner can neglect your attachment or relationship needs. Becoming your own source means that you are cultivating your own capacity to source within, meet your own needs instead of being solely reliant on external sources for filling you up, giving you value or meeting your needs for you. Each bullet point can be done in order or as a standalone exercise, depending on what aspects resonate the most with you.

- Like all the previous exercises, take a few minutes to center and ground yourself in a way that feels good to you.
- Pick an experience or attribute, such as love or power, that you would like to feel within yourself instead of as something dependent on external conditions. Connect with a time when you felt that attribute. For example, think of a time when you felt love for another person or animal, a time when you felt like you were in your own power, or a moment when you felt happiness. Even if these memories were connected to other people, or were temporary situations such as laughing and connecting with a friend, winning an award or completing an important project, that's OK. We're using the memory of the positive quality as a prompt, even if the experience you are using was originally more externally than internally sourced. Breathe and bring alive the feeling of this

quality in your own body. As you remember an experience of something like love, happiness or power, imagine
that it is filling up your entire body, penetrating deep
into your bones and bathing all of your cells. Amplify this
quality as much as you can. Tune in to the sensations
you feel as you connect with this quality within yourself
and enjoy it for a few breaths, or for as long as you like.
Realize that it was you who generated this entire experience. Even if you used a memory, it was your own mind,
heart and body that generated the memory and brought
alive this quality within you—and no one else. At first, it's
OK to use the props or prompts of an external exercise in
order to connect with these qualities within yourself, but
remember that your experience of this quality was just
sourced from within your own consciousness.

- Another way to do this exercise is in a more abstract
  way, where you forgo using any specific external stimuli
  or past memories of the quality you are wanting to feel
  within and instead repeat the quality you are trying to
  experience again and again, feeling it come alive in your
  own body. In this context, you can use statements such
  as "I am love," "I am happiness," "I am connection," "I
  am health" or "I am peace," and then feel them come
  alive within yourself, or you can get a felt sense of what
  you're trying to experience and conjure it up from
  within. Use your breath to amplify and expand this
  quality throughout your body and enjoy the sensations
  that arise.

- One more way to do this exercise is to imagine a ball of
  light somewhere in the center of your body, either your
  chest or abdomen. Imagine this ball of light or energy
  represents the intelligence that guides all life: the invisible intelligence that forms planets and galaxies, turns an
  acorn into a tree, and divides individual human cells to
  create an entire human. This level of intelligence resides
  within every atom, molecule, cell and system in your

body. Experience the aliveness within your own body as you reconnect with this creative power, remembering it is the source of everything and that it lives within you, fully accessible whenever you need it.

From Enmeshment to Differentiation in Partnership

Circling back to Polyamory School's article about the importance of differentiating as a couple before opening the relationship, we find a list of some very practical things couples can do together to get the ball rolling. While they actually use the word "disentanglement" instead of "differentiation," their useful suggestions include things like each person picking a different night throughout the week to go out on their own. The logic here is that partners can get used to doing things separately, as well as start training their nervous systems to normalize the other person having adventures without them. They also suggest partners start intentionally asking each other out for date nights. This has the dual purpose of reintroducing more chemistry into the relationship, while also dropping the assumption that you own each other's time. Another suggestion is putting off going on an actual first date with someone new until couples have done the previous steps for a few months. They thoughtfully remind us of the importance of initially going slow, methodically opening up to dating other people perhaps one day per month for a while, then maybe adding a kiss a little down the road.

While I genuinely appreciate these suggestions and definitely agree that most partnerships would fare far better following this kind of advice, the clients Dave and I typically encounter in our work have had dramatically different experiences. The few couples that have actually sought out our help before opening up their relationship have typically prevented a lot of pain and complications. However, most people we work with have already opened up their relationships by the time they come to see us, and they realize in hindsight that they have issues with enmeshment or codependency. Unfortunately the realization has only come after significant conflict, hurt and paralyzing confusion have already occurred. This advice also does not address CNM partners who were never monogamous together, but still find themselves or their relationships in a tangled-up, codependent web.

Another dilemma is that most people simply do not have the patience or desire to take five to six months before getting a goodnight kiss, nor do they typically encounter other potential partners who want to wait for the preexisting relationship to go through the differentiation process before really getting things started. These types of dynamics can cast new potential partners in the role of props for the couple's own process, missing or minimizing the needs of the new people they are dating. So while some people may be up for going extremely slow with a person who is going through the differentiation process with another partner, I would say this is rare, and in certain situations it could even be unethical to ask new people to solely yield to and submerge their own wants to the original relationship.

As you can probably already surmise, the process of differentiation is a big one. It takes time, and there are usually many fumbles, backslides and humbling lessons along the way. For some partnerships, this process feels like it is ripping them apart—which in some ways it is—with the severity of that sensation ranging from having a bandaid quickly pulled off to a limb being torn from the body. The level of complexity and difficulty also increases depending on the number of people involved in the process. For example, it's one thing to realize that you personally have yet to differentiate from others and to decide to take on a process of doing so for your own personal growth and development. It is quite another to, in an attempt to recreate yourselves as well as your relationships, dive into the process of differentiation with the person or people you have been enmeshed with. Then multiply those same challenges exponentially when considering the full-time work of revamping your original relationship while simultaneously exploring a new, nonmonogamous paradigm of relationship. By no means do I want to be discouraging here; it's just the reality that many people are facing as they open up. We are emphasizing these challenges so that you can ultimately have more empathy and compassion for yourself and your partners as you reflect on the fact that both the process of opening up *and* of differentiation are each in and of themselves endeavors that require a significant amount of mental and emotional bandwidth.

Taking Ownership for Your Part in the Enmeshed Dynamic

When Dave and I opened up our marriage, we were faced with several uncomfortable realities regarding the ways we were enmeshed and codependent. What's interesting is that before opening up, neither of us would have ever identified codependency as a problem in our relationship. I would've said that we both had a fair amount of freedom, autonomy and independence, and yet, as we later discovered, codependency still factored into our dynamic in everyday, less overt ways. For my part, I was in the role of the house administrator. I managed most of our logistical life and financial details, and even took on the responsibility of planning trips or arranging special activities. I also liked to vacuum and do most of the laundry. Dave, on the other hand, played the part of the custodial technician and house culinarian, always cleaning the bathroom and kitchen and cooking the majority of the meals.

On the surface, it can be hard to tell the difference between a prudent division of labor based on our individual strengths or preferences and an imbalanced way of relating. For example,

Dave always cleaned the bathroom because I hated to, and I balanced the checkbook because I genuinely enjoy organizing and keeping track of details. To us, this felt like a smart way to allocate our limited resources, and we were both grateful to avoid doing the tasks neither of us liked. However, this seemingly sensible division of household duties unwittingly crossed the line in certain situations where I would actually be overfunctioning and Dave underfunctioning. For example, my managerial inclinations would bleed into codependent behaviors whenever I would look at Dave's open email inbox on our shared laptop, see a potentially important message from his boss and then tell him he should tend to his time-sensitive emails. To some, a comment like, "Hey babe, your boss, Barbara, wrote to you about changes in the schedule today" could seem like I'm just being a helpful partner. However, in actuality I was over-concerning myself with what was essentially Dave's responsibility to keep track of. Even though we weren't tracking the impact of these kinds of codependent patterns back then, we were sowing the seeds of a classic adult/child dynamic where the blurred lines would eventually yield unhealthy doses of resentment, judgment and frustration.

Dave here!

In monogamy, our patterns were invisible to us, and things seemed essentially good. However, as we opened up, we quickly came face-to-face with the fact that many of our taken-for-granted arrangements were problematic. As Jessica started seeing other people, she began spending more time tending to the needs of other partners. The surplus of time that previously went to helping me with my own scheduling and technical issues was now being diverted to other relationships, and, seemingly all of sudden, she didn't have the time or desire to do those kinds of tasks for me anymore. Her cessation of the overfunctioning behavior interrupted a pattern that I had unconsciously grown accustomed to for over a decade. My nervous system registered the change as an unwelcome vacuum of support, and I felt left to manage aspects of my own life that I never had to worry about before. Honestly, in moments it felt nearly impossible not to interpret the healthy changes she was making as a kind of abandonment.

The further we went into practicing nonmonogamy, the more we uncovered even deeper layers of our own codependency. Without a doubt one of the most eye-opening revelations was that several of our patterns were actually extensions of old childhood survival strategies. For example, as a very young child, I experienced several significant health issues for which my mother felt personally responsible. Her guilt over my delicate state of being meant that she felt the need to overfunction in the caretaker's role, and she shielded me from certain elements of life that she probably shouldn't have. Because of that dynamic I subconsciously internalized the message that receiving love from a female attachment figure essentially looked like putting a woman in charge of managing basic elements of my daily life. This unfortunate predisposition merged perfectly with Jessica's own programming. Her story was in some ways the opposite of mine, where survival meant overcompensating for the lack of support and presence from her caretakers. She quickly learned that she needed to become completely self-reliant, with few to no needs of her own, and that the way to get some semblance of closeness, attention or validation was by taking care of others.

While it certainly doesn't represent the totality of our life together, it was pretty humbling to recognize the ways these strategies had played out in our relationship. Part of my attraction to Jessica's organizational skills and logistical savvy was an extension of my survival strategy, which suggested I needed a competent woman at the helm of my administrative existence. And part of Jessica's draw to me was the unconscious belief that she needed someone to take care of in order to feel like she was worthy of love. From this perspective, we were able to see how my adult struggles with a severe autoimmune condition gave our relationship both a tremendous amount of meaning *and* codependency.

As polyamory put a spotlight on our codependency and lack of differentiation, we were forced to reexamine several of our original arrangements and expectations and begin to deliberately explore more balanced and conscious ways of relating. We found ourselves in a challenging but ultimately important process of not just reallocating domestic duties and household chores but also reconsidering the ways we did or didn't take responsibility for ourselves as individuals, for each other and for the relationship in general. In the course of this process, not only did we expose various unspoken and previously unexamined narratives about how each of us should be showing up for the other, but we also confronted the need to completely redefine the relationship in nonmonogamous and less hierarchical terms. We both realized that we could no longer relate to each other through the lens of a monogamous couple as we had done for just over a decade, and that each of us now had to take responsibility for course correcting our own part of the codependent dynamics that were playing out in our relationship.

For newly opened couples, the process of confronting enmeshment and codependency in the relationship can be particularly dramatic—as was the case in our situation—because it is likely the first time you are having to really look at these things together. And yet the importance of identifying these patterns and adequately assessing your need for more healthy differentiation is relevant in all relationships, at any point along your CNM journey. It is the nature of relational transitions, be they opening up for the first time, introducing new partners into the mix, escalating attachments or commitments, or dismantling hierarchical structures, that some of the more glaring imbalances in your preexisting relationships get exposed. While it probably won't feel like much of a blessing, at least initially, the process of identifying and addressing any issues related to enmeshment or codependency before they become terminal can actually be the thing that saves a relationship. The trick is to become familiar with the potential patterns that are playing out in your relationship and then be willing to explore how you could benefit from introducing more differentiation and interdependence into the partnership. The following table identifies some of the more common codependent behaviors that partners struggle with. More specifically, it highlights the ways we do or don't share our own inner experience with our partners, the degree to which our communication is more avoidant or anxious, and the level of responsibility we take for ourselves, the relationship and our partner's experience.

Codependent behavior	Explanation	Interdependent skill or behavior to apply
Holding in	The way you relate to your internal reality is by holding it in, containing or keeping in things that need to be expressed, as well as concealing, minimizing or denying your experience and reality.	Sharing your inner world in a way that reveals your truth, opinion, feelings and needs. Speaking up and advocating for yourself when timely and appropriate.
Venting out	The way you relate to your internal reality is by pushing it out, making it known to everyone around you, dumping it onto others or exaggerating and dramatizing it.	Learning how to hold your own experience with an appropriate level of containment that can share what you're going through but does not put it onto others.

Codependent behavior	Explanation	Interdependent skill or behavior to apply
Pulling away/ withdrawing	Taking a posture in a relationship that is too far back: disengaging, avoiding, disconnecting, not touching, too little contact.	Learning how to lean into and reach for your partner and interpersonal interactions.
Pushing into/grasping	Taking a posture towards a partner that is too far in: steamrolling, clinging, constant texting, too much contact.	Learning self-regulation skills so you can soothe yourself in moments of anxiousness.
Overfunctioning	Too much responsibility for the relationship or your partner, too much emotional or practical labor, rescuing, being someone's coach or therapist, thinking you're responsible for your partner's reactions or feelings. Thinking you can fix what's happening for others.	Look at the ways the strategy of caretaking your partners interferes with or overrides your ability to tend to your own needs. Recognize any discomfort you may feel when seeing partners struggle with life challenges and resist the urge to rescue them from their difficulty or pain. Respect their autonomy as individuals and their need to cultivate personal agency.

Codependent behavior	Explanation	Interdependent skill or behavior to apply
Underfunctioning	Not taking responsibility for what's yours or what the relationship needs to stay healthy, blaming others for your difficulties or pain. Getting stuck in a victim narrative.	Acknowledge the areas of your life where you have made a partner responsible for some aspect of your personal wellbeing— physical, emotional, financial, administrative, etc. Assume the responsibility for this element of your experience unless otherwise negotiated.

TABLE 5.1: Examples of codependent behaviors and their antidotes.

EXERCISE **Your Part in Your Enmeshed or Codependent Dynamic**

The following experience is meant to support you in more fully owning your part in an enmeshed or codependent dynamic. With each behavior of your own that you identify, you will explore the benefits and costs of this behavior, what changes you are willing to make and what changes you want to request from your partner.

What is my enmeshed or codependent behavior?	How is this behavior serving me (or what benefits am I deriving from this behavior)?	What is the cost of this behavior to me and my partners?	How can I use a new behavior to correct or change the pattern?	What can I request of my partners, or how can I communicate my intention to change?
Example: Letting Dave know that I see important emails in Dave's inbox that he should read.	I reduce my own anxiety that Dave will miss important work things that could lead to him losing his job and me having even more responsibilities if he is jobless.	I'm doing too much for him and not focusing on my own projects. This leads to feelings of resentment. Dave is not developing the skills he needs to manage his own job.	No longer looking at Dave's inbox, and letting that be his responsibility. Managing my own fears and anxiety.	"Dave, I've realized that I'm participating in a codependent pattern by keeping track of your work emails for you. I've been doing this to help you, but also to manage my own anxiety about you keeping up with your work emails. The impact is that I get resentful and I have less time for my own projects. I'm not going to do this anymore."
Example: Not asking for help when I need it.	I don't have to be too vulnerable or deal with the possible disappointment of Dave not showing up for me. If I explicitly keep asking and he repeatedly doesn't show up for me, I have to face the potential end of the relationship.	Feeling overwhelmed, alone and resentful. Feeling less attracted to Dave.	Asking for help when I need it while also knowing that no one can help me 100% of the time.	"Hey, Dave. I'm starting to feel overwhelmed about the logistics for our upcoming trip and it would be really helpful for reducing my stress and anxiety if you could be the one to take on putting our meals together beforehand."

After going through the above chart and mapping out your own process, you may also want to explore your own personal history to see where these behaviors come from. Just as we mentioned before with our process, it was extremely helpful for Dave and me to connect the dots between our codependent behaviors and the early childhood experiences that created the precedent for them. Since self-differentiation can be a process that takes time, I also suggest seeking professional support to more deeply understand the roots of the codependent adaptations you needed to make based on the events of your past and then decide how to move forward more fully as yourself.

Here are some additional questions to support taking responsibility for your part in a codependent dynamic:

- Given the behaviors you listed above, if you saw these behaviors were coming from a "part" of you (see chapter two for inner parts work exercises), what name or title would you give your codependent part or survival strategy? For example, it could be the Overachiever, the People Pleaser, Constantly in Crisis, the Damsel in Distress, Flying Under the Radar, I Need You to Need Me, the Tough Guy, etc.)
- What were the circumstances of your upbringing and life that created this codependent strategy or part?
- How has this strategy helped you to get certain needs, like love, attention, connection, meaning, safety or security, met?
- In what ways has this strategy protected you?
- Have a conversation with this part, or write a letter to this survival strategy, thanking it for all of the ways it's been a support and protector to you. Honor this part for helping you get through the challenges and difficulties that you were faced with as you were growing up. After offering genuine gratitude to this part, let it be known that you are no longer in the same survival situations from the past and that this part does not have to play the same role that it did. You can imagine letting this part go,

or you can update its role to what's more relevant to you now as an adult.

████████████

Reinventing Your Relationship in Nonmonogamy

When two people enter a monogamous relationship, certain cornerstones of assumptions and expectations lay the foundation for them being together. These may include ideas such as "It's only us," "We're number one to each other," and "We'll be together forever," just to name a few. These cornerstones are often the larger cultural and societal narratives of the monoromantic ideal to which we may or may not have fully consented. The bricks and stones that form the rest of that foundation are the more specific aspects of this particular relationship that drew you to each other. These could be things like shared interests or hobbies; humor; attraction; shared religious, spiritual or political beliefs; or visions for the future. For example, I can clearly state what is special and unique about Dave and that no one on the planet makes me laugh like he does, and we both have a deep interest in the psycho-spiritual. From day one we've shared a unique, easy connection and a nonjudgmental openness to each other's personal processes. We have our own special brand of shit talk, we both love to watch stand-up comedy and dance shows, and we will always have a lifelong commitment to co-parent our son together. These bricks would be the compatibility factors that make us a good match.

However, some of our relationship foundation bricks are less conscious, and are based on the pairing up of our individual survival strategies—or what Gay Hendricks and Kathlyn Hendricks call "unconscious commitments." According to them, these are when partners make the unspoken agreement to stay locked in unconscious patterns, where:

> The basic contract is: If I allow you to sleepwalk through life, you won't make me wake up either. If I agree not to grow, you won't either. If I don't insist that you change your bad habits, you won't leave me or make me challenge my bad habits.

When enmeshment and codependency have been at play in a relationship, often the very foundation of your relationship needs to be recreated. This does not mean that everything you've created together needs to be discarded, but it is important to assess what aspects of the ways you have been relating to each other no longer serve your relationship, which ways of relating are important to keep and what new ways of relating you want to add.

Here are some questions for you to consider as you recreate your relationship in CNM:

- What part of our relationship foundation do we want to keep? What works for us and why?
- What aspects need to be let go of or recreated? What hasn't worked and why?
- What aspects need to be rebuilt for one or both of us (e.g., trust, safety, security, friendship)?
- What decisions are more autonomous now, and what decisions are still shared decisions or now need to be shared?
- What roles or acts of service do we still want to offer each other, and which ones do we want to recreate or no longer do?
- Who do we want to be to each other now?
- What would the ideal version of our relationship look like now?

Allowing the Grief of Nonmonogamous Differentiation

Once when I was struggling with a difficult choice to make as to whether or not I should stay in a certain relationship that I really cared about but that was not compatible with some of my core values, my therapist emphatically said to me that "with every decision there is always an incision." She was acknowledging that with every choice we make, we are saying yes to certain things, and we are also cutting out, letting go of and saying no to other things. Every decision comes with its gains as well as its losses, and it can be helpful to acknowledge what we are both saying *yes* to as well as *no* to when transitioning to nonmonogamy or changing the ways we are practicing CNM with our partners.

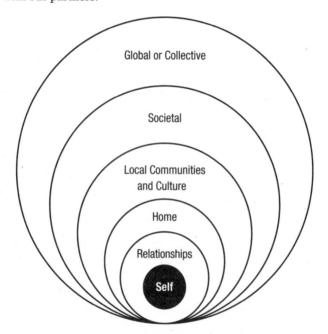

FIGURE 5.1: The Nested Model of Attachment and Trauma

When people choose the nonmonogamous paradigm of relationship, they are inviting more growth, expansion, people, love and support into their lives, and there are also notable losses that come with this, too. In *Polysecure* I introduced the Nested Model of Attachment and Trauma (see above), where I present the different dimensions of our human experience: self, relationships, home, local communities and culture, society, and the collective, and I explain how all these different levels can be impacted when transitioning to nonmonogamy. While each level comes with new advantages and benefits when someone is nonmonogamous, there can also be the painful and consequential losses of people, privileges and rights. More specific to this chapter, when partners go through CNM transitions that bring up the need for more differentiation, they can encounter many positive gains, but they also lose the comforts and conveniences that came from their enmeshed, symbiotic, exclusive or more hierarchical life together, and this loss can produce grief. Even if all partners fully want to move forward with a certain CNM transition, they still lose certain monogamous, primary partner or time-based advantages and the associated future they envisioned.

Some potential griefs you may be experiencing:

- Loss of telling each other everything and being each other's go-to person for most things.
- Loss of emotional exclusivity or primacy.
- Loss of sexual and romantic exclusivity or primacy.
- Loss of the perception (or reality) that your partner is mostly available to you.
- Loss of certain levels or access to or inclusion in your partner's life.
- No longer playing a certain role in your partner's life, or vice versa.
- Loss of ease around scheduling and availability.
- Loss of decision-making power.
- Loss of what was.
- Loss of the future that you thought was going to be.

Another facet of grief that we can experience in our CNM relationships is not so much about the sorrow or loss of what *was*, but rather the sadness and grief of what *will never be* (or at least is very unlikely to ever be, given the current constellation of life circumstances and relationships). When we fall in love with new partners or share certain meaningful points of connection with people, we can experience the heartache of what we can't have with this person that, potentially, we could have had in the context of monogamy or in a different CNM structure. It can be painful to acknowledge that certain experiences are off the table with a particular partner because of being CNM, and it's important to give space for this pain so it doesn't go underground and later resurface in unskillful or hurtful ways that undermine our relationships.

Some potential CNM griefs you may experience include:

- Not living together.
- Not being able to merge your lives in a certain way.
- Not knowing each other's friends or family of origin.
- Not being able to be out or in public with this relationship.
- Not having children together.
- Not traveling or having extended time together.
- Not doing certain sexual acts, enjoying types of kinky play or having unbarriered sex.
- Only having time that includes other partners.
- Not having time that includes other partners or metamours.
- Not being able to get married or have a commitment ceremony.
- Not being able to offer or share certain types of structural support such as finances, health insurance, inheritance rights or child care.

EXERCISE   Naming Your Grief

As your relationship paradigm changes, grief is normal, and denying or minimizing your or your partners' grief can be detrimental to making the changes ahead. Allowing and acknowledging your and your partners' grief lets you better come to terms with any big or small losses and make sense of your new reality. For this exercise you will start by making a list of the losses you are experiencing based on transitioning either from monogamy to nonmonogamy or from your current CNM situation or style to another. These can be losses related to time, resources, attention, status or prioritization, as well as visions and hopes for the future.

Take the time to first acknowledge the sense of grief and loss you're experiencing. Allow yourself the time to feel whatever arises. You may need to cry, move your body, or journal your feelings or talk them out with someone. When you are ready, share the losses you are experiencing with the partner you are going through these changes with. You can refer back to Dave's Restorative Relationship Conversations process from chapter four if you would like to make this a more structured conversation.

EXERCISE   Acknowledging and Adjusting to the Changes

Use the following prompts for each one of the losses that you named in the previous exercise. The goal of this exercise is to acknowledge what you are saying goodbye to or letting go of in your relationship and then coming up with what adjustments you need to make internally and externally to best support these changes for yourself and your relationship.

- What are you saying goodbye to or letting go of for now?
- How does this change or loss make you feel?

- What positive experiences do you hope this change will bring into your life and relationships?
- What are the new adjustments and changes you are taking on? These could be changes in daily routine, change in identity, new roles or responsibilities, new beliefs or worldviews, etc.
- What are two or three things you can do on a daily or regular basis that will support you in these changes?
- What requests can you make of your partners to support you in these changes?

Nonmonogamy as a Preventive Measure

As we continue to become more sensitized to the prevalence of relational abuse and trauma in our society, our willingness to consider new ways to deal with it expands. People with trauma histories can be codependent, and enmeshed dynamics are common symptoms of abuse and trauma, so having relationship structures that reduce or prevent the development of these patterns can be extremely helpful. Interestingly, being nonmonogamous can actually be a way for some people to manage their previous codependent tendencies, recognizing that they simply can't function in a monogamous relationship without succumbing to the gravitational pull of enmeshment. For these people, being nonmonogamous gives them a practical way to shape their relational life without falling into the codependency trap, while still allowing themselves closeness, connection, intimacy and commitment in a way that maintains their healthy sense of self and autonomy.

One example is a client of mine who had three very intense emotionally and physically abusive monogamous relationships in a row. After a decade of relationship trauma, she decided that she didn't want to intertwine her life entirely with her romantic partners anymore in order to preserve a certain level of space and autonomy. Previously, all of her relationships played out completely on her partners' terms, which ultimately came at the expense of her own wants, needs and safety. As she recognized her need for more alone time and the importance of having the space to tune in to her own feelings and thoughts, she realized that being solo polyamorous was the antidote to her tendency to give herself over to her romantic relationships. In this way, solo polyamory allowed her to ease into intimacy on more of her own terms, and in the two years we worked together, I saw her make tremendous strides in her ability to differentiate herself from her partners and maintain the deep connection, commitments *and* freedoms she wanted in her intimate relationships.

§

Despite the fact that differentiation is a healthy and necessary step in the evolution of adult relationships, in our experience, we see that relatively few partners (both in monogamous and nonmonogamous relationships) have actually made it through this phase of their relationship. Because our mono-centric culture has done such a good job of idealizing the essential elements of symbiosis and conditioning, many of us equate this initial stage of relationship development with true romantic love, and it has become genuinely difficult not to see the departure from symbiosis as anything other than threatening or problematic. While we do think CNM and the variety of subcultures that intersect with it have made a great deal of progress towards deconstructing the influence of these overly simplistic romantic ideals, the degree to which so many adherents of CNM still struggle with the issue of codependency and enmeshment seems to suggest that the romanticizing of symbiosis that is so prevalent in couple-centric culture is one of the most difficult remnants of monogamy to shed. Explicitly identifying differentiation (along with all its uncomfortable growing pains) and naming its importance in the journey through the stages of a healthy adult relationship can help a lot of people contextualize some of the more perplexing challenges they have faced in their partnerships. While it can certainly feel scary at first, the process of creating more space and independence within our relationships can serve to deepen our connection and intimacy with our partners in the long run.

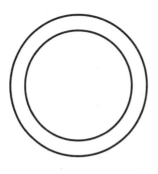

CHAPTER SIX
DEALING WITH DIFFERENCES

When I was 14 years old, my first love was Tony. Our love was intense, exciting and passionate, and yet we couldn't have been more different. Tony was gregarious, while I was more reserved. He was obnoxious and unfiltered, whereas I was cool and circumspect. He was slapstick; I was witty. His big personality made him audible within a two-block radius and mostly intolerable to those around him, whereas I was generally liked and trusted by my friends' parents. Tony was a social bull in a china shop, while I strived to be a gazelle. From an outsider's view we didn't make any sense, but I figured if Paula Abdul and that cartoon cat from the video "Opposites Attract" could make it work, then why couldn't Tony and I? Our love was palpable, and in my partial defense, Tony would reveal a tender, sweet side of himself to me that was rarely seen by others. I also admired how uninhibited he was, and he had a fierce, protective hunger for me which was exactly what I needed as a neglected teenage girl with no father in sight.

Even though Tony's and my differences created a fiery polarity, they also drove us nuts, provoking late-night screaming matches in my bedroom where he would destroy my art projects, and in retaliation I would throw the gifts he had made me in his woodshop class from my third-story apartment window. Our differences, which drew us together like two opposing magnets, eventually became combustive and destructive because some fundamental aspects of compatibility were missing for us. Tony was my first lesson in how love is not all you need, and how love and chemistry alone are definitely not enough to maintain a relationship—or keep your artwork from being destroyed. Years later when I would run into Tony or hear about him from mutual friends, it was crystal clear that while he will always hold a special place in my heart as my first love, our lives were undoubtedly destined to go in very different directions because of how different and incompatible we were.

As an adult, I have had several (albeit less dramatic) iterations of this early lesson about how the power of attraction and love can keep us drawn to and bonded to someone without guaranteeing a healthy relationship. When we are under the influence of the mind-altering haze of NRE, we tend to minimize differences between ourselves and our partners and focus mostly on the similarities. The rose-colored glasses of the hormonal honeymoon phase distort our perception, and we can often mistake red flags for red roses. As the hormones begin to subside, our dissimilarities can become increasingly more apparent.

Also, once we begin to differentiate as a couple—whether that differentiation coincides with the waning of new relationship energy or happens later down the road—the differences between us as partners can start to have more of an impact on our connection. Many of the differences we have with our partners can be complementary, positive and even necessary. These kinds of differences can keep us stimulated, inspire novelty and encourage us to grow beyond our individual perspectives and comfort levels. Differences can create chemistry. But there are other differences between partners that make a relationship untenable or can leave you feeling like there is just too much incompatibility for things to really work out.

The issue of compatibility in relationships can be tricky and confusing. Some experts swear by the necessity of compatibility factors, which would be the things that individuals have in common, such as your favorite books, music and shows;

your personality profile; or your political views and religious beliefs. Dating apps have algorithms to rate your percentage of compatibility based on how similar or dissimilar your answers are to questions that gauge your personality and interests so that you can best match with your next mate. Professional matchmakers and dating coaches will even advise you to ask your date questions regarding their hobbies or favorite musical artists, not just as good icebreakers, but also as ways to determine whether you should even consider a second date.

Other relationship experts suggest that these kinds of more objective compatibility factors have little impact on relationship health and sustainability, and instead assert that it is the presence of more subjective values and process-based compatibility factors that actually determine its viability. Examples of these subjective factors include things like the partners' level of commitment and effort to make the relationship work. Similarly, others in this camp focus on how partners treat each other, whether or not they can create shared meaning together, their capacity to support each other as individuals, how they handle conflict, whether or not they actually enjoy spending time with one another, and the presence or absence of respect in the relationship.

At this point in my career, I can safely say that I've seen enough partnerships to build a case in either direction in terms of whether the objective measures of compatibility do or don't matter. For some people, objective personality measures, such as shared extraversion or introversion, bear no weight in the relationship, whereas for others they absolutely do. If one person's life or career is devoted to a certain interest, having a partner that doesn't share that interest with them can eventually become a dealbreaker, because without that shared interest they will either have little to connect on or too much time apart. And most relationships struggle without the more subjective and process-based compatibility factors such as mutual respect, admiration, willingness to repair after conflict and clarity about commitment level.

In the same way that we talked about how CNM transitions can expose the cracks in the foundation of your relationship, so too can they create a heightened awareness of the differences between you and your partner. The paradigm shift has a way of shaking up your differences and turning your compatibility inside out. In relationships that were initially monogamous, sometimes these differences already existed before opening, but they were either less noticeable, or were more tolerable in the context of monogamy. But now, in nonmonogamy, they have become more substantial—and intolerable. Similarly, in relationships that are already CNM, certain changes, such as the levels of priority or the addition of new partners, can unmask certain differences between partners that can become overwhelming. Ways that people felt themselves to be highly complementary, like peanut butter and jelly, now become like oil and water. In other situations, the CNM transition itself creates brand new incompatibilities that now challenge the feasibility of the relationship altogether.

When Virtue Becomes Vice

As discussed in the previous chapter on differentiation, both the monogamous romantic ideals of our culture and the relationship stage of symbiosis encourage downplaying differences between partners and promote the fusion of selves within relationships. While in most cases, I don't think people are completely unaware of the bigger, more challenging differences between themselves and their partners, I do think this romantic ideal of monogamy, along with the safety and security that higher degrees of hierarchy can provide, have a way of getting people to ignore, minimize or even justify the things about their partners that feel fundamentally incompatible. Understandably, people don't want to address the differences that could rock—or capsize, for that matter—the boat of the relationship. Naming and acknowledging the differences between us and our partners is always risky, regardless of the type of relationship we're in. Differences threaten our security in the relationship. Will my partner still love me if they find out I see things differently? However, to keep a relationship healthy and growing, we need to be courageous enough to rock the boat, bring up difficult conversations when necessary, and try to figure out how to bridge some of our differences, accept them or talk about options for moving forward in new directions.

The transition to nonmonogamy or to less hierarchical or couple-centric forms of CNM can have some interesting consequences for the way partners experience their preexisting differences. For example, in one couple, Dawna was originally drawn to her wife, Alexis, because of her spontaneity, sense of adventure and zest for life. Alexis's qualities brought Dawna alive in ways she'd never experienced before, initiating spontaneous day trips for them, exposing Dawna to foods she never would have tried on her own and even planning epic surprise birthday parties for her. Even though Dawna did have some complaints about Alexis's impulsive spending habits and more mercurial temperament, they were overshadowed by the benefits Dawna experienced as a result of her wife's exuberance. Alexis, on the other hand, expressed being drawn to Dawna precisely because of her more practical, grounded disposition. Dawna was present, reliable and sensible, functioning as the stable rock in Alexis's more capricious life.

Fast-forward to the opening of their relationship. The very same attributes that were once complementary and experienced as life-enhancing in a monogamous context now become chasms that felt unbridgeable in the new polyamorous one. Dawna, who had previously drawn a lot of meaning and purpose from being her wife's rock and anchor, now felt neglected and even used, as Alexis channeled her vibrant and creative spontaneity into other relationships. Dawna was overwhelmed by how fast Alexis was falling in love or having sex with new partners, and she began to feel like all the ups and downs of Alexis's other relationships were giving her emotional whiplash. Alexis's more carefree side led her, on more than one occasion, to break their relationship agreements, which began to erode Dawna's trust.

Additionally, Dawna no longer wanted to be just the safe haven for Alexis, which in the polyamorous context meant that Dawna was often playing the role of therapist or crisis manager for Alexis's other relationships, Dawna also wanted the chance to be an interesting and exciting play partner, receiving the same level of high-intensity attention that Alexis was doling out to others. On the other hand, Alexis felt that her once-dependable rock of a wife had become an immovable weight, preventing her from any forward momentum with others. Alexis now experienced Dawna as controlling, difficult and inflexible, with no respect or consideration for her own unique pacing. Dawna's more grounded nature had turned into stagnation and resistance, and the more she tried to slow Alexis down, the more Alexis responded by asserting her freedom.

In the case of Dawna and Alexis, the differences they once appreciated about each other, which enhanced their sense of harmony in their monogamous relationship, quickly turned into disharmony when they opened up. In the transition to polyamory, Alexis's spontaneity and willingness to try new things was interpreted as a recklessness that overwhelmed Dawna and undermined her trust. And Dawna's stability and steadfastness, which had previously provided safety and security for Alexis, was now a source of intolerable restriction, impeding her ability to explore new relationships on her own terms. This is a prime example of how sometimes the differences that are initially attractive and connective for partners in the context of monogamy can quickly become objectionable and antagonistic in nonmonogamy. Likewise, what feels harmonious in more hierarchical forms of CNM can later turn into a CNM cacophony if primacy is dismantled. This kind of radical, 180-degree shift in our experience of the qualities that we once found appealing in our partners can be extremely jarring and call into question whether there is enough compatibility to continue the relationship.

When the Previously Manageable Becomes Intolerable

Another variation of this dynamic is the situation where preexisting differences between partners go from manageable to unmanageable as they transition from one paradigm to the other or change the style of CNM they are practicing. Cases like these are different from the previous example, because here the original difference was already experienced as problematic—albeit more tolerable—before their CNM transition (instead of originally being seen as something positive). An example of this dynamic is the case of Monica and Frank. When they started dating, they were both CNM, each of them having mostly casual relationships with others. Monica made it clear that two of her most important relational values were honesty and transparency. Any omission or alteration of the truth could be interpreted as a betrayal and cause a lack of safety and trust. Frank had a different relationship to honesty, which meant there were times when placating or telling "white lies" was acceptable and appropriate, believing there were certain situations when it was actually better to tell people what they "needed" to hear in order to save face or avoid unnecessary conflict. Occasionally Monica would hear Frank dip into this gray area in conversations with friends, his kids or clients, saying things that felt dishonest to her. She didn't like it, but when she would question him on it, he would always reassure her that he wasn't hurting anyone with his behavior and that he was always completely honest with *her*. Even though Frank's micro-dishonesties with others made her feel uncomfortable, Monica tolerated it, and she reassured herself that he wouldn't do this with her, especially since she was his main squeeze.

Later, when Monica wanted to become more serious with another partner and change her style of CNM to being more solo polyamorous with two non-nesting primary partners (Frank and this other partner), Frank's flexibility with the truth eventually became a deal-breaker for Monica. To compensate for the changes Monica initiated, Frank increased his tendency, when dating other women, to downplay the significance of his very close and involved partnership with Monica so these women wouldn't get cold feet or be spooked by his level of commitment. On the other hand, with Monica, he would reveal information about his dates with other women in ways that didn't always add up to her. He would omit certain details to avoid making Monica upset or trigger her jealousy, and this over time started to create suspicion and mistrust. In their new version of less-hierarchical CNM, safety and trust became even more important to Monica, as she was now required to actively grapple with higher degrees of insecurity and jealousy with Frank and his other partners. Her vigilance of the relational landscape with Frank was intensified, and she was more sensitive than ever to anything that seemed "off" in their communication. In their previous CNM structure, where they were functioning more as each other's primary partners and there wasn't the same need to be as alert, she was able to tolerate the difference between their respective relationships to honesty. But as Frank connected with more partners, putting Monica's secure attachment to the test, she could no longer hold the same space for this behavior. As she continued to uncover discrepancies in his accounts of situations with other partners, she realized she needed to exit the relationship.

In nonmonogamy, where the relational complexity is greatly increased and the stakes can feel much higher, the importance of being transparent, maintaining open communication, keeping our word, sticking to our agreements and staying in integrity cannot be overstated. Because nonmonogamy can already be inherently more challenging for many of us, our threshold for shenanigans and questionable behavior can be much lower. Successfully managing multiple romantic relationships requires more emotional and mental energy than we're used to putting out, and when we are working with reduced emotional bandwidth, the ways we weren't in alignment with our partners can now seem exponentially more taxing, and what was previously manageable about our partner can become intolerable.

You're Talking on Mars, I'm Talking on Venus, and We're Lost in Translation

Another big difference between partners that can become problematic occurs in language and communication. Obviously misunderstandings and miscommunication happen in all human relationships, but in CNM, it seems as though the potential for misinterpreting our partners' words increases exponentially. As we negotiate the terms of new relationships and make agreements about what's permitted and what's off limits, suddenly it's as if partners are speaking two different languages, even though they're actually using the very same words! Running the gamut from amusing to baffling to outright enraging, these vastly different interpretations of what we tell our partners can have significant consequences for the relationship.

After Dave and I separated romantically, I went through a period of solo polyamory, which I loved. However, when I met my partner, Will, I had just gone through two significant breakups a few months earlier, and my heart and nervous system needed the time to create a secure foundation with just one person. Will and I decided to have an initial period of exclusivity together, but I was clear with him that my polyamory was inevitable. We became nesting partners and since we both had a high level of communication and skill, I was extremely surprised that when we opened up, we began to have repeat communication breakdowns right out of the box. In one situation in particular, Will was going out of town with my son for the weekend. I was excited to host a date at my house with my new partner, but I wanted to make sure Will and I were clear about the details of what that would look like. Before Will left for his trip, I distinctly remember saying to him, "Since you'll have the car, I'm going to have Ethan (my new partner) come here for our date, but he's *not* going to stay the night." Ethan and I had yet to have a sleepover, and I wanted to reassure Will that even though Ethan was coming over to our house, I wasn't escalating to an overnight, especially without talking about it first.

The following day after my date with Ethan, Will and I spoke on the phone, and he asked how the date was. When I replied that it was great, and that it was really nice to have Ethan over at the house, Will was surprised and hurt. It turns out we both had a very different idea of what the concept of "have Ethan come here" meant. For more context, Ethan lives over an hour away from us, so Will assumed that "here" just meant here in the city of Asheville where we live, and that Ethan and I would go out on the town for the evening. However, when I said, "I'm going to have Ethan come *here*," I had literally meant *here*, at our house, precisely where I was standing with Will as we were having the conversation. It turns out that Will also did not hear me say that Ethan would not be sleeping over, which obviously fed into the misunderstanding. Regardless of the fact that Ethan did not sleep over, Will was emotionally unprepared for the fact that Ethan came to our house and that he and I had sex in my bedroom. Even though I thought I couldn't have been more clear in what I said, and I was being a "good" polyamorous partner doing my best to prepare and inform him, Will felt completely blindsided on the phone as we talked about how my date went.

Later it dawned on me that, a few weeks before this situation, my son had had two of his friends over for a playdate, and at some point I'd told Will that the boys were spending the night. A few hours later, when it was getting close to bedtime, Will asked when the boys' parents were coming to pick them up. I reminded him that the boys were having a sleepover, and he vaguely remembered me mentioning it earlier. It was a similar situation to my previous example, but obviously the implications of not hearing me mention the sleepover part were vastly different. Our son having friends sleep over

is a situation with low stakes emotionally and no real consequences for our relationship. But not catching that Ethan was
not intending to sleep over, which would have put "I'm going
to have Ethan come here" into a greater context, had much
higher stakes and consequences. For us, it would have meant
an escalation in my relationship with Ethan that excluded Will
and Will's need to have some emotional prep time before I had
sex with someone else in our house.

Often the meanings of particular words that seem absolutely clear or obvious to both people later turn out to have
been interpreted in very different ways. The meanings of
key words or phrases that play a central role in agreements
between partners can get lost in translation, and this can have
serious repercussions. Things like "having protected sex," "I
won't be out too late," or "we're just going to hang out" may
seem to carry little ambiguity on the surface, but can in fact be
construed drastically differently by each person.

One of my favorite anecdotes regarding this CNM phenomenon is a situation in which, in my therapy practice, I've
had, not one, not two, but three different couples complain
about their differing interpretations of the phrase "Go have
fun!" For simplicity, I'll share the story from just one couple's
perspective. In this relationship, one partner (Jake) was polyamorous and the other (Rick) was monogamous. Jake told
Rick that a mutual friend of theirs had just expressed interest
in him. Rick was excited by this news because he trusted this
particular friend, and it felt like an emotionally safer situation
for him than some of the previous people Jake had been with,
whom Rick hadn't known as well. As Jake was leaving for his
date, Rick cheerfully sent him off with an enthusiastic "Go
have fun, baby!" After Jake got home from the date and shared
that he had had sex with this trusted friend, Rick was shocked.
In response to Rick's dismay, Jake said, "But you told me to
go have fun!" to which Rick replied, "Yeah, but 'fun' means
go have a good conversation over some coffee or tea, not sex
the first time you meet up!" Perplexed, Jake finally retorted,

"When you said 'Go have fun!' I thought you were giving me your blessing to do whatever I wanted. Coffee and conversation are nice, but not fun. For me, sex is fun!"

Typically, this kind of miscommunication is not intentional or even conscious, since we naturally hear what we want to hear or distort what we hear to fit our personal hopes or expectations. The desire to have a particular experience can become a powerful filter through which we process our agreements with partners, and when we think we're getting what we wanted, we're probably not going to stop and look the gift horse in the mouth. However, one of the big lessons of these unfortunate breakdowns in communication is that we need to do exactly that: slow down and make sure everyone has the same understanding of the agreement we just made and intentions we just stated. Success is in the details, and it can save everyone involved a lot of heartache and hard feelings to verify that you are truly on the same page before going out on a date with someone else. When it comes to agreements, specificity is worth its weight in gold, along with writing down agreements; clarifying what vague terms like *fun, safe, play, sex, kink* or *later* mean; and holding an attitude of open curiosity and collaboration.

Name Your Differences

Getting familiar with and naming the differences that show up in our intimate relationships is an important way to proactively engage them and, ideally, defuse the tension or disconnection they might be causing. First, it can be helpful to think about differences in terms of categories: for example, there can be differences in personality, such as between introverts and extroverts, or between people who are verbal processors— needing to talk through everything—and people who primarily integrate information quietly in their heads. Situational differences may arise when partners have significantly different incomes, or one partner struggles with a chronic illness while the other person is healthy. Partners can have wildly different attitudes and relationships to money and spending, which often create challenges. Key differences in pacing may also come up in terms of how fast or slow partners move in their new relationships and form new attachments. Additionally, partners can have very different risk tolerances around things like sexually transmitted infections or other infectious disease risks, or about being with someone who is or isn't vaccinated. Think about some of these differences between you and a partner, and how being in the context of monogamy or non-monogamy, or with higher or lesser degrees of hierarchy or priority, made some of them easier or more challenging.

Another, lesser-known difference between partners that I see show up as more challenging in CNM is what I like to call the difference of sequencing. As individuals, we all tend to have our own unique sequence of how we perform the three basic human behaviors of *think, feel* and *act*. While obviously we all do these fundamental things countless times throughout the course of any given day, the sequence in which we do and prioritize them can differ significantly depending on who we are. For instance, if you are a feel-act-think type, you will typically respond to situations by first having a strong emotion or feeling, which then propels you into action, after which—once everything is all said and done—you will reflect on the impact of your actions. However, if you are a *think-act-feel* type, you will first ponder the implications of your potential decisions and then act accordingly, without a clear sense of how you actually feel about your decision until after the fact.

People have their own tendencies to work through these three stages in specific sequences, with our first attribute typically dominating our decision-making process. Obviously each particular sequence can have its own advantages and disadvantages, but the interesting consideration for us is the way these differences in our sequencing can affect our partnerships. For example, if you are someone who thinks first and you are paired with an act-first type, their tendency to jump into action before weighing all the consequences could eventually drive you up the wall. This could be especially true in a scenario where, after newly opening your relationship, your act-first partner flies into action with someone new, too excited to stop and think about the agreements you'd made together and the potential emotional impact on you.

The presence of these differences can bring some partners to ask themselves whether they should stay, or leave the relationship. In the examples we have just named, the recognition of these differences can even make us question if we even like or respect our partner anymore. Shining a light on our incompatibilities can bring up a lot of uncertainty about whether we actually still want to be with the other person. I often pose the question to partners: "Would you still choose your partner if you were just now meeting them for the first time?" and it's fascinating to hear their answers. As we come to terms with the recognition of our core differences, our perspectives and our felt sense of the relationship can change dramatically.

Sitting down with your partners and doing an inventory of your respective similarities and differences can be a very helpful exercise for bringing potentially challenging dynamics, as well as points of appreciation and celebration, to the surface of your awareness. As you see and name these similarities and differences in a supportive space, hopefully you can all learn to recognize them as unique attributes that, despite their sometimes grating nature, make you who you are instead of simply being the bane of your partner's existence.

Here are some questions to consider in these conversations:

- What are the ways that you and your partners are similar?
- How are your similarities supportive? How are they challenging?
- What are the main differences you can identify between you and your partners?
- Which of those differences typically create challenges between you?

- Which ones are more complementary and supportive?
- Can you identify the origins of those differences? Did they used to be sources of attraction or appreciation, but now seem to only cause friction?
- Were they things that you definitely noticed previously but that were only mildly bothersome or problematic before opening your relationship or going through a CNM transition?
- Do some of these differences feel bridgeable, and if not, would changing the structure of the relationship make some of these differences manageable?

New Paradigm, New Differences

The differences that can shake up a relationship aren't always preexisting issues or personality traits that later become intolerable. Sometimes it's the transition from monogamy to non-monogamy itself that generates new, unanticipated differences between partners. As you explore the world of CNM, you may be exposed to a much wider range of relationship ideas and concepts, many of which you will have never encountered, considered or given yourself permission to explore. While it's certainly possible to be monogamous and interested in things like BDSM, nonbinary consciousness, erotic blueprints, healing attachment wounds, interpersonal conflict resolution skills, conscious communication, relationship check-ins, and so on, these things are typically more prevalent and promoted within the context of different CNM communities, forums and media. Exposure to the concepts and ideas embedded in these areas of interest can awaken completely new passions, desires, questions, and trajectories of personal exploration that radically change the way you fundamentally see yourself and your relationships. These changes can mean big shifts in terms of your personal standards, expectations and values, and these shifts can in turn have consequences for your preexisting relationships.

As it stands, our mainstream culture is not particularly interested in or focused on raising our relational consciousness very much, and so you can easily enter a monogamous relationship without really having much relationship savvy or competency. Apart from seeking help with the occasional conflict or crisis, it will typically not occur to many monogamous couples to actively engage in continuing education for their relationship. One of my close friends actually joked that her recent attempts to go back to exclusive relationships after being CNM for years were unsuccessful because she was having trouble finding any monogamous partners with enough communication skills to make it worth her time! And as cliché as it may sound, I can't tell you how many (typically) women in heterosexual marriages I've seen roll their eyes at the thought of their husband ever considering therapy or even reading a relationship book together.

I have found that people who already experience some kind of marginalization or identify as not fitting neatly into the parameters of conventional society are much more likely to gravitate to spaces where challenging and deconstructing social norms is commonplace. In general, this is especially true within different CNM communities. These arise from dynamic intersections of various subcultures that attract unique individuals who, aside from nonmonogamy, are often also interested in things like—among others—sex positivity, different sexual orientations, gender fluidity, understanding neurodiversity, therapeutic use of psychedelics, tantra, and issues concerning race, class and privilege. This means that if people who are curious about CNM start to engage with nonmonogamous communities at large, they are inevitably introduced to much more than just the ins and outs of consensual nonmonogamy. They are also initiated into a whole universe of new ideas and experiences that can have a profound impact on their basic sense of who they are. As partners get a taste of the new and expansive possibilities that are available to them through this exposure, they can change in totally unpredictable ways that can disrupt the status quo of their relationships.

In the next chapter I go into more depth about the personal awakening that can happen as a result of exposure to the multiverse of CNM, and the various ways that awakening can unfold. But for now, I want to focus on a few of the differences that can arise between partners as they dive into and embrace the paradigm of nonmonogamy, as well as how these particular differences can present unique challenges for relationships.

New Partners, New Differences

In the same way that the paradigm of CNM can create entirely new ways of being and self-expression for people, so too can new CNM partners have a paradigm-altering effect on your worldview, personality and identity. To be clear, I'm not just referring to the phenomenon of NRE and its power to make you act in unpredictable ways, but instead to the way that being in a relationship with particular people can tangibly change you into someone new. Some of these changes can be a boon for all of your relationships. Just as a rising tide lifts all boats, the growth and evolution that you experience directly from your new relationship can have a positive impact on all of your relationships. As one partner inspires you to be a better version of yourself, this new and improved self has the potential to positively influence every aspect of your life. As one of my own partners once said to me, "You're inspiring me to be a better person, which is making me be a better husband to my wife and father to my kids." #polyparadise

On the flip side, sometimes the person who emerges in response to new partners is the product of changes that you would probably have preferred never happened. As your partner enthusiastically soaks up all the novel experiences and ideas that come their way via their newest partner, you cringe in dismay as you start to question who the hell they are becoming. It's possible to watch your partner, under the influence of their latest romance, take on new religious beliefs, political views, substance use habits, sexual preferences, attitudes or opinions that begin to alienate you and create a gulf in the relationship. Or maybe it's a question of safety, where your partner starts to engage in risky, unhealthy or destructive behavior, and you have genuine concerns about their or your own wellbeing in relation to this "new person."

In other instances, it could be the case that your partner stays exactly the same with you, but they turn into an amazing person with someone else. Similar to the phenomenon of justice jealousy that I discussed in chapter three, this is the infuriating situation in which one of your partners becomes the kind of person you've always wanted to experience in the context of a completely different relationship. As one client of mine described, after successfully navigating an open marriage of 18 years with her husband, everything changed when he met a new woman, with whom he started to present as a completely different human being. As my client indignantly watched from the sidelines, she had to digest the fact that whenever the new partner was around, her partner was markedly much happier and more attentive, caring, fun and enthusiastic about everything. However, in the new woman's absence, the husband would revert back to his old, ho-hum demeanor, completely losing all the spark and *joie de vivre* that he displayed in her presence. The painful question that my client was left pondering was, "Why is he able to turn that kind of energy on for her, and not for me?" It's a fair question, and one that is echoed by many people in the same situation.

In cases such as this, the partner who is changing in new ways is often not totally aware of their behavior, or at least of the impact of their behavior on existing partners. It's easy to get caught up in the invigorating energy of a relationship that still hasn't accumulated all the weight of shared history and lose sight of the way we are affecting our other relationships. Having to watch a partner morph into someone different under the influence of a new relationship can create strong feelings of resentment, frustration and confusion, and can even provoke the sensation that we are no longer desirable or important. If left unaddressed, this can start to create toxic patterns in the relationship that are hard to overcome. However, if partners are willing to recognize and acknowledge the ways their new-found personality traits, mannerisms, hobbies, attitudes, or behaviors are negatively impacting their original relationships and can find genuine ways to reattune to the needs of their initial partners, they can restore balance to the connections.

Finally, new partners can also create new differences by creating game-changing relationships. These are the people we meet who create an unprecedented shift in how we view the world, ourselves and, especially, our relationships. They don't just change how we ourselves show up in the world; they also change what we want and expect from our other partnerships. A game-changing relationship is a unique situation that may open our eyes to previously unimagined depth, intimacy and connection on an intellectual, emotional, sexual and poten-tially even spiritual level. We may experience being listened to, empathized with and supported in ways we may never have before, and the relationship may end up raising our relational bar so high that everything else falls short in comparison. It's both amazing and horrible, a transcendental romance and a tragedy all at the same time, depending on which side of the game-changing experience you end up on.

In the world of CNM, the topic of game-changing relation-ships can be taboo. I believe this is one of the big reasons that CNM is often feared in general. In monogamy, the assumption (not necessarily the reality) is that once we've found our per-son, we stop looking elsewhere. This same rationale is even applied to people who are nonmonogamous, suggesting they will give up CNM once they have finally found their one "right" person. If our partners are no longer dating others, we think we can relax, because it's hard to find what you're no longer looking for. Of course, game-changing relationships can show up regardless of whether you are monogamous, celibate or nonmonogamous, but undoubtedly, people who are CNM seem more likely to stumble upon a game-changing relationship if they are actively dating or open to meeting new partners. While the nonmonogamous paradigm is not about continuing to date until you find the "one" or endlessly searching for "better" partners, I do think the higher potential for game-changing relationships is often a contributor to the underlying anxiety that many CNM people grapple with consistently. While in principle, monogamy can attempt to shield us from this uncomfortable possibility, in CNM, there is no pretending that such a risk does not exist.

Instead, here are some questions and suggestions to consider: Is your current CNM relationship style being influenced by fear of you or one of your partners experiencing a game-changing relationship? If so, how has this fear been impacting you, your partners and your style of CNM? Work on accepting that this is part of the risk that comes with *any* relationship, and it is not something you can control or prevent, especially when it comes to your partners. Accepting this allows you to better relate to your fear and choose how to engage with the risk of game-changing relationships.

If you are experiencing a game-changing relationship, be honest about it. Get clear within yourself what this means for you, and how it impacts your preexisting relationships. Have direct and kind conversations with your partners about the changes you are experiencing through this new relationship, and how the changes within you are initiating changes within your relationships. Be honest about the level of relationship that you want with your partners now and what you are realistically able to offer. Take responsibility for your actions and acknowledge the impact this has on your partners. Do not compare your partners to each other or blame your preexisting partners for the game-changing relationship you're having.

If one of your partners is experiencing a game-changing relationship and is changing in ways you find undesirable, or is less available to you, ask yourself if these changes are compatible with who you are and what you want in relationships. If you are feeling mistreated by your partner as they engage in this relationship, are they able to acknowledge, address and repair the hurt with you? Are you still receiving the level of time and attention that you need or want from them? Sometimes, the changes that come as a result of your partner's new relationship can leave you needing to accept and grieve the loss of certain aspects of the relationship. In other cases, you may find that you need to make specific requests of your partner in order to feel like the relationship is still viable. The important thing is not to fall into the trap of blaming yourself for your partner's behaviors, or for the fact that they had a game-changing relationship. Remember that their experience is not indicative of a deficiency in you.

Nonmonogamy as Lifestyle Versus Nonmonogamy as Relationship Orientation

As people practice and explore nonmonogamy, the ways they make sense of their CNM preferences and behaviors, and the meaning they give to their CNM identity, can vary. There is much debate as to whether being nonmonogamous is an orientation or a lifestyle choice, and because of this, I intentionally focused dozens of my interviews on this very topic, asking people about whether they experienced their monogamy or nonmonogamy as a lifestyle choice versus an orientation, and then digging more thoroughly into what that really means for each of them. Several years ago I also began to include this question in my initial intake with clients, offering me even more insight into hundreds of people's experiences as they would describe to me how they have come to define and understand themselves regarding being either monogamous or nonmonogamous.

What I found is that being monogamous or nonmonogamous was not a rigid binary or typology, but a spectrum. On
one end of the spectrum we have monogamy, where people are
more mono-amorous and mono-sexual, and on the other end
we have nonmonogamy, where people are more polyamorous
and polysexual. I do not think that any of the locations on this
spectrum are necessarily permanent or static, but what I have
encountered is that the people who are on either of the further
ends of this spectrum describe their version of monogamy or
nonmonogamy as an orientation. For them, being either
monogamous or nonmonogamous does not feel like a choice
they are able to make; they experience it as how they are wired
to be regarding romance and sex.

Lifestyle Choice

Orientation

In the middle of this spectrum we find a whole range of
individuals who, for a variety of reasons, are drawn to being
either more monogamous or nonmonogamous, but do not
identify with it in the same way as the "by orientation" folks.
While they also resonate more with the principles and philosophy of either the monogamous or nonmonogamous paradigms,
they see their placement on this spectrum more as a choice
they are making, which, depending on the life circumstances
in which they find themselves, could change at some point
in the future. As couples open up, there can be disparity in
how each person identifies their nonmonogamy. Some people
identify being nonmonogamous as a lifestyle choice because,
for them, like any lifestyle, it can change, ebb and flow, and
come and go—unlike the orientation folks, who feel CNM is a
fundamental expression of who they are. As people open up
or date each other within the CNM context, these differences
can create obstacles, in particular, when you have a lifestyle
partner paired with more of an orientation partner. This

pairing can be particularly challenging to deal with because each person can have some significantly different needs and desires in regard to how their process with CNM unfolds.

What I learned is that people who identify more with nonmonogamy as a lifestyle choice can vary greatly in terms of their interest and enthusiasm. For many, it was an empowering choice they made as part of exploring themselves and learning more about their romantic and sexual preferences. In such cases, their relationship to nonmonogamy was usually dictated more by where they were in life (such as a post-divorce experimentation phase, or being in their 20s or 30s and dating in the 2010s when exclusivity was no longer assumed in the same way it had been for previous generations), what their needs were in the moment, or who their current partners were than any deeply held conviction that they "needed" to be nonmonogamous. Others who explore nonmonogamy as a lifestyle choice would not have made the choice to embrace it if it hadn't been for the influence of someone else, typically a lover or spouse interested in exploring CNM. For them, the choice to enter nonmonogamy didn't feel as empowering as it did for others, but they were willing to give it a try and eventually found that it genuinely worked for them.

People who identified as nonmonogamous as orientation described their relationship to being nonmonogamous as being just who they essentially were and the fullest expression of their love or sexuality. As one person described, he was faithful in all of his monogamous relationships, but no matter how hard he tried, he always fell in love with other people, feeling like he had to deny important aspects of himself just to stay with one partner. As he described:

> I was able to play the monogamy game for a long time, but one day I realized it was killing me to deny myself like this. Literally! I was having unexplainable health issues, and my doctor eventually told me to go get therapy, because there was no physical explanation

for the pain I had. One day a friend introduced me to a woman who was polyamorous, and she told me about what her life was like, and I began to cry on the spot. I knew what she was describing was who I was supposed to be, and I couldn't pretend anymore. It was like a cork was pulled out of the bottom of me, and all of the physical pain drained away. All the monogamous baggage left me, and I was finally free to be me.

One of the main dilemmas that partners encounter when one identifies with being CNM as more of a lifestyle and the other as an orientation is that they have to confront how differently they both perceive the importance of nonmonogamy in their lives. When the question of nonmonogamy is framed as "this who I am," it essentially becomes nonnegotiable: "How can you deny me the chance to be myself?" A complicating factor in this dynamic is also that many nonmonogamy-as-orientation people feel like they have already waited years to start living out this aspect of their identity. They may or may not have had multiple relationships at the same time in the past, but they certainly intuited there was another way of doing relationships that was more in alignment with their felt sense of self. For them, finding the structure and practice of nonmonogamy is a tremendously powerful validation of something they have wanted for potentially a long time. The experience of having already delayed living out their preferred relational identity helps explain why the pacing can often be so different for the members of these couples.

For the "nonmonogamy as lifestyle" individuals, the faster pace of their partner can be extremely difficult to handle. Since they don't have the same zeal for nonmonogamy, the urgency of their partners can be confusing and a source of hurt. Another important consideration is that the lifestylers still have at least one foot in the monogamous paradigm. The axis of their identity either still pivots around the narratives of monogamy or is positionally closer to monogamy than their partner's, which often means they can be quicker to question the value of nonmonogamy in their lives when things get hard. For them, monogamy might always be a viable option in their back pocket, or at the very least seem like a reasonable request to make of their partner when they are struggling with the transition.

Conflict can arise here because partners can have very different needs in terms of how CNM plays out in their relationship. As each partner in this pairing interprets the other's perspective through their own position on the spectrum, they can both feel unseen, misunderstood and hopeless about how to make it work. Both individuals can feel torn between taking care of themselves and taking care of the relationship. For the nonmonogamy-as-orientation partner the dilemma is, "I want the freedom to explore, but it hurts you when I do, and I don't want to hurt you," and for the nonmonogamy-as-lifestyle partner the conundrum is, "I don't want to stop you from getting your needs met or being happy, but I can't emotionally handle your process."

So how do we navigate these differences of relational realities? They can create a painful, even unbearable dynamic where we feel torn between meeting our own needs and being whole and complete as a person and meeting the needs of a relationship we value or a person we greatly love. The way we frame and approach this tension is critical for addressing this issue without escalating conflict. First, just becoming aware of this difference can be a big help for partners. If partners are dealing with some version of this combination of nonmonogamy as orientation and as lifestyle, recognizing that their behavior has more to do with their position on the spectrum than an attempt to thwart needs or control their partner can hopefully help them see each other with more compassion and understanding.

Another consideration that can be helpful for these kinds of pairings is how to best address the issue of pacing. Partners really need to decide *together* how to answer the question of how fast or slow to go with new relationships. As partners date other people, it's incredibly important that they maintain a sense of shared reality within their own relationship. Dating new people can be destabilizing for current relationships and trigger a number of deep-seated insecurities for both partners. Attachment fears can get easily activated, and it's particularly important that we make decisions with a lot of awareness, care and sensitivity during this delicate phase of going through a CNM transition. Moving too fast—or too slow—can give partners the sense that the process of the CNM transition we are in is no longer a shared process and that our relational realities are getting too far apart.

Partners need to really stay open and be willing to hold space for the potentially big differences in each other's experiences. We need to undertake honest explorations of what really underlies the requests we make of our partners. If I make requests for you to not do certain things initially with new partners, such as overnights or oral sex, are my requests actually a question of pacing, or an expression of a need to control your process? Sometimes a request to pump the brakes comes from a legitimate need to give our nervous systems a chance to recalibrate and integrate all the new changes. And sometimes the ask to slow down is a strategy to postpone exposure to the discomfort of seeing our partner with other people.

On the other side of things, it's important to recognize when our desire to have new experiences with new partners is a healthy expression of our own differentiation and when it starts to become a one-sided pursuit of our needs at the expense of the connection with our partner. It requires a great deal of self-awareness and trust between partners to authentically distinguish between these two possibilities and make genuine compromises on both sides. It's also important to be able to tell the difference between the feeling that you have to ask your partner for permission to have the experiences you want to have and having the consideration for your partner's feelings and needs, along with a willingness to temper your pace for the sake of the relationship. Granted, it can often be very difficult to strike a balance between these two perspectives, and not always easy to know when we should err on the side of advocating for our own needs or for the health of the original relationship.

Differences in Approach to CNM and Relationship Structure

There are many different ways to practice CNM, and as couples open their relationship or people in CNM relationships date new partners, it's very common that they either want or end up wanting very different CNM styles. This is yet another challenge that can emerge after the transition to nonmonogamy has been initiated for people new to CNM, and it is a recurring experience for the seasoned CNM practitioner. What I observe is that people typically fall along two intersecting lines of possibilities in terms of their personal preferences for how to do nonmonogamy. The first relates to the degree of togetherness or separateness with which they want to share their nonmonogamous experiences with their partners, and the second relates to the degree of hierarchy—or lack thereof—that they want in their relationships. When partners are not in alignment around either of these two issues, the differences can be hard to overcome. Let's take a closer look at what each of these differences entail.

The Degree of Togetherness and Separateness in CNM

For some people, the journey into CNM is something they genuinely want to share with a spouse or primary partner. For these individuals, their experiences have more meaning when done together and serve to strengthen the bond between them and their partner. Exploring CNM in tandem can also feel safer for some because there are fewer opportunities for independent bonds to be formed. There are fewer unknowns and less uncertainty to grapple with, which can alleviate, or at least reduce, some of the anxiousness or insecurities that can arise. A gamut of possibilities are available to people who want a more shared CNM experience, and these can include swinging, threesomes, group sex, triads or quad relationships, and even *garden party* or *kitchen table polyamory* (see glossary, page 304).

The opposite of the shared experience is when partners want to keep their sexual and relational experiences more separate. The desire or need is to experience CNM on their own terms as an individual, apart from the context of their other relationships. This more independent approach, the extreme of which is commonly referred to as *parallel polyamory*, can be helpful for people coming out of an enmeshed or codependent dynamic, where the need is to differentiate from their partner instead of further intertwining their realities. This preference can also have nothing to do with someone trying to circumvent getting too enmeshed or someone trying to assert their autonomy, but can be based on connection styles, such as being more introverted and preferring to see people one-on-one, or just pure scheduling realities, such as that, when you only see someone once every week or so, you want time with just them, not in a group dynamic. Also, some people feel a desire to discover new parts of themselves through different relationships, and they feel that including their partners in their other relationships would only inhibit this discovery. As one person I interviewed said, "I tried having all my partners hang out together, and they hated each other. Eventually, I realized I didn't need to have all my relationships overlap, and that I actually like to have partners that represent very different aspects of myself. Keeping my various connections separate allows me to embody those different selves in a way that wouldn't be possible if they crossed over."

While it's certainly possible for partners to want a combination of these two approaches—for example, I currently have both a nesting kitchen table dynamic with Dave and my current nesting partner, as well as a parallel relationship outside of our poly family dynamic—the difficulties typically arise when individuals in a particular relationship or polycule want opposing styles. Some partners only feel comfortable when they share sexual or romantic experiences with their partners, and other partners really prefer to have their dates be separate. This dynamic can be extremely difficult to navigate unless there is some willingness to negotiate or find some kind of compromise that meets the needs of everyone in the dynamic for separateness and shared experiences. If each person's preference for togetherness and separateness is too far apart, it is important to figure out how each of you can compromise, finding a way to get enough of your needs met, knowing that none of you will get exactly what you want.

Relationship Hierarchy

The topic of hierarchy in CNM relationships can be tricky, confusing and often quite polarized. Some people adamantly want it, while others determinedly don't. For some, it is unimaginable to do CNM without some aspects of hierarchy, whereas for others it is offensive to even use the word. As a therapist, I have seen hierarchy used both in ethical and transparent ways in CNM relationships and as a tool to limit and control other people's behavior. On the other end of the spectrum, I have seen people practice nonhierarchical CNM in ways that honor and respect everyone involved, but I have also seen people cause significant harm in the name of being nonhierarchical. I have had clients tell me in no uncertain terms they abhor the use of terms like *primary partner*, expressing their ardent belief that relationships shouldn't be categorized in hierarchical structures. And I've also had numerous people timidly admit in the safety of our confidential session that they actually want some form of hierarchy but are too ashamed to ask for it in the context of their relationships, fearing judgment and backlash from their partners or their CNM communities.

When referring to hierarchical CNM in this book, we are talking about the practice of ranking romantic and sexual relationships into a hierarchy of importance, where certain relationships are considered more valuable than others. Typically, words like *primary*, *secondary* and sometimes *tertiary* are used to describe the various levels of significance, commitment and influence that each relationship can have in people's lives. In this case, a primary partner would be at the top of this structure and generally afforded certain privileges such as more time, support or decision-making power, or even rights to set the rules for other relationships. This configuration usually reflects a dynamic in which the people in secondary or tertiary relationships have little to no input about how their relationship unfolds, or are subject to vetoes and rules from their metamours who are at the top of the hierarchy.

To further nuance our understanding of hierarchical relationships, in their book *More Than Two* Eve Rickert and Franklin Veaux point out an important distinction between *prescriptive* and *descriptive* hierarchy. Prescriptive hierarchy describes the practice of explicitly naming a particular relationship as primary and prescribes all future relationships subordinate to it. In this context, the primary status usually means that each member of a couple has the right to put certain restrictions or limits on how strong, deep, intense, or committed their partner's other relationships can become. Descriptive hierarchy, on the other hand, is less about prescribing the container of a specific relationship or the possible connections with other people, and more about recognizing that the circumstances shaping our lives can organically create different levels of priority, commitment and even power among partners. In descriptive hierarchy, a dyad could function very much like a primary relationship in the sense that they are more domestically, financially or emotionally intertwined with each other than with other partners, but there is still an openness to allowing the nature of relationships to change, or to integrating new people into the relationship constellation.

In nonhierarchical CNM, relationships are not arranged within the structure of a hierarchy or ranking of partners. No one person has the right to hold sway over another person's relationships, regardless of whether partners live together or have a longer relationship history. Ideally, everyone gets a voice and has the space for their needs and wants to be considered. Each relationship is given the chance to evolve according to its own dictates. Functionally, many nonhierarchical relationships look like descriptively hierarchical relationships, and you'll see people arguing that the difference is largely a matter of semantics. And despite the fact that, in some cases, nonhierarchical CNM may include prioritization of certain relationships or different levels of investment and commitment, the nonhierarchical structure does not promote power differentials, advocating instead for flexibility in terms of how decisions are made and how relationships can change over time, according to the lived circumstances of the individuals in those relationships. Terms like *nesting*, *anchor* or *inner circle* partner have been adopted by some CNM people instead of the label of primary partner, which give more nuance to the nature of these relationships while at the same time acknowledging there are still varying degrees of investment, commitment or descriptive hierarchy present.

Given the differences between hierarchical and nonhierarchical relationships, it's easy to see why this issue can cause challenges for partners who find themselves on opposite sides of the fence. Sometimes these differences can reflect potential incompatibilities between fundamental values, wants and needs that could threaten the relationship, and this, in turn, can make talking about this issue very scary for people. What I often see is partners getting stuck in philosophical or intellectual debates about the validity of their respective points of view, or falling into the trap of shaming or pathologizing each other for leaning towards one end of the hierarchy spectrum or the other. Far from changing a partner's mind, this kind of headbutting typically creates more disconnection than mutual understanding. The fear of losing the relationship can also create distortions that greatly limit our capacity to hold space for a partner's perspective, feeding the story that their position on hierarchy is not only inferior to our own, but the principal cause of our potential incompatibility. In such cases, I find it helpful to temporarily put the debate aside and explore the attachment needs underlying these positions, adopting a willingness to talk about this issue in a way that is more relational and collaborative.

In *Polysecure*, one of the things that felt helpful to people was bringing the concept of attachment-based relationships into the context of CNM. Having an awareness of the powerful influence that our emotional attachment systems can have on our fundamental sense of safety and security in CNM relationships gave people a useful framework with which they could better understand their relational needs, and thus feel more empowered to advocate for those needs. *Polysecure* also gave people more tools for thinking about how to create secure attachment than just relying on hierarchical structures. When talking about attachment-based relationships, we are referring to relationships where you are deliberately cultivating the behaviors that foster and support the development of secure emotional attachment with a partner. This includes things like demonstrating consistent emotional attunement, loving presence and regular responsiveness to your partner's needs and wants. In these relationships, we feel that more than not we can count on our partner's support when we feel hurt, scared, overwhelmed, or in need of connection, comfort, reassurance or celebration. Attachment-based relationships can be forged regardless of your degree of hierarchy or lack thereof; however, they do imply some level of commitment to regularly being available and attentive to each other.

One salient distinction to make is between having a *secure connection* with someone versus being in an *attachment-based relationship*. Secure connections are with people or partners who may come in and out of our lives with greater degrees of fluidity, but with whom we still feel a great deal of closeness and intimacy. The connection we have with such people can feel very secure, and this connection could be deeply meaningful, special and important to us, but we wouldn't necessarily invest the same level of time and attention into the relationship as we would with an attachment-based relationship. Having the conceptual framework of secure connections and attachment-based relationships expands our options in terms of how we think about what we need and want from our CNM relationships, particularly with regard to issues of emotional safety and security. Sometimes what happens is that partners are asking for more hierarchy, but really they're just wanting the experience of a more attachment-based relationship. I have seen numerous clients initially use the idea of hierarchy to feel more secure in their CNM relationships, then later realize what they actually wanted was to have a partner put more energy into tending to their emotional attachment needs. On the other hand, sometimes partners are saying they want less hierarchy, when what they actually mean is that they want less of an attachment-based relationship and more of a secure connection.

Of course, it does not have to be one or the other, where you either want more hierarchy because you want more of an attachment-based relationship, or you want less hierarchy because you want less of an attachment-based relationship. People can still want an attachment-based relationship and also want less structural hierarchy, or more balance between how they experience connection and autonomy in their relationship. Having more clarity about these potential differences between ours and our partners' needs for more or less attachment-based connection can sometimes alleviate the tension around whether or not hierarchy is a relevant consideration in a particular relationship or constellation of relationships. While it doesn't always resolve the issue, it does, at least, bring more nuance and precision to the conversation and help illuminate what is an issue of genuinely wanting different levels of relationship, or wanting a different type of relationship altogether.

The point of examining this issue of attachment needs is ultimately to help partners tease apart the often confusing tangle of viewpoints that swirl around the question of hierarchy in CNM relationships. My observations are based on the real examples of clients who, after learning about attachment needs and attachment-based relationships, were able to recognize that what they previously thought was an issue of more or less hierarchy was actually a need for more or less focus on their attachment system. By no means am I suggesting that the desire for more hierarchy in your open relationship, in and of itself, is somehow problematic, or means you are clinging to relational structure for safety and security. It is an absolutely valid want that can sometimes be exactly what people need to do CNM in a way that genuinely supports themselves and their partners. I also do not mean to say that everyone with the conviction to do nonhierarchical CNM is necessarily wanting a relationship with less emotional attachment. As I said before, the absence of hierarchy in no way precludes attachment-based relationships, and nonhierarchical styles of CNM can offer people important ways of relating that allow them to be in alignment with many of their core relational principles and values.

However, with all that said, it is important to recognize that some people *do* use hierarchy to control their relationships and avoid feelings of insecurity or uncertainty, while others *do* use the concept of nonhierarchy as a way of avoiding commitment or being considerate of their partners' needs. If you fall into either of these two categories, it's important to recognize this and be as honest as you can with yourself about it. If you are using the concept of more or less hierarchy as a substitute for something like attending to your attachment-based needs and wants or being honest about the level of involvement you really want in a particular relationship, you will most likely find yourself in relationship dynamics that continue to leave you feeling unfulfilled and dissatisfied, and your partners and metamours confused and hurt. However, if you are clear on what level of hierarchical structure and attachment-based experiences you want for yourself and with your partners, you will be much better equipped to negotiate these differences, or to come to terms with the incompatibilities they create in your relationships.

Sometimes the differing degree of hierarchy, or lack thereof, that partners want *is* incompatible, and one partner always feels their freedom is limited while the other can never get enough safety and security. When partners fall squarely on opposite ends of the hierarchy spectrum like this, I rarely see things work out. The gulf between the respective wants and needs is too great, and no amount of negotiation will bridge it. However, when people are a bit closer on the spectrum, and the possibility of inching towards your partner's position can be done in a way that doesn't leave you overly compromising yourself or your own needs, then there is a chance to find a middle ground. While this may mean that you have to sometimes manage circumstances that are not always ideal or easy for you, your love for each other and your desire to be together ultimately make it worth it. Similarly, the fact that your preferences for attachment-based connections are different from a partner's doesn't necessarily mean the end of the relationship. If partners agree to wanting an attachment-based relationship, then it's important to explore the differing needs around freedom, exploration, emotional attunement, safety and connection in order to recognize and adjust expectations accordingly. Therefore, when talking to partners about how you want hierarchy to show up—or not—in your relationships, get clear on exactly what you are agreeing to and asking for. Here are some helpful questions to guide your process:

- Based on your history and experiences, when has hierarchy been helpful for you or your partners? When has it been challenging or harmful for you or your partners?
- Based on your history and experiences, when has nonhierarchy or less hierarchy been helpful for you or your partners? When has it been challenging, hurtful or harmful for you or your partners?
- What aspects of hierarchical structure do you want in your relationships?
- What aspects of hierarchical structure do you not want?
- What attachment-based experiences would support you in feeling more secure in your relationships?
- Why are hierarchy, nonhierarchy, an attachment-based relationship or a secure connection important to you?

  Some best practices would be:
- If you want hierarchy, articulate why you want it, and how it connects to your values and understanding of yourself and what you need.
- Don't use hierarchy to control your partner or their partners.
- Don't use hierarchy to avoid your own feelings of jealousy or the uncertainty that inevitably comes with being in any relationship, regardless of structure, but particularly in CNM.
- If you do have aspects of prescriptive or descriptive hierarchy, get clear on why this is most aligned for you, and do your best to communicate this to partners.

The Differences That Make Less of a Difference

In this last section, I want to shift gears a bit and talk about the cases where differences with partners actually become *less* of an issue when we are nonmonogamous. Sometimes within CNM we can become more accepting of the differences between us and our partners because the criteria for what we want in a relationship changes, allowing more space for those differences. Many people know that it's not possible to get all of our needs met by one person, but the prevailing monogamous narrative still suggests that it's reasonable to expect one partner to meet the majority of our emotional, intellectual, sexual and practical needs. This weighty expectation puts us in the peculiar situation where our criteria for potential partners has to include an exhaustive list of everything we could possibly want in a relationship, because if our chosen partner doesn't check one of our boxes, we're basically doomed to live without it for the rest of our lives. A beautiful benefit of CNM is that it can release the tension to get all your needs met by the same person. The result is frequently that they experience even more acceptance and appreciation for who their partners are and the gifts they bring to their life, because now they can focus less on what they are not getting.

Furthermore, in CNM the new relationships that we explore can have much more flexibility in terms of the criteria and standards we have. For example in a non-nesting relationship, the differences and incompatibilities that could be problematic in exclusive or nesting relationships are often inconsequential. This frees us up to have connections we wouldn't otherwise entertain. Without the expectation that we will be intertwining our lives in the same way we would with a nesting partner, we can allow more differences to be present, and this in turn gives us the chance to experience genuinely novel things with these new partners. In these kinds of relationships, the differences between ourselves and new partners can actually represent refreshing contrasts that expand our sense of who we are.

§

As partners explore nonmonogamy together, they are simultaneously presented with the gift as well as the potential threat of contrast. When new to CNM, sometimes these differences are exactly what we needed to bring more awareness to our relationship dynamics and make the necessary changes to keep growing as individuals and as partners. In other cases, they spell the end of a relationship that was already riddled with issues and simply waiting for the right detonator to finally end things. Either way, the transition from a monogamous to a nonmonogamous paradigm can be a tremendous catalyst for either growth or dissolution, depending on the nature and degree of the differences that arise as a result, as well as how partners choose to deal with them.

Similarly, for those of you already steeped in CNM, the process of taking on new partners, changing how you prioritize certain partners, or making significant changes to your style of CNM or level of hierarchy can create stark differences between how you and your partners want to experience sex and romance, which can bring a lot of unexpected things to the surface: attributes that were originally endearing can become intolerable, questionable characteristics can turn into dealbreakers, and even the language we use to make agreements can be rendered inscrutable. Also, as we begin to intimately engage with new and interesting people who are different from us, we can be inspired to live our own lives in new ways. We can discover new relational possibilities and freedoms and experience levels of compatibility and attunement that we didn't even know were possible. This new perspective forces us to see things we may not have seen before and often makes many of the things we weren't paying much attention to come to the forefront of our awareness. For better, and sometimes for worse, the new vantage point that we gain through the differences that emerge in our new relationships forever changes the way we see ourselves and our relationships, and what we ultimately want from them.

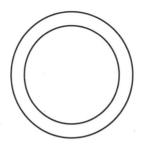

CHAPTER SEVEN
SELF TRANSFORMATION

My first memory of experiencing awe was at nine years old while standing in the dimly lit Hall of North American Forests exhibit at the Museum of Natural History in New York City. With my hands and forehead pushed up against the glass showcase of a diorama depicting the scale of humans in comparison to the great redwood and sequoia trees of California, I skeptically asked my mom if a place like that actually existed. When she said it did, I was wonderstruck with disbelief: "But the people are so tiny, and the trees are so big!" Growing up in Brooklyn, my experience of the natural world was minimal, and my only point of reference for towering giants was the concrete skyscrapers of the city skyline. Even though I could hardly conceive of such untamed towers growing in the forest, I knew I had to see those majestic trees with my own eyes one day, and it was this experience that planted the first seed within me to eventually leave New York and one day move out West.

As I got older and the deadline for college applications quickly approached, I thought only of schools in California. From a relatively early age, I recognized I didn't completely gel with the ultra-urban culture of New York City, even though I was never 100% sure why. Intuitively, I just felt like the West would be a better fit. It represented a place where I would finally feel a sense of deep resonance, belonging and even relaxation in my body. Part of me was starting to get a glimpse of the constant hypervigilance that my East Coast nervous system had grown accustomed to, and I was beginning to see little cracks in the calloused emotional armor that had allowed me to survive as a young girl growing up in the housing projects of Brooklyn. I also think some part of me knew that I would never escape the enmeshed dynamics of my family if I stayed put. However, despite my ardent desire to leave and start a new life in sunny California, the inescapable realities of poverty meant I was ultimately destined to pay in-state tuition at a New York state school.

After graduating from college at 22, I reclaimed my intention to go West and decided to attend an alternative healing arts school in Northern California—the place where Dave and I would eventually meet. As I made my way across the country, I made sure that my first stop on the West Coast was the old growth forests of northern California. As someone who had previously prided herself on never crying, I cried at the sheer beauty of nature's redwood cathedrals. Looking up hundreds of feet, I felt an even greater sense of awe than the little nine-year-old me had experienced in the museum that day. With my own eyes I finally knew that trees of this magnitude were real, and it cracked me open. My body reverberated with an overwhelming reverence for the magnificence of life and the greater order and intelligence of nature. It was there and then that I first felt the power of an experience that I had previously only heard associated with church. A new version of myself had emerged.

In the years to follow, I continued to be astonished by the vast differences between East and West Coast culture in the United States. In California, and later in Colorado, the pace of life was slower and more manageable, the physical environment was beautifully distinct, and people talked about things like "relating to each other from the heart," mindful listening and even mindful eating. There was also easy and abundant access to incredible nature, health food stores, and any kind of dance, yoga or alternative medicine modalities you could conceive of. It was the first time in my life where I was meeting people who were genuinely open-minded and prioritized their physical, emotional and mental health in a sincere way—not merely for aesthetics.

It was there, living and breathing in a totally different culture, that I could really see just how unhappy, shut down and guarded I had been in my native New York. I realized that who I was there had been more of a reaction to my environment and a performance of what I thought I was supposed to be rather than an authentic expression of who I was. The unbounded expansiveness of the West Coast paradigm naturally invited more of me to come forward, and I experienced parts of myself that I never would have known without leaving Brooklyn. The powerful magnetism of those first images in the museum called me to the West, and it was only there, in a place so different from where I was from, that I could actually see all the ways I had been conditioned by my environment to be out of sync with myself.

Similarly, for some people it is not until they have "moved away" from and stepped outside of monogamy that they start to see new and different parts of themselves come alive. The different worldview and beliefs of nonmonogamy, paired with the new experiences that occur through having multiple relationships, can wake people up to newer versions of themselves that were either previously unavailable or only partially accessible. What I have observed over and over again is that the transition from monogamy to nonmonogamy is not just a transformation of people's relationships; it can also catalyze a genuine awakening of the self. When people describe this experience to me, they talk about how living in a new paradigm activates, stimulates and rouses new and old parts of themselves, leaving them feeling fortified and enlivened, finally in connection with their true or authentic self. I categorize this aspect of the transition from monogamy to nonmonogamy as being a more expansive *awakening of the self* aspect that can give people a new sense of clarity, meaning and purpose in their life.

Moreover, as the contrast between our newer nonmonogamous experiences and previous monogamous ways of being become more obvious to us, we are faced with all the ways we have potentially been inauthentic, disconnected or even in denial about who we are and what we have really wanted for ourselves and in our relationships. These reflections about ourselves can call our sense of identity into question and open us up to new levels of uncertainty. Also, if we explore the many subcultures that make up the tapestry of the different nonmonogamous communities, we may be exposed to additional concepts, lifestyles and identities, which can further challenge our previous sense of who and how we are in this world. One of the consequences of this unique deconstruction of the self that can happen as a result of embracing nonmonogamy is the realization that you may have previously been living a life that was never really your own, and this can evoke intense feelings of grief, guilt or shame. In my experience, very few people are prepared for this kind of dismantling of their identity.

Awakening of the Self

As I listened to the people I interviewed for this book and heard my clients' stories about how their sense of self was shaken or even radically jolted in either their initial transition to nonmonogamy or in certain CNM transitions, they continually alluded to the concept of *awakening* to describe their own experiences. They used various metaphors to describe a process of going from a sleeping state to an awakened one, being reborn, experiencing the activation of their previously dormant authentic self, having a veil removed from their eyes, being a hermit crab leaving behind its shell, and even being toothpaste that can no longer be put back in the tube. As one interviewee said, "It's the classic once-I-was-blind-but-now-I-can-see experience." Of course, the narrative therapist in me was fascinated by their repeated use of these analogies to describe what to them was a remaking of who they once were into a new self. After hearing several anecdotes of this kind, I was reminded of the consciousness-altering process described by Robert Kegan in his Theory of Adult Development, where he outlines the transitions that individuals go through as they progress from one stage of psychological development to another. Robert Kegan is an American developmental psychologist and researcher who enumerated five stages of human psychological development.

Like all models, theories of human psychological development can offer important insights and create interesting frames of reference for better understanding our behavior and ways of relating. However, they can also have significant limits and drawbacks. For example, many developmental theorists have been rightly critiqued for being gender biased, equating "higher" levels of psychological development with more "masculine" qualities and "lower" stages of development with more feminine qualities. Another concern is a pronounced bias towards a Eurocentric or capitalist point of view in many of the theories, where attributes like freedom, individuality and personal autonomy are touted as hallmarks of the "highest" developmental stages, whereas the values of more collectivist and socio-centric cultures such as many in Africa, Asia or the Middle East are seen as reflecting "lower" stages.

Compared to other developmentalists, I have found Kegan to acknowledge that stages are influenced by the culture and history from which they arose and may not be applicable to all cultures throughout time. Kegan's theory has also tended to stay away from making binary claims rooted in gendered viewpoints, and his final stage of development includes qualities typically associated with both masculine and feminine archetypes, as well as individualistic and collective values. I chose Kegan's theory because it complemented the way my clients and interviewees described their personal growth experiences, and my intention is to offer his model as a useful way of framing the way we interact with the world, which to me is culturally and contextually dependent, and by no means absolute.

Stage of Development	Typical Ages and Percentage of the Adult Population	Associated Traits	Focus	Capacities Under Conscious Awareness	Capacities Still in Progress or Under Development
Stage 1: The Impulsive Mind	Early childhood. Approximately 2–6 years old.	Learning about the objects of the world. Trouble understanding others' perspectives or opinions. Needs to be repeatedly reminded of social rules.	External	—	Impulses and perceptions.
Stage 2: The Imperial Mind	Adolescence 6 years to teens (6% of adult population).	Self-centric, self-protective and opportunistic. Tendency to view relationships in utilitarian terms. Limited ability to take others' perspectives. Seeks out and follows unchanging universal rules.	Internal/ individualistic	Impulses and perceptions.	Feelings, needs, interests and desires.
Stage 3: The Socialized Mind	Post-adolescence (58% of the adult population).	"I am my relationships, and I follow the rules." Oriented to maintaining affiliation with group or family. Capable of goal-setting, planning, self-reflection and empathy. Able to think abstractly and reflect on others' actions. Can be diplomatic or conformist.	External/collective An outside-in approach to understanding and defining one's self.	Feelings, needs, interests and desires.	Interpersonal relationships, mutuality.

Stage 4: The Self-Authoring Mind	Adult (35% of the adult population).	"I have an identity. I make choices." Identifies values and aims to contribute meaningfully. Able to identify the need for and nurture affiliations. Self-guided, self-evaluative, conscientious and responsible.	Internal/individualistic An inside-out approach to understanding and defining one's self.	Interpersonal relationships, mutuality.	Self-authorship, identity, ideology.
Stage 5: The Self-Transforming Mind	Adult (1% of the adult population).	"I hold many identities. I embrace paradox." Able to regard multiple perspectives simultaneously. Able to think systematically and embrace complexity. Attentive to multiple levels (self, collective, systemic).	Both external / collective and internal / individualistic. An integration of both an inside-out and an outside-in approach to understanding and defining one's self.	Self-authorship, identity, ideology.	Dialectic among ideologies.

TABLE 7.1: Kegan's stages of development. Adapted from *The Evolving Self* by Robert Kegan, 1982.

According to Kegan, adults—just like children—go through different stages of psychological development, and these sometimes do not correspond directly to our biological growth. These stages in and of themselves constitute whole new paradigms, entire worldviews and novel ways of mentally constructing our lived reality. For Kegan, becoming an adult is not just about learning new things, gaining more skills or acquiring more knowledge. Instead of simply adding things to the "container" of the mind, he suggests maturity is more about changing the actual form of our container, changing the *way* we know and understand the world. This means there are vast qualitative and perceptual differences between the various stages that make it extremely difficult for individuals inhabiting different stages to really get each other. Also, because the transition between each developmental stage represents such a big change in our fundamental way of understanding the world, the process of going from one to the other can be expansive and illuminating, tumultuous and turbulent, or somewhere in between.

As we progress through the developmental stages, we alternate back and forth between a more internal or individualistic focus and an emphasis on being more external and collectively oriented. Kegan was clear that people who occupy the later stages of the model are in no way superior or more advanced than people in earlier stages. He asserted instead that the process of moving through the developmental stages meant that we experience a significant increase in our own psychological complexity, and this allows us to reflect on ourselves and the world with new, expanded intellectual awareness and emotional capacity. As we increase our capacity to think and analyze in more complex and multidimensional ways, we gain more agency to deliberately chose the kind of relational realities we want.

I find that Kegan's model is most useful to the degree that it gives us greater insight into our own lived experiences and helps us imagine new possibilities for our relationships. Instead of suggesting fixed or rigid levels of development, I see these stages as frames of reference that can help contextualize the often-bewildering array of possibilities within CNM. As we consider the varying stages of Kegan's model, our intention is not to pigeonhole or diagnose the essence of a person's character or personality by associating their attitudes or behavior with a particular stage. The stages should not be weaponized or used as a means for categorizing, labeling, pathologizing, essentializing, dismissing or diminishing ourselves or our partners.

Reflecting on the testimony of my clients, I was able to track their different experiences and thought processes and link their expression to the corresponding stages of Kegan's model. While there were clearly individuals whose process indicated they were in the transition from stage two (imperial mind) to stage three (socialized mind), as well as people moving from stage four (self-authoring mind) to stage five (self-transforming mind), the majority of personal anecdotes reflected the transition from stage three (socialized mind) to stage four (self-authoring mind). Because the first stage, the impulsive mind, represents the stage occupied by children and was not representative of any of my clients' or interviewees' descriptions of their experiences, I will only focus on stages two through five in this chapter.

Another important consideration is that these stages do not represent static states of being that are achieved once and for all. It's actually possible to display the characteristics of certain stages in certain circumstances, or in particular relationships and not in others. For instance, as an adult, when you spend time with your family of origin or go home for the holidays, you might find yourself taking on aspects of the adolescent imperial mind typical of stage two, while in your work or with a trusted friend or partner you could present more as the self-authoring mind of stage four. The important thing is to be able to track and recognize your own process and ways of being in your intimate relationships in order to decide on which stage you want to be functioning in.

Stage Two: The Imperial Mind

Stage two, the imperial mind, is mostly associated with adolescence. The description of this stage is not meant to pathologize or reduce all teenagers into the superficial or pejorative stereotypes commonly promoted by North American culture, which suggest they are completely narcissistic or selfish. Obviously, teenagers are complex, multifaceted, and capable of a wide range of behaviors and traits, many of which include thoughtfulness, sincerity, empathy and altruism. However, from a strictly developmental point of view, I do think it is appropriate to make some generalizations about the evolutive impetus driving this stage of human psychological development. In North America, one of the primary functions of adolescence is to begin defining and asserting our own individuality and identity as distinct from our familial systems of origin. This drive to figure out who we "really are" in a larger social context creates a necessarily "me"-focused orientation. Granted, when this self-first perspective is not tempered by appropriate role models and is taken to extremes, it can become shadowy and self-serving in ways that are potentially destructive. But in its essence, the need to focus primarily on oneself during this phase is a critical step in the process of figuring out who one is and where one fits in their particular social reality.

Regardless of their age, some adults remain squarely rooted in this psychological stage. In stage two, the primary emphasis is on one's own needs, interests and agendas. It is very individualistic, and relationships with others are mostly valued in terms of their utility: the advantages that can be gained by maintaining them. Relationships are therefore more a means to an end than an end in themselves. The transactional quality of stage two relationships means it can be difficult for individuals to have a real sense of shared reality with a partner. They are more preoccupied with what they are getting and how others perceive them than with how their partners actually feel, and this preoccupation is typically concerned with the possible consequences that other people's perceptions of them could have on their own experience. For example, a person occupying stage two would avoid lying to a friend not because honesty and transparency are important in and of themselves, but rather out of fear of the consequences of lying, or of possible retaliation. The core values of the stage two consciousness are personal comfort, convenience, reputation, self-satisfaction and unfettered freedom. Furthermore, stage two individuals may follow rules, express allegiance to certain principles or ideologies, and even act in accord with policy and protocol, but they will only do so to be liked, rewarded, or avoid being punished. If they are faithful in a romantic relationship, for instance, their loyalty comes from fear of being caught by their partner, and not because cheating goes against their personal values. As one woman in this stage said to her husband, "It's fine if you cheat on me, but just don't leave me."

Stage Three: The Socialized Mind

In stage three, the socialized mind, our focus shifts outward to others, and we no longer view relationships as simply a means to an end. We can consider other people's opinions and perspectives, not just because of the potential consequences of those opinions but because we are open to and care about other points of view. However, despite our capacity to take other people's thoughts and feelings into consideration, it is the ideas, beliefs and norms of the systems around us—family, culture, institutions and society—that most influence our behavior and make up the center of our moral and ethical compass. Our point of reference for making decisions and judging the value of our actions is the conditions and expectations of our external social environment.

Statistically, most adults stay at this stage. Part of the challenge of this stage is that we lack the connection to a strong, independent sense of self apart from these larger systems we are embedded in. The need to conform to these external standards makes it difficult to recognize and embrace the aspects of ourselves that challenge the status quo. As a consequence, when faced with conflict, we can have a hard time connecting with and asserting any of our wants and needs that run counter to social norms and can actually hide, deny, repress and even criticize the parts of us that seem "socially unacceptable," if we're even aware of them. Because people at this stage derive their sense of self from external validation, their need for approval is very high, and they tend to spend a lot of effort projecting the image of themselves that others are expecting to see.

Stage 4: The Self-Authoring Mind

The transition into stage four, the self-authoring mind, represents the next developmental shift, from unquestioning conformity to social rules and norms to taking responsibility for creating one's own life and reality. External sources of authority are dethroned and replaced with internal sources as we take on the task of authoring the stories that shape our experience. While we can clearly recognize and acknowledge that we still belong to a particular culture that impacts us, we have an inner compass that allows us to critically evaluate its beliefs and discourses, and we can decide for ourselves their value or relevance in our lives. As we prioritize our own opinions and viewpoints, we have more agency to change and influence our life according to what's true for us, and we can let go of the ideas from our culture, religion or parents that have held us back.

At this stage the question is no longer "who should you be?" but rather "who do you want to be?" Our aim is not to please others, but to live out our values and author a unique, personal sense of purpose. At this stage of development, we can objectively evaluate the conditions of our social environment and choose to either move with or against the stream of collective consciousness. The freedom to live in alignment with our own thoughts, feelings and values is a liberating experience for most, which is often described as a personal awakening. As a socialized mind, showing who we really are is risky. A significant disadvantage of this wariness is that because we never feel comfortable or safe showing who we are, we can never fully trust the love we receive from others. This is because the love we receive is meant for the socially acceptable projection we present to the world, and not the complex, dynamic selves of our lived experience—and thus, it is partial. Therefore, to be fully loved for who we are, we must first know who we are, and then be able to express that self-authored self to others.

Stage 5: The Self-Transforming Mind

In stage five, the self-transforming mind, the ability to consciously write the story of our lives through the self-authoring process of stage four takes the next leap forward, with the burgeoning capacity to simultaneously embrace our individuality as well as our relational and collective realities. Now we realize we are not tied to *any* particular identity or role, even the ones we create for ourselves, and we wake up to the possibility of continuously recreating ourselves in the context of new relationships and life experiences. This stage reflects elements of the Buddhist concept of the impermanence of self, a self that is not inherently fixed or static, but in constant flux in response to the circumstances of the moment. As we come to realize that all identities are relative to some social context— and therefore socially constructed—we lose our attachment to any particular narrative or role and instead pick and choose whatever resonates with the circumstances in which we find ourselves. We are no longer confined to the restrictions of any one particular identity. We can see and hold the complexities of life, recognize that all identity constructs are limited, and continuously pivot to meet the needs of the current situation.

From the freedom and autonomy of the self-transforming mind we can question external authority *and* ourselves,
scrutinizing our own thoughts and beliefs as well as those of
any systems we're a part of. We do not believe that "truth" can
be contained or expressed by any particular point of view or
strategy. We intentionally choose the filters through which we
evaluate the information coming to us from others, and we are
open to change ourselves by developing new filters as necessary
or desired. We are comfortable holding multiple, even conflict-
ing, thoughts, emotions, identities and ideologies at once, and
we can understand things from various perspectives. Thanks to
this perceptual agility, we are able to embrace paradoxes that
would seem impossible from earlier stages of development.
The number of individuals who transition into this stage is
relatively small in comparison to the previous stages.

Monogamy and Kegan's stages	Nonmonogamy and Kegan's Stages
Imperial mind	Imperial mind
Adolescent mentality/self-centered. I do what I want, when I want. My needs are the only ones that matter. I don't cheat because I'm afraid to get caught, but I would probably cheat if I thought I could get away with it.	I'm reclaiming the primacy of my needs and wants. My need for freedom is more important than your need for safety. Any request for me to slow my pace is an imposition on my freedom. I will honor our agreements only when it's convenient to do so or fits with my needs.
Socialized mind	Socialized mind
I am monogamous because that is what is acceptable in my world. I am a respectful and loving partner because that is how I was raised. I respect your needs because that is what "good" partners do. I believe cheating is morally wrong even though I may have the desire to be with other people.	I identify as nonmonogamous and I follow the "rules" of CNM. We must negotiate our needs because that is what we do as CNM partners. CNM culture says agreements are important, so I make them with my partner and strive to follow them, and I feel like a bad person when I don't. CNM culture says prescriptive hierarchy is bad even though I want it, and I feel bad for not being CNM enough.

Monogamy and Kegan's stages	Nonmonogamy and Kegan's Stages
Self-authoring	Self-authoring
I have considered the possibilities of (and maybe even experienced) other relationship structures, and I consciously choose exclusivity. Monogamy meets my needs, and I feel happiest in a monogamous relationship. I am clear about my personal values and monogamy is in alignment with them, but my exclusive relationship will have elements that are less traditional, such as travel apart, fluid gender roles or sleeping in different beds.	Despite the fact that CNM is not generally accepted, I choose to be in an open relationship. Through my experiences with CNM, I constantly learn more about myself and my needs. The philosophy and principles of CNM are in alignment with my own as an autonomous, free-thinking person.
Self-transforming mind	Self-transforming mind
I don't necessarily identify as monogamous, I'm simply not interested in more than one relationship at this point in my life. I recognize that monogamy is only one of many valid relationship structures but I choose it for myself. I recognize the potential shortcomings or pitfalls of monogamy and choose the elements that suit me and my relationship and leave out the ones that don't.	I don't necessarily identify as nonmonogamous but the authentic expression of my needs in this moment are served by some form of CNM. I see nonmonogamy not as an identity but rather as a stepping stone along a bigger journey of self-discovery. I recognize the potential shortcomings or pitfalls of nonmonogamy and create my own unique version of it, tailored to my particular path as an individual, knowing it could change at any point.

TABLE 7.2: Applying stages two through four of Kegan's developmental stages to monogamy and nonmonogamy.

Applying Kegan's Stages to Nonmonogamy

Table 7.2 gives us a look at the four stages of Kegan's developmental model that we have been exploring thus far, filtered through both a monogamous and nonmonogamous lens. The statements associated with each stage are reflective of the perspective of someone occupying that particular stage of development. Even though Kegan's five-stage model of adult psychological development was never specifically intended to be applied to nonmonogamous relationships, I find it incredibly useful for mapping out the different places where people are on their CNM journey. Recognizing the underlying motives and values that characterize each stage can support a better understanding of our own behavior and that of our partner, and it also gives us a road map for the possibilities that lie ahead. When we can see our actions and feelings as the expressions of a series of stages that can change over time, we have the opportunity to not only make more sense of our relational challenges as we journey through a nonmonogamous paradigm, but to also be much more engaged in our own personal development. This model helps explain why even though two people may be practicing the same CNM style, it can look very different depending on what developmental stage someone is in—and just because someone is CNM doesn't mean that they are living it through the same values, awareness, capacities and perspectives.

Another reason Kegan's model is so useful is because it can help us map out the different places where individuals start their journey into CNM. As individuals begin to make the shift to CNM, they don't necessarily make a direct, horizontal move from their monogamous stage of development to the corresponding stage in nonmonogamy. For example, it is quite common for people who have entered the stage of self-authoring in the monogamous paradigm to actually fall back into earlier stages as they start to experiment with nonmonogamy. The integration of consciousness that allows someone to move from one stage of development to another within a particular paradigm often does not translate across paradigms. This is especially true when the paradigms in question are significantly different in terms of their inherent complexity and dynamism.

For instance, the differences between the monogamous and nonmonogamous paradigms can be so stark that the self-awareness and emotional intelligence garnered through monogamous relationships is often insufficient to successfully navigate the inevitable challenges that arise in nonmonogamous ones. This means that as people make the transition to CNM, they are often quickly confronted with the realization that they need to expand their relational intelligence in order to meet the demands of the new paradigm. I see this discrepancy between the stages across paradigmatic lines as an unanticipated and shocking CNM surprise, especially when you see your partner suddenly acting like a teenager, becoming more self-focused or deferring to authorities in ways you've never seen before. Having Kegan's model to put some of that paradigm shock into perspective can be incredibly supportive. In order to better understand why the developmental stages of Kegan's model do not always cross over cleanly from the monogamous to the nonmonogamous paradigm, though, let's take a look at each stage and explore how the experiences and narratives of individuals can change as they make the paradigm shift.

Imperial Mind

When someone makes a purely lateral shift from the monogamous imperial mind to the nonmonogamous imperial mind, their behavior is relatively easy to understand. The more self-focused mindset simply does what it has always done, focusing exclusively on itself and its own needs. It is simply the case that in nonmonogamy, there are more people in the equation to get caught in the crossfire of a consciousness that cannot fully see the impact of its behavior on others. The motivations underlying the imperial mind's behavior are relatively simple. Its main prerogative is to avoid negative consequences. For example, "I don't cheat because I don't want to get caught," or more specifically "I don't want the hassle of the consequences of being caught." Similarly, "If I *do* cheat, it's because I know I can't get caught and likely won't get punished," "I will say I'm following our CNM agreements, but sometimes I don't, or I try to get by on a technicality," or "I *do* really care about you, but my freedom comes first."

However, where things really become interesting is when someone from a later stage of development makes the shift to nonmonogamy, and all of sudden they start to exhibit the traits of the imperial mind. This can be one of the most jarring and difficult transitions to manage for partners going through a CNM transition together. It can also be a huge disappointment when dating someone who initially presents as a very conscious, mature CNM partner, but is later discovered to only be cloaking their self-centered and immature behavior in the name of CNM friendly principles like freedom and autonomy.

When someone takes on the behavior and posture typically associated with the imperial stage, it looks very much like what we'd expect from the shadow of adolescence: a sense of entitlement to do whatever you want, whenever you want, regardless of the impact on your partners. From this place, there can be a strong urge to approach CNM like a free-for-all or open buffet, striving to have as many encounters with new people as you possibly can. You become hyper-focused on your desires and freedoms, and you essentially function like a single person with no commitments or accountability to anyone else. You may feel bad that your partners are hurting or unhappy with your behaviors, but it doesn't necessarily stop you. Any attempt to rein in your enthusiasm, acknowledge the impact of your behavior or slow your pace is met with defensiveness and interpreted as manipulative or controlling, similar to a teenager pushing back against their parents' restrictions. In cases such as this, you may be proclaiming yourself to be *ethically* nonmonogamous, but you are actually using your nonmonogamy unethically, as a way to absolve yourself of responsibility, care or consideration for others. Unfortunately, this is the kind of behavior that is often associated with CNM, which leads to the justification of some very skewed and negative stereotypes. However, it's not truly reflective of nonmonogamy per se, but rather of the stage of psychological development of the person who is engaging in CNM.

And yet despite all the potential pitfalls of this stage, this can actually be a very important, necessary and even healthy phase for some people to go through. The trick is learning how to give this part of ourselves the freedom to explore and satisfy its needs while balancing that exploration with a grounded, relational awareness of our partners. What really makes the imperial mind stage an important stepping stone in the personal journey of so many people transitioning to CNM is the fact that it provides a powerful counterpoint to several of the imbalances that frequently exist in monogamous relationships. For many, living in accord with the rules of society often means we must fragment ourselves, suppressing or denying certain needs and wants. In particular, we often find ourselves in relationships where the expectations of our mononormative culture say we should put the needs of our spouse, kids, community, family of origin and even our work above our own. To do otherwise would simply be selfish.

Because of this, many people never even had the opportunity to go through the imperial mind stage, and thus never developed the strong sense of "me" that could stand its ground and advocate for itself. By skipping or only partially making it through the imperial stage, they potentially entered into the subsequent stages with several pieces of their psychological development still unintegrated. Then, as they later transition into CNM, the allure of the freedom promised by open relating unleashes a flood of pent-up energy as the frustrated martyr, overworked caregiver, obliging spouse or exhausted parent realizes, possibly for the first time in their lives, that their needs matter too! They are emboldened by the idea that they, too, have the right to do what they want as a person and can, at last, shed the oppressive shackles of the socialized self. The problem is then that this rush of newfound personal freedom swings too far. The desperate feeling of living years—possibly decades—under the yoke of self-denial creates a blinding desire to make up for lost time, which in the end distorts our perception and eclipses our relational awareness. We get lost in our pursuit of fulfilling longstanding desires at the expense of our relationships.

Socialized Mind

Whether in monogamous or nonmonogamous relationships, people anchored in the stage of the socialized mind are primarily identified with the values and norms set forth by the social systems to which they belong. Right and wrong are determined by external sources of authority rather than one's own personal experiences, and obeying the dictates of the community is the main concern. If you are monogamous, then being exclusive is what is considered right, and so you strive to be faithful. From the socialized perspective, cheating is morally wrong and a breach of the commitment to be loyal. If someone in this stage does cheat, they will feel a tremendous amount of guilt and shame about it, and they may even consider themselves a lesser person for doing so. Monogamous individuals at the socialized stage can struggle with their desire for sex or love with more than one person and experience a lot of internal turmoil around the discrepancy between their personal desires and the dominant social expectations. However, despite the inner tension caused by this discrepancy, these individuals will affirm the rightness or legitimacy of the monogamous narrative while dismissing their own wants or needs.

On the other hand, people at the socialized stage who have made the transition into nonmonogamy are liberated from that particular moral dilemma. But while they can enjoy the freedom of their nonmonogamous experiences, they are nevertheless subject to the standards, norms and expectations of whatever CNM subculture they are operating in. Within the CNM paradigm there are various subcultures, each with its own particular ideas about what to do and not to do. For example, within some nonmonogamous communities the idea of having prescriptively hierarchical relationships is absolutely counter to the philosophical tenets of CNM, and nonhierarchical relationships or relationship anarchy are considered more favorable models of human relating, whereas other CNM styles assume or prefer couple-centric, prescriptively hierarchical relationships. As the socialized mind encounters these kinds of extreme positions, it can struggle with thinking critically about the relevance of them for its own experience and simply take them on as its own. The tendency to defer to what non-monogamous "experts" say will override their own thoughts and opinions, and they will still conform to the ideas of others.

Another challenge that the socialized person can often face in nonmonogamy is the overwhelm that can come from trying to please not just one partner, but multiple partners all at the same time. Since people at this stage often have diffi-culty knowing themselves and staying grounded in their own needs and wants, they often fall into the trap of taking on the responsibility of juggling the needs of everyone else. Instead of being able to assert their own boundaries and preferences, they quickly yield to their partners' rules and expectations, which can eventually become unsustainable. When conflict arises in their relationships, these people can often take on negative identity labels, struggling with feelings of unworthiness or a sense of not being good at CNM. They interpret the bumps in the road as signs that they are somehow failing to live up to the standards of their relationships or their community.

Self-Authoring Mind

Entering the stage of the self-authoring mind represents a significant transition in individual consciousness. We have left behind the self-centeredness of the imperial stage and are no longer bound to the dictates of social constructs as we were in the socialized stage. We are ready to claim the freedom and responsibility of deciding for ourselves who and how we want to be in the world, making our decisions based on what feels most in alignment with our own lived experience. Because we have embraced the personal autonomy and power implicit in this stage, we are open to entirely new realms of possibilities that were previously unimaginable from earlier stages of development. It is an exciting and dynamic transition, filled with new learning and sometimes radical changes.

From the vantage point of the self-authoring mind, I would suggest that practiced monogamy is no longer the default monogamy that most people ascribe to, but rather a conscious exclusivity that reflects the actual needs and wants of the people who choose it. This kind of monogamy represents an upgrade from the traditional monogamy that most couples engage in and can be quite expansive, even revolutionary, for some people. Someone in the self-authoring stage can deconstruct mainstream monogamy and its limiting beliefs and intentionally sift through what works for them, leaving behind what doesn't. For instance, they might recognize how monogamy has traditionally aided patriarchal control of women, their bodies and their sexuality, and so instead create a partnership that is more egalitarian, where the domestic, financial and parenting responsibilities are more equally shared regardless of genitals or gender. Partners at this stage who choose to be exclusive may decide to sleep in separate bedrooms, craft a commitment ceremony that best expresses their unique union, or decide not to get legally married—or even to live together at all. They may also still choose to have elements of traditional monogamy in their relationship, but to them, this is a conscious choice as opposed to conformity with an external standard.

For the people who have integrated the self-authoring stage into their exploration of CNM, the experience is most often described as nothing less than an awakening of self.

They report new and emergent identities capable of holding more love, joy, pleasure and even heartache. As they open up their relationships, they commonly note a parallel awakening of their sexuality, which for some releases decades of sexual repression. For some people, the introduction to things like kink, BDSM or bisexuality inspires new erotic desires and preferences that offer previously unimagined horizons for sexual exploration. For others, the transition grants them the permission—possibly for the first time in their lives—to simply be a sexual being with their own unique wants and desires.

However, reaching this kind of awakening in the context of CNM usually takes time, experience and, typically, a lot of mistakes. Unfortunately, we don't arrive there instantly, and as previously stated, the fact that you have entered the stage of self-authoring in your monogamous relationship doesn't always mean you will begin your CNM journey with that as your starting point. Another potential downside of this stage is that we can become over-identified with a certain style of CNM. In the expansiveness of our newly awakened self, we can quickly become attached to particular forms of CNM and start to think "This is who I am now!" Choosing to embrace something like solo polyamory or open marriage may be an accurate reflection of our personal journey at the moment, and thus a valid expression of self-authoring, but if we cling to the constructs of a particular style or form of nonmonogamy, we can fall into the trap of becoming too rigid or inflexible.

Self-Transforming Mind

For people in the stage of the self-transforming mind, the need for structures, labels and identities holds less sway. Here, the constructs of monogamy and nonmonogamy may have little importance in and of themselves, and merely serve as symbolic points of reference. Choice is the hallmark of this stage, and people in this stage can demonstrate a tremendous amount of relational responsiveness and flexibility. From the self-transforming mind, we can recognize all relationship structures as relative, and so appreciate their strengths and weaknesses. We can appreciate the benefits of monogamy as well as acknowledge its limitations, and we can enjoy the many advantages of nonmonogamy without assuming we will be in nonmonogamous relationships for the rest of our lives.

The self-awakening that began in the self-authoring stage expands to encompass a sense of self that can identify with something bigger than itself. In this sense, the stage of self-transformation gives us an expanded capacity to identify with the whole of the human community. We can hold the complexity of being both an individual with our own particular needs and wants, and an inseparable part of the social collective in which we find ourselves, without tension or contradiction. This ability to fluidly go back and forth between a personal and social consciousness gives us a perceptual flexibility that allows us to pick and choose the ideas with which we create our sense of self. Since we no longer feel a sense of obligation to ideological dogmas or constructs, we have a tremendous amount of freedom to create our relationships according to the values and principles with which we most resonate.

In this sense, the stage of self-transformation is like a spiritual awakening, where the possibility of a love unencumbered by artificial constructs becomes the very thing we are awakening to. Our relationships become vehicles for more than just the satisfaction of our personal needs or the fulfillment of social expectations: they are the unfettered expression of our capacity to love with our whole being. They serve the purpose of increasing our capacity to love in ways that are not hampered by the social programming that previously dictated our relational choices.

Through the self-transforming lens, CNM could be seen as a path to states of consciousness where love is given and received without clinging to structures or outcomes, or conversely, that exclusive commitment feels expansive and inspires devotion when it is no longer encumbered by monogamous obligation.

In the ebb and flow of multiple relationships, one might learn how to allow connections to be defined by the uniqueness of the individuals coming together and what is best for that particular combination of human beings—eventually arriving at a place where one can truly love others for who they really are, and not just for the needs they satisfy. We can also appreciate that love does not always conform to our ideas about it, and that its nature is to change and evolve over time. This allows us to keep letting go of the urge to control our relationships and to surrender to the natural rhythms of love, which include inevitable phases of more or less connection and disconnection.

It should be noted, however, that none of the aforementioned description of the self-transforming mind is meant to negate the importance of intentionally cultivating emotional safety and security in CNM relationships. We do not mean to suggest that people occupying the self-transforming stage operate with a disregard for the attachment-based needs of their partners. If anything, the deepened ability to attune to our own needs and wants that comes with the self-transforming stage will actually enhance our capacity to tune into our partners, as well. Without the influence of the limiting beliefs or ideas that come to us from society about who or what we, our partners or our relationships are supposed to be, or what needs and wants are reasonable and legitimate, we are much more likely to create relationships that genuinely suit the needs of everyone involved.

The Interaction of the Stages

In chapter five we discussed Bader and Pearson's Developmental Model of Couples Therapy to better understand the various stages relationships can go through. Specifically, we saw that differentiation is a natural step in adult relationships. As we applied that model to CNM, we were able to see some of the challenges partners face when they occupy different stages at the same time: for example, when one person wants to

create more differentiation while the other continues to crave
the comfort of symbiosis. In the same way that a mismatch
in stages between partners can create problems in terms of
differentiation, so too can a disparity between partners' levels
of development within Kegan's model test a relationship. This
potential for incongruity is even more likely when we remember that as people go from monogamy to nonmonogamy, they
can revert back to earlier stages of development. For instance,
it's possible for monogamous partners to begin with both of
them squarely rooted in the self-authoring mind, but in their
transition to nonmonogamy, for one partner to maintain their
position within that stage while the other reverts back to the
imperial mind. These kinds of divergent experiences make
an already challenging transition even more difficult and can
leave people feeling like they don't know who their partners
are anymore.

People can also have the experience that their different
relationships function in different stages of development.
Because relationships with various partners can be so different, it's not uncommon to find oneself in one stage with a
particular partner and a totally distinct stage with another.
The relationship we create with each partner—and thus the
particular stage of the relationship as a whole—reflects the
unique constellation of our personalities, life circumstances
and experiences.

One client of mine observed that, in the context of his
domestic life with his nesting partner and their two children,
he felt expected to play a more traditional and socially defined
role, and so he experienced himself squarely grounded in the
developmental stage of the socialized mind. But with his non-
nesting partner, where there wasn't the same rigidly defined
relational structure or expectations, he identified more with
the self-transforming mind. While he appreciated feeling the
different developmental facets of himself expressed through
his different relationships, his nesting partner often com-
plained of justice jealousy. Seeing him show up in new and

expansive ways with his non-nesting partner while remaining contained and reserved with her and their family created hurt and resentment. In this particular case, our work was to deliberately connect with the desirable attributes of the self-transforming stage that he experienced with his non-nesting partner and begin to integrate them into the context where he was used to residing in more a socialized self. Recognizing that he could connect to this more enlivened side of himself and intentionally bring elements of it into the relationship with his nesting partner was a revelation for him and very healing for that partnership.

It can also be the case that a particular partner's stage of development can have more to do with the overall stage of the relationship than just the life circumstances in which the relationship is anchored. When one of our partners is firmly grounded in a different stage of consciousness, their influence can have a profound effect not only on us as individuals, but also on the relationship as a whole. This can be one of the most exciting and compelling aspects of a particular relationship—especially with a partner experiencing the self-authoring or self-transforming mind—because we can experience new levels of relational awareness that were previously unknown or unavailable to us. The exposure to the more expansive and creative aspects of these stages can be exhilarating and genuinely life-changing. Challenges, however, can arise when we find ourselves having to go back and forth between various stages as we engage in our different relationships. Having to constantly adjust our relational experiences to fit the parameters of contrasting emotional and intellectual environments can be confusing and disorienting.

Another way that discord between Kegan's stages can present itself is in situations where relationships themselves are presenting as being in different stages simultaneously. This is most common when couples have opened up their relationship but, for various reasons, feel the need to continue appearing as a monogamous partnership to the outside world.

Privately, partners are consensually practicing nonmonogamy, but socially they maintain the appearance of a monogamous couple. For some couples, straddling both worlds is
not a problem, and they are able to navigate between their
respective monogamous and nonmonogamous identities with
relative ease. But for others, the split in realities can create
a tension that eventually becomes problematic, whether it is
because one partner no longer wants to hide who they are, or
because one or more of their other partners no longer wants to
be kept a secret.

The challenge of being in the nonmonogamous closet can
also become more challenging when couples struggle with
conflict or have difficulties with jealousy. The need for secrecy
and discretion means that people have very little, if any, emotional support from their social networks in times of duress.
This can leave them feeling isolated and alone in their process
and put even more pressure on the relationship. In situations
like this, what I typically see is that individuals are either still
very much anchored in the socialized stage but are wanting
to move from monogamy to nonmonogamy, or they are occupying an emerging self-authoring mind, but because of life
circumstances (work, family of origin, religion, community,
etc.), they find themselves obliged to maintain the veneer of a
socialized lifestyle.

Deconstruction of the Self

Up to this point, we have been getting familiar with Kegan's
model of human psychological development, exploring the
various stages and seeing how they apply to both the monogamous and nonmonogamous experience. What we've seen so
far is that as we move from the imperial mind towards the self-
transforming stage, we begin to approach life and relationships more and more from the inside out instead of from the
outside in. Simply satisfying our adolescent needs for instant

gratification or making everyone else around us happy starts to take a back seat as we learn to follow our own inner guidance and allow more of our personal truth to come front and center. We have also seen that a monumental shift occurs when we begin to transition away from the socialized mind towards the self-authoring mind, which in turn initiates a powerful process of questioning the rules and expectations of our upbringing. We've also talked about how this shift can often leave us feeling more awake, alive and aligned than ever before, and we've even gotten a glimpse of the profoundly expansive state that can accompany the final stage of self-transformation.

However, there is still another side of this progression through Kegan's stages, and it is less glamorous. While we have already named several benefits that accompany the process of moving from one stage of development to another, we also need to acknowledge that for some, the transition into new and very different selves can be frightening, bewildering and very destabilizing. As we move between the stages, our fundamental sense of self can undergo radical changes. Many of us are not prepared for this kind of internal upheaval, and it can feel as though the very existential, tectonic plates of our being are moving beneath our feet. In the space that opens up between the previous and emergent stages, it is not uncommon to feel as though your fixed, reliable sense of self starts to fray at the edges and becomes unstable. As the familiar ideas and beliefs of earlier stages come more and more into question, you can face uncertainty that is often uncomfortable. The transitions between stages are incredibly vulnerable periods of our lives where deep insecurities and past traumas can bubble up to the surface, creating confusion as to what is up and what is down. I call this process the "deconstruction of the self."

As we progress through Kegan's stages, our susceptibility to this kind of self-deconstruction increases. Every time we transition from one stage to another, we must endure the nebulous space between them as we simultaneously let go of one while striving to integrate the other. When crossing this threshold from the old to the new, we cannot fully embrace or identify with either, and this can leave us feeling like we don't know who we really are. While this in-between place has the promise of eventually leading to the reconstruction of a new, more expansive and integrated self, there can be a significant gap between the dissolution of the old and the emergence of the new that leaves people feeling afraid, anxious and unwell.

Often the questioning that accompanies this gap is not limited to one particular area of one's life, but can fan out in multiple directions at once. For instance, challenging the constructs of monogamy could be just the beginning, for some, of a much larger process of questioning all the other dominant paradigms, ideas and discourses that have been deeply internalized around gender, sexuality, individualism, ownership, patriarchy and colonialism. Or maybe your entry point into this process of deconstruction was something else, like your race, sexual orientation or gender identity, and CNM was simply one of the paradigms that later emerged on your journey towards the next stage. Regardless of when CNM entered the picture for you, the process of pulling apart not only the essential building blocks of your personal identity but also the very paradigmatic framework of your social reality can be genuinely terrifying and is an experience for which very few of us have any kind of precedent. It is also the case that, for some people, the move from one stage to another could imply very real consequences, such as the loss of relationships with family or friends, negative consequences at work, loss of social status or legal rights, and even mental health issues.

As I write this, I am reminded of a story told by one of my clients about her own process of deconstruction of the self. Through the process of opening her marriage, she was confronted with all the ways she had not been her own person. For decades she had defined herself as a wife and mother, unconditionally supporting her husband's career, focusing on the kids, and investing her time and energy in the projects they shared as a couple. Her sense of self and security, as well as her personal worth and value, came from being in a monogamous marriage. She even admitted that she had sublimated herself, giving up many of her own professional hopes and dreams just to be in that relationship. When she and her husband eventually opened their marriage, she was completely unprepared for the ways it dismantled the entire foundation upon which she had built her personal identity. As she began to move forward with dating, she asked me, "What am I supposed to write on a dating profile about myself, if my whole life has been about everyone else but me?" The subsequent vacuum left in the wake of that deconstruction sparked a grieving process that forced her to acknowledge the irrevocable loss of her monogamous identity and the fear of facing an uncertain future.

Part of the challenge is that we can't just reconstruct our new, nonmonogamous self on top of the foundation of an old, monogamous identity. All the old stories, tricks, strategies, masks and defenses no longer fit. We have to recognize the ways we have been complicit with the narratives and beliefs that kept us small and disempowered, and we have to be willing to undergo a process of detoxing from the social constructs that limited our potential as dynamic and creative beings. Like the woman from the previous anecdote, sometimes we need to consciously grieve our past, holding space for all the ways we diminished or dismissed ourselves and our own needs just to be "OK" in relationships. We also need to be ready for the vacuum of meaning that can accompany the deconstruction process and learn to reframe this void as a creative space, rich with potential, instead of as merely overwhelming or threatening.

Dave's Deconstruction of the Self

Dave here!

Over the years I have had a healthy dose of experiences that have challenged my sense of self and initiated various processes of deconstruction. From very early on I was exposed to racial violence and discrimination in the urban public schools of my youth; I have explored altered states of consciousness through years of psychedelic journeying; I have suffered two near-death experiences; and I have even endured a significant chronic illness since I was 19. All this to say: I am not someone who is wholly unfamiliar with the process of deconstructing and recreating the self. And yet I have to admit that, even with everything I've just mentioned, I was not prepared for what I faced when Jessica and I first opened our marriage.

I can vividly remember the searing anguish I felt in those first few weeks after opening up. As a couple who had maybe two or three explosive fights in the first decade we were together, all of sudden we were now having arguments almost every other day. We were experiencing some of the hardest moments of our marriage, and I just couldn't stop my jealous outbursts. It felt like my life was breaking apart and everything that mattered to me was slipping away. By the time I put my fist through a door for the second time, I realized something had to change.

As someone who considered himself relatively self-aware, I was honestly shocked by the volatility of my reactions to Jessica dating other men. If she was intellectually or emotionally intimate with them, I was fine, but throw sex into the mix and I became a fucking lunatic. I would have literal panic attacks when it was time for her to go on a date, and I would say to myself, "This is crazy! I'm not the kind of guy who is possessive or gets jealous. I'm no slave to the patriarchy!" Oh, how wrong I was. Through the madness of my primal attachment panic, I watched as the mechanisms of internalized patriarchy played out through the toxic narratives of masculinity that relentlessly ran through my anguished brain: "This is destroying our family! If she loved me she wouldn't be fucking some other guy! I'm worthless as a husband!" All of the unconscious ideas about what it meant to be a monogamous husband and father of a nuclear family came rushing to the surface like rabid attack dogs. And in the worst moments, I couldn't even turn to her for comfort because, as far as my disorganized attachment was concerned, she was simultaneously the key master of my emotional wellbeing *and* the source of my torment.

A huge part of what I was forced to come to terms with was the way several unconscious ideas about sex and love had completely infiltrated my masculine identity. For one, I wasn't aware at the time that monogamy had instilled in me the idea that sex and love were inextricably fused. If there was sex there was love, and vice versa. The merger of these two things in my mind gave each of them an inflated sense of importance that made it impossible to hold the nuances of different possibilities. For instance, I could not conceive of Jessica having a sexual relationship with someone else without that necessarily meaning she was completely in love with that person. I couldn't hold the possibility that maybe she was simply exploring her own sexual identity or wanting to expand her erotic experience through other connections without that implying she was *in love* with these other partners.

In the cases where she *was* feeling love for someone with whom she was having sex, the two-dimensional idea of love that still dominated my romantic operating system could not help but feel threatened by that. It felt as though whenever Jessica was having sex with another person, she was taking love away from me—like mom giving the boob to someone else, robbing me of my share of mother's precious milk. This is essentially why I melted down every time I had to confront the reality of Jessica being physical with other men. I couldn't separate the two things in my mind, and I couldn't hold the possibility that she could genuinely continue loving me to the same degree if she were giving love to someone else.

In the hetero-monogamous paradigm of my culture, the act of sex has long been considered the consummation of any "legitimate" or "serious" relationship. While it is much less common these days that couples will actually wait until marriage to start having sex, the singular and disproportionate importance we have awarded sex still lingers in the crawl spaces of our collective psyche. What complicated matters for me was the fact that Jessica's and my sexual relationship had been struggling during this phase of our marriage. While certainly not just a man's issue, I have seen in my work with partners a disproportionate number of men struggling with a similar dynamic. Because of society's influence, many men feel a profound disconnect from their own emotions, and the places where we are allowed to be genuinely vulnerable can be extremely limited. One of the few spaces where we can safely let down our guard is in the bedroom. This is why, for so many individuals, sex has taken on such huge significance: aside from physical pleasure and intimate connection, it has also become one of the only safe places to be fully ourselves with our partners. This puts a tremendous amount of undue pressure on the sexual relationship, as it is required to serve not only as the release of sexual desire but also as the emotional refuge for masculine angst.

The trifecta in this recipe for disaster was the (for me) very unexpected influence of masculine narratives about competition and sexual performance. While I certainly remember being competitive with my brother around sports when we were kids, outside of that, competition was never really something that motivated me, especially not in the realm of personal relationships. As a husband in a monogamous marriage, I never had to face competition with other men. If men looked at Jessica while we were together it was, if anything, flattering, because it simply meant they recognized I was with a beautiful woman. At the end of the day, she was always going home with me. But after opening up all that changed, and the interest of other men became a legitimate threat to my status as the most important man in Jessica's life—or so I thought.

My identity as a more "evolved" or "conscious" man started to unravel as I found myself measuring my own self-worth in terms of how often she and I were having sex. If she had more sex with a partner in a week than she had with me, I would interpret that as a sign not only that she loved me less, but also that my very integrity as a man was being called into question. I would wonder if he had a bigger cock than me, or was perhaps better in the sack? Was she with him because I wasn't man enough to give her what she needed sexually? Everything became a possible trigger for the masculine insecurities that, quite frankly, I assumed I had transcended long ago. It seemed like I was actually devolving as a person and becoming everything I had worked so hard to let go of as a man in my culture. On top of navigating all the other challenges of opening up the marriage, which is already a big deal in and of itself, I also found myself dealing with the deconstruction of patriarchy, toxic masculinity and my own self-worth as a man, as well as a ruthless and unrelenting attachment anxiety.

The extremity of my situation created an almost desperate urgency to figure out how to deal with this deconstruction of self. Jessica and I were in constant conflict, things were slipping through the cracks at work, my relationship with my young son was suffering, and my emotional and physical health were declining rapidly. Without a clear path to follow, I was forced to improvise and try whatever seemed like it had the potential to help. The turning point came when I decided to go to Peru and participate in several ayahuasca ceremonies with a group that a close friend had recommended. In the context of the shamanic work used in those ceremonies, I found a much-needed conceptual framework with which I could start making sense of my own journey. In the shamanic tradition, the metaphor of death is used to describe all of the significant transitions that we experience as human beings, framing them as "little deaths," or as the symbolic death of aspects of ourselves that no longer serve us. Like the caterpillar's transformation into a butterfly or the shedding of a snake's skin, we, too, continually pass from one self to another along a path of constant change and growth.

Doing that work in Peru gave me a clear sense of the parts of myself that I needed to let go of in order to take the next step in my healing. While ayahuasca didn't actually take away the emotional pain of my experience, it did give me powerful insights into the specific narratives about monogamy and masculinity that were fueling my suffering. I was able to see how many of the ideas that I internalized as a boy about what it meant to be a man and a husband were still influencing my sense of identity as an adult, and how most of those ideas were impeding my ability to give and receive the kind of intimacy I deeply longed for. I also realized that in order to really move forward in my process, I needed to let go of the idea that I had to handle everything on my own and accept that it was OK to ask for help.

After returning to the States, I began a feverish search for the necessary resources and support not only to continue navigating the deconstruction of my old self but also to rebuild a new, more preferred self: one that was truly in alignment with the wants, needs and values of the person I wanted to become. I did MDMA-assisted psychotherapy to heal anxious attachment wounds, used EMDR and somatic therapy to release trauma from the past, worked with traditional talk therapists to unpack the influences of my family of origin, joined men's groups to create circles of accountability, explored kink and sex positivity to reprogram my relationship to sex and intimacy, and continued engaging in new relationships to experience the different parts of me that had never felt truly integrated into the context of my marriage. Over time, I was gradually able to regain my confidence and begin integrating all the different pieces of my process into a coherent narrative of what, for me, a healthy masculinity would look like. This new, more expansive vision of myself marked the end of a long and difficult process of deconstructing a self that was still partly anchored in the stages of imperial and socialized mind, and ushered in the emergence of the self-authoring stage.

The point of my story is to highlight the ways that, for many, the process of deconstructing the self that accompanies the transition to CNM can be extremely difficult and painful. Instead of the expansive and awakening journey that some people experience, it can also be a harsh reflection of all the baggage of our monogamous, socialized self that still remains in the dark little corners of our minds. While your triggers may look different than mine, deconstruction is the same process of peeling back the layers of our identities to see how the social narratives about sex, possessiveness, purity culture, race, gender roles and control continue to inhibit the free expression of our preferred selves. In order to cross the threshold of the self-authoring stage and experience the freedom that comes with it, we must first peek into our shadows and recognize the parts of ourselves that still cling to the structures of repression and conformity. Choosing CNM is a choice to seek personal growth through the path of multiple loves. However, this path can break your heart wide open and expose the ways you have been out of alignment with who you really want to be. The invitation that lies just beneath the pain is to use this shattering as a powerful catalyst for creating a more awake, relationally fulfilled, integrated and expansive you.

§

By applying Kegan's model of human psychological development to both the transitions from monogamy to nonmonogamy and those within preexisting CNM relationships, we are presented with a new way to think about the challenges that arise in these transitions. In the journey from the socialized to the self-transforming mind, we have the opportunity to let go of the socialized mind's tendency to model our sense of self according to limiting social norms and expectations, and to gradually shift our inner compass towards the true north of our most preferred and authentic self. In the context of CNM, this journey through the stages promises deep personal growth and learning as we navigate the complexities of multiple relationships. As we learn to trust more and more in our own experiences and intuition, eventually we can have an awakening of the self: a state of conscious connection with the authentic self that emerges in the stage of self-transformation, characterized by immense freedom and expansiveness.

However, in contrast to the beauty and freedom that some people experience through the awakening of self, the journey through Kegan's stages can also create quite an opposite experience. As we move through the various stages, the transitions themselves can have a very destabilizing effect on our sense of identity. This destabilizing effect is often accompanied by an acute period in which various fundamental aspects of ourselves are called into question and we struggle to find a clear and safe sense of center within our own being. This deconstruction of the self can be a terrifying and painful counterpoint to the awakening of self even though they both share the same underlying capacity to provoke tremendous self-growth and inner transformation.

CONCLUSION

My favorite professor in college was Dr. Needham. I took every course he offered, was his teaching assistant for his experimental psychology class, asked him to be my college advisor and even took an independent study with him in cognitive psychology. All this meant that I spent many hours in his office: chatting, listening, asking—and staring at his walls as he tended to other students. Covering his office walls were beautiful photographs of orange- and pink-colored canyons in Arizona, shelves of books I wish I had the time to read, framed diplomas, and handwritten Post-It notes on corkboards that I could barely make out. But what received most of my attention was an old poster of a cute cartoon monster in a library with half-eaten books strewn all around it and the Francis Bacon quote: "Some books are to be tasted, others to be swallowed, and some few to be chewed and digested."

Initially I was amused that such a distinguished man would adorn his office walls with something so, well, adorable—something you would imagine finding in an elementary school reading nook, not a psychology professor's office—but as my college years passed and I spent more and more time in Dr. Needham's office, I came to appreciate the genuine wisdom of that poster. As someone who rarely finishes books, this quote gave me permission to not judge myself so harshly, since the books I never finished might have just been for the tasting.

I was liberated to dabble in the ideas that caught my attention and not force myself to read what didn't hold my interest. As semesters came to an end and I found myself cramming for exams, I better understood how books that were swallowed too quickly often caused mental indigestion, or the information was quickly forgotten after it was mindlessly regurgitated onto a test. As I came to the end of my senior year, I had a much greater appreciation for what it really means to learn something, to internalize a field of study, or to say that I've acquired any semblance of knowledge or expertise on a topic. For me, it meant reading something not once or twice, but usually many times over before it was thoroughly chewed and digested.

Years later, when I received the offer to write my first book, I took a walk to my favorite bookstore in Boulder, Colorado, to contemplate whether I would accept the offer. As I walked through the bookstore, I wondered what it would be like to see my own name on one of those shelves. But as I paused and stood among the hundreds and hundreds of books, I started to feel completely overwhelmed as various parts of myself began raising their voice in protest. My insecure parts screamed in fear, claiming I would have nothing of value to offer the world. I was assailed by my critical part, who adamantly reminded me how I was dyslexic and couldn't even write a book if I wanted to. An apathetic and defeated part looked around at all the books already on the shelves, questioning whether or not the world needs anymore frickin' books. Thankfully, a wiser inner part chimed in and reminded me of that lovable book-eating monster on Dr. Needham's wall. If I wrote something that was tasted and swallowed by some, that would be amazing, and if I wrote something that was actually worth chewing and digesting to even just a few, it would be worth it!

In this book we focused on the power of paradigms to shape our reality—in particular, our relational world. Specifically, we examined some of the key differences between monogamous and nonmonogamous paradigms and the importance of recognizing that many relational challenges with CNM are related to the lingering influence of monogamy, along with its central archetype, the couple. We also saw how grounding your focus on the concept of paradigms can support you in troubleshooting your resistance to either making the transition to CNM or successfully navigating a significant change in preexisting CNM relationships. We explored how certain cracks in the foundation of your existing relationships could get exposed in the context of CNM or make the dynamics of current relationships seem even harder. We introduced Dave's important work with Restorative Relationship Conversations and learned that a fundamental paradigm shift is needed not just from monogamy to nonmonogamy, but also from an adversarial to a restorative approach in the context of our interpersonal conflict. He also gave us a unique model to start working through conflict and healing past relationship ruptures with more grace and ease. Later, we looked at the challenge of codependency and the importance of differentiation, and how differentiation is actually a healthy step in any relationship even though it is often misinterpreted as problematic or threatening. Afterwards, we saw the role that differences among partners can play in CNM, and finally, we examined the phenomenon of the awakening and deconstruction of the self, and how different stages of adult psychological development can impact our growth or stagnation in relationship to CNM.

Depending on your particular style of CNM, the amount of time you have been living it, the variety of your experiences and the nature of your relational challenges, different parts of this book will have more relevance than others. Although we tried to cover as much ground as we could, representing the most common obstacles and challenges that we see CNM relationships face on a regular basis, inevitably there will be things we missed, or perspectives we haven't spoken to. If you have made it this far in the book, my hope is that there have been at least a few things worth being tasted and swallowed. Ideally, there have also been things worth taking the time to digest. Because integration is an ongoing process, the concepts and exercises in this book are meant to be practical tools that you can use whenever you feel you need them. Our intention was to offer a legitimate resource that people struggling with their relationship to CNM could come back to over and over again, as a point of reference. Although polywise will look different to everyone, in its essence, it is an ideal worth striving for, an affirmation that you can have the kind of relationships you really want, if you're willing to do the work to get there.

If you want to make it to the top of Mount Everest and revel in the lofty views of its majestic peaks, you don't simply buy plane tickets for Nepal, grab your warmest winter coat and set off at your earliest convenience. That would be suicide. It can take literally years of preparation, both physically and psychologically, to reach the point of readiness for such an endeavor. Even after you have successfully made your way to the base of the mountain with all your gear and provisions assembled, you still can't rush your way up to the top in one shot. You have to move in phases, first setting up basecamp and getting used to the new air, then later ascending in slow increments, constantly taking stock of the ever-changing climatic conditions, always stopping to acclimate to new altitudes. Sometimes your journey is slowed or even halted by unpredictable storms or accidents that make the path forward untenable, forcing you against your will to descend to safer grounds until you can start up the mountain again. You have to adapt and be flexible in conditions and situations that are ultimately beyond your control, and, above all, you have to know your limits.

While I recognize that the transition to CNM is probably not as perilous as an expedition to the top of Mount Everest, there are some useful parallels that can temper one's perspective and encourage a more realistic approach. Like the spectacular views that accompany the journey upward, being nonmonogamous can offer new and expansive points of view that were previously unimaginable from where we started. Being polywise is akin to being the seasoned climber who, through years of experience and hard lessons learned along the way, has developed a deep respect for what it actually takes to safely make the trek. They recognize the importance of going slow, acclimating to new heights, paying close attention to the conditions in which they find themselves and relying on their own self-awareness, intuition and experience, as well as the tools they've brought with them. They have a keen sense that *how* you climb is even more important than *how far* you climb, and that being present to the adventure every step of the way matters so much more than just making it to the top. Above all, they have a healthy sense of their own limits and are willing to take a step back when necessary. In the same way, being polywise means that you are grounded in the self-knowledge that allows you to do what actually works for you, honoring your personal self-limits and desires. It is also the willingness to learn from those who have come before us, considering their mistakes, reflecting on their trials and integrating their hard-won wisdom.

To this, we bid you the best of support, love and skill on your polywise journey.

Jessica Fern and David Cooley

GLOSSARY

Compersion
The positive feelings experienced when a lover or partner is having a positive experience with one of their other lovers or partners.

Consensual nonmonogamy (CNM)
The practice of having or being open to multiple sexual or romantic partners at the same time, where all people involved are aware of this relationship arrangement and consent to it. CNM can take forms such as polyamory, swinging, open marriage, open relationships, solo polyamory and relationship anarchy.

Garden party polyamory
An approach to polyamory where metamours only spend time together at social events, such as a mutual partner's birthday. In such cases, these metamours will usually have cordial and respectful interactions or even a friendly connection, with little contact outside of these events.

Kitchen table polyamory
An approach to polyamory where partners and metamours are friendly or close with each other, all comfortable sitting at the literal or metaphorical kitchen table together. Metamours tend to cultivate their own friendship with one another, and partners are open to their children or extended family spending time together.

Metamour
Two people who share a partner but are not romantically or sexually involved with each other. For example, if you have a partner who also has a spouse, you and their spouse would be metamours, or if you have a boyfriend and a girlfriend who are not involved with each other, the two of them would be metamours to each other.

Monogamy
The practice of having one sexual or romantic partner at a time.

Mononormativity
A term coined by Marianne Pieper and Robin Bauer to refer to the societal dominant assumptions regarding the naturalness and normalcy of monogamy, where political, popular and psychological narratives typically present monogamy as the superior, most natural or morally correct way to do relationships.

Parallel polyamory
CNM relationships where a person's different relationships have little to no interaction.

Polycule
A combination of the words *poly* (for polyamorous) and *molecule* referring to a connected network of partners and metamours in CNM relationships.

Polysecure
Experiencing secure attachment with yourself and your multiple partners. A person who is polysecure is both securely attached to multiple romantic partners and has enough internal security to be able to navigate the structural relationship insecurity inherent to nonmonogamy, as well as the increased complexity and uncertainty that occurs when having multiple partners and metamours.

Relationship anarchy
A relationship style that applies political anarchist principles to interpersonal relationships. Relationship anarchists seek to dismantle the social hierarchies dictating how sexual and romantic relationships are prioritized over all other forms of love, and so people who identify as relationship anarchists make less distinction between the importance or value of their lovers over their friends or other people in their life, and they do not only reserve intimacy or romance for only the people they have sex with.

Solo polyamory
An approach to polyamory that emphasizes personal agency. Individuals do not seek to engage in relationships that are tightly couple-centric or financially or domestically entwined. People who identify as solo polyamorous emphasize autonomy, the freedom to choose their own relationships without seeking permission from others, and flexibility in the form their relationships take. It is a common misconception that people practicing solo polyamory are either more casual or less committed in their relationships; this is not necessarily the case. Solo polyamorous folks can be deeply emotionally involved and committed in their relationships, but they typically choose not to take on the traditional roles that some partners assume, such as living together, having shared finances or doing domestic duties (at least not as a relationship expectation or obligation).

REFERENCES

Dossie Easton and Janet W. Hardy, *The Ethical Slut: A Practical Guide to Polyamory, Open Relationships and Other Freedoms in Sex and Love*, third edition (Berkeley, CA: Ten Speed Press, 2017).

Daniel L. Everett, *Don't Sleep, There Are Snakes: Life and Language in the Amazonian Jungle* (New York: Vintage Books, 2008).

Jessica Fern, *Polysecure: Attachment, Trauma and Consensual Nonmonogamy* (Portland, OR: Thorntree Press, 2020).

Jessica Fern, *The Polysecure Workbook: Healing Your Attachment and Creating Security in Loving Relationships* (Victoria, BC: Thornapple Press, 2022).

Amy Gahran, *Stepping Off the Relationship Escalator: Uncommon Love and Life* (Boulder: Off the Escalator Enterprises LLC, 2017).

Barney G. Glaser and Ansel M. Strauss, *The Discovery of Grounded Theory: Strategies for Qualitative Research* (Mill Valley, CA: Sociology Press, 1967).

John Gottman and Nan Silver, *The Seven Principles for Making Marriage Work* (New York: Crown Publishers, 1999).

Julie Gottman and John Gottman, *10 Principles for Doing Effective Couples Therapy* (New York: W.W. Norton & Company, 2015).

Donald O. Hebb, *The Organization of Behavior: A Neuropsychological Theory* (New York: John Wiley and Sons, 1949).

Gay Hendricks and Kathlyn Hendricks, *Conscious Loving: The Journey to Co-Commitment* (New York: Bantam Books, 1990).

Robert Kegan, *The Evolving Self: Problem and Process in Human Development* (Cambridge, MA: Harvard University Press, 1982).

Thomas S. Kuhn, *The Structure of Scientific Revolutions* (Chicago: University of Chicago Press, 1962).

Mystic Life, *Spiritual Polyamory* (Lincoln, NE: iUniverse, Inc., 2004).

Terrence Real, *The New Rules of Marriage: What You Need to Know to Make Love Work* (New York: Ballantine Books, 2007).

Eve Rickert et al., *More Than Two: A Practical Guide to Ethical Polyamory* (Portland, OR: Thorntree Press, 2014).

Scott A. Spradlin, *Don't Let Your Emotions Run Your Life: How Dialectical Behavior Therapy Can Put You in Control* (Oakland, CA: New Harbinger Publications, 2003).

Florence Williams, *Breasts: A Natural and Unnatural History* (New York: W.W. Norton & Company, 2012).

INDEX

ABOUT THE AUTHORS

Jessica Fern is a psychotherapist, public speaker, and trauma and relationship expert. In her international private practice, Jessica works with individuals, couples and people in multiple-partner relationships who no longer want to be limited by their reactive patterns, cultural conditioning, insecure attachment styles and past traumas, helping them to embody new possibilities in life and love.

David Cooley is a professional restorative justice facilitator, diversity and privilege awareness trainer, and bilingual cultural broker. He is the creator of the Restorative Relationships Conversations model, a process that transforms interpersonal conflict into deeper connection, intimacy and repair. In his private practice, David specializes in working with non-monogamous and LGBTQ partnerships, incorporating a variety of modalities including trauma-informed care, attachment theory, somatic practices, narrative theory and mindfulness-based techniques.

ALSO FROM THORNAPPLE PRESS

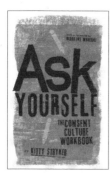

Ask Yourself: The Consent Culture Workbook
Kitty Stryker
With a foreword by Wagatwe Wanjuki

"*Ask: Building Consent Culture* editor Kitty Stryker invites readers to delve deeper, with guest experts and personal anecdotes, to manifest a culture of consent in one's own community that starts at the heart."
— Jiz Lee, editor of *Coming Out Like a Porn Star*

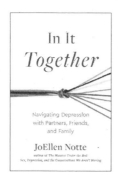

In It Together: Navigating Depression with Partners, Friends, and Family
JoEllen Notte

"Am I allowed to say I laughed and had so much fun reading about depression? Read this book and you'll feel seen — and you'll walk away with a real-life guide to helping loved ones without sacrificing your own mental health."
— Meredith Goldstein, Boston Globe Love Letters advice columnist, podcast host and author of *Can't Help Myself*

Better Halves: Rebuilding a Post-Addiction Marriage
Christopher Dale

"Christopher Dale gives us an insightful and meaningful contribution to one of the most under-discussed topics of the addiction crisis: marriage. *Better Halves* is a well written and prescriptive read for any person or couple navigating the trials and tribulations of addiction and recovery."
— Ryan Hampton, national addiction recovery advocate and author of *American Fix* and *Unsettled*

Nonmonogamy and Jealousy: A More Than Two Essentials Guide
Eve Rickert

A revised and updated guide to handling jealousy in nonmonogamous relationships. "How do you deal with jealousy?" It's the first question many people ask when they hear about consensual nonmonogamy. Tools for dealing with jealous feelings are among the most basic resources in a well-equipped polyamorist's toolkit. Eve Rickert, author of the popular book *More Than Two: A Practical Guide to Ethical Polyamory*, presents *Nonmonogamy and Jealousy*, a distilled guide to troubleshooting one of the most universal challenges in nonmonogamous relationships.